NUCLEAR ARMS

NUCLEAR ARMS

Ethics, Strategy, Politics

Edited by

R. JAMES WOOLSEY

ICS PRESS

Institute for Contemporary Studies
San Francisco, California

Inquiries, book orders, and catalog requests should be addressed to ICS
Press, Suite 750, 785 Market Street, San Francisco, California 94103—
(415)543-6213.

Library of Congress Cataloging in Publication Data
Main entry under title:

Nuclear arms.

    Includes bibliographical references and index.
    1. Atomic weapons—Addresses, essays, lectures.
2. United States—Military policy—Addresses, essays,
lectures. 3. Arms race—History—20th century—Addresses,
essays, lectures. 4. Deterrence (Strategy)—Addresses,
essays, lectures. 5. Strategic forces—United States—
Addresses, essays, lectures. 6. Atomic weapons and
disarmament—Addresses, essays, lectures. I. Woolsey,
R. James, 1941–
U264.N79   1984   355'.0217   83–26580
ISBN 0–917616–56–1
ISBN 0–917616–55–3 (pbk.)

CONTENTS

IV

Arms Control and Politics

V

The Nonnuclear Dimensions of Strategy

VI

Space and Defense

VII

Conclusion

PREFACE

Since the beginning of this decade, no issue of national policy has engaged public attention more urgently than the question of nuclear arms. The Reagan administration's responses to Soviet weapons deployments on both the strategic and intermediate-range levels have provoked unprecedented controversy here and abroad. As a consequence, previously recondite issues of defense policy and military strategy have become subjects of the broadest public concern.

At no point in our peacetime history has there been such need for clarification of our basic strategic circumstances and alternatives. In particular, it has become essential to illuminate once again the critical relation between moral thinking and military necessity.

In an attempt to elucidate these vital questions, the Institute for Contemporary Studies asked R. James Woolsey, former Undersecretary of the Navy under President Carter and currently delegate-at-large to the Geneva arms talks, to bring together a distinguished bipartisan group of experts for a comprehensive review of the issues. These essays, assembled in the wake of the pathbreaking report of the Scowcroft Commission on the MX missile, reflect the best and the latest thinking on the whole range of ethical, strategic, and political concerns that bear on the problem of national defense in the nuclear age.

This book is the latest in a series of Institute publications dealing with crucial issues of national defense and foreign policy. In 1977, the Institute co-published with Basic Books *Defending America,* edited by James R. Schlesinger. This volume was followed in 1980 by *National Security in the 1980s: From Weakness to Strength,* edited by W. Scott Thompson, and most recently by

Beyond Containment: Alternative American Policies Toward the Soviet Union, edited by Aaron Wildavsky.

This book will provide to citizen and policymaker alike an invaluable guide to the freshest responsible thinking on an issue of the first importance.

Glenn Dumke
President
Institute for Contemporary Studies

I

Introduction

1

R. JAMES WOOLSEY

Introduction

Whatever one's views about strategic matters and arms control, it has not been a particularly good decade.

In the years 1973–83, those primarily concerned with the relative strategic balance have seen a substantial buildup in Soviet strategic nuclear forces — equaling and, in some areas, surpassing the U.S. buildup that principally occurred in the 1960s. Those primarily concerned with U.S.–Soviet tensions and the lack of arms control agreements have seen an increase in such tensions and no congressionally approved agreements during the same time. Following President Ford's negotiation of the Vladivostok accord in 1974, each of the two succeeding American presidents has opposed and significantly departed from the arms control approach of his predecessor and has made major changes in his predecessor's strategic modernization program. Technological trends have significantly increased the long-run vulnerability of fixed targets on land, such as intercontinental ballistic missile (ICBM) silos. The U.S. domestic debate over strategic issues has grown more and more divisive — rhetoric about prevailing in a nuclear war on the one hand, the nuclear freeze movement and the recent

American Catholic bishops' pastoral letter on the other. Equally, important elements of the antinuclear movement in Europe present strong opposition to NATO theater nuclear force modernization, even in the absence of the Soviets' willingness to limit their own parallel systems.

During the same period the Soviet strategic grip has tightened both directly (Afghanistan) and by proxy (Poland, South Yemen, Angola, Ethiopia, Vietnam, Nicaragua). International terrorism, and the vulnerability of Western societies to it, has increased— and apace with it the risk of proliferated nuclear weapons' or chemical and bacteriological weapons' falling into the hands of terrorists or renegade states such as Libya. Outer space appears to be becoming a major frontier of U.S.–Soviet military competition as well.

In short, dwelling on an extrapolation of current trends is not a recipe for peaceful sleep.

The authors of the following chapters sketch different portions of this somewhat gloomy strategic picture of the recent past and try to point out some steps we can take so that the future may be painted in somewhat lighter hues. It is, at the very least, a demanding task. For although one can see in some individual areas how improvements would be plausible, it is difficult to see any general improvement in our strategic condition without a greater domestic consensus on both the dangers and the solutions.

Over most of the last decade that consensus has become increasingly frayed. The backdrop has been the relative improvement of the Soviet strategic position—both in nuclear weapons and in the vigor of the expansion of its influence through its proxies. Such developments produce at least one essential ingredient for dissension and confusion in the West—fear. Indeed the range of domestic argument and dissension on strategic questions today is probably most parallel to that existing at the end of the 1950s, just after Sputnik, when the front-page issues were different— civil defense, the missile gap, U.S. inferiority in space, and ban the bomb—but the fears and anxieties were very similar to today's.

The range of debate over strategy and arms control today is broader than it was in the late 1950s and early 1960s. In part this is because the early 1980s debate has involved questioning of the fundamental notion of deterrence—by no less than the American

Catholic bishops. Today's debate has also seen a national nuclear freeze campaign that, although its congressional supporters have held firmly to a bilateral approach, was tilted perceptibly towards unilateralism by noncongressional leaders at their national conference in February 1983. At the same time some publications of impeccable liberal credentials (e.g., *The Washington Post, The New Republic*), while not mincing their criticism of some aspects of the Reagan administration's strategic and arms control policies, have stood strongly for deterrence and against the unilateralist trends in the freeze movement. And President Reagan received some crucial and, to many, surprising help in 1983 from several members of the House Democratic leadership and from other prominent Democratic as well as Republican congressmen when he obtained approval to produce the MX missile as part of a package including a shift toward small ICBMs and a new approach toward arms control recommended by the bipartisan Scowcroft Commission.

The underlying strategic concerns of the United States have recently been in transition in other ways as well. It is becoming increasingly apparent that "strategic" does not mean solely "nuclear" and that "nuclear" does not mean solely "Soviet." The days are past in which the United States could deter a Soviet attack by relying on Strategic Air Command and Polaris submarines and feel that its strategic concerns were fully met. First, the role of our strategic nuclear forces in deterring an attack upon our allies has been constrained by the Soviet nuclear buildup. Hence the particular political importance of the decisions in 1983 about deployment and negotiations concerning intermediate-range nuclear forces in Europe. At stake is the credibility of the overall U.S. guarantee to NATO—in many senses the fabric of the Alliance itself.

Moreover, the vulnerabilities of our own energy distribution system and other networks (food, communications) in this country raise the possibility of terrorist attacks' creating serious disruptions—especially if nuclear, chemical, or bacteriological weapons are used. Proliferation of these weapons adds to the opportunity of their use by terrorists acting on their own, supported by outlaw states such as Libya, or supported covertly by the Soviets. The question whether outer space should be a region for arms control, competition, or a mix of both is another example of the expanded definition of U.S. strategic interest—an expansion that adds to the current range of disagreement.

Appropriately, then, the range of current issues explored by the authors of the following chapters encompasses a far greater span than is normal in our debate on these issues. In the newly prominent moral and ethical dimension of the debate, Charles Krauthammer, Patrick Glynn, and Michael Quinlan survey deterrence in light of the current skepticism about it, and each finds considerable utility in the old doctrine, for somewhat different reasons. Brent Scowcroft sets out a framework for thinking about strategic nuclear forces that is designed to sustain deterrence and promote strategic stability, both because of the types of forces built and the types of arms control pursued. William Perry, in an updated version of a paper published two years ago, explicates the technological trends underlying the Scowcroft Commission's 1983 recommendations. Richard Burt, writing in the midst of negotiations over intermediate-range nuclear forces that have since seen a Soviet walkout, highlights the underlying strength of the NATO Alliance and the advantages to it of the decision to both deploy and negotiate. Walter Slocombe and Colin Gray present thoughtful cases—without claiming too much for their respective positions—for what can and cannot be accomplished by arms control.

There then follow four essays on two new dimensions of U.S. strategic thought—our domestic infrastructure and space. Amory and Hunter Lovins and Robert Kupperman set forth the reasons why the former, especially in an age of terrorism, must have its strategic weaknesses assessed. Hans Mark and Newt Gingrich (the latter together with John Madison) set forth from a technical and a political perspective how one might begin to approach thinking strategically about the new high seas of space. Finally, Senator Sam Nunn delineates, in the first annual David M. Abshire Lecture given at the Center for Strategic and International Studies, Georgetown University, in 1983, a comprehensive view of U.S. strategy—and an approach to reduce reliance on nuclear weapons through conventional force improvements and a shift in the responsibilities of our allies.

The primary political question is whether, in light of all these issues, the United States can find a framework for a consensus—

about strategic modernization, an approach toward arms control, guarantees for our allies, and ways to limit threats from terrorism and from military dangers from space—that will let us deal with the Soviets and the rest of the world with some degree of cohesion and consistency over time. The objective may not be impossible even though such a consensus may be far from complete and may not extend to many other issues of national security and foreign policy. In the late 1940s and early 1950s, for example, Republicans and Democrats, Congress and the president were deeply divided about many crucial issues of national security that were fought out vigorously and often in a highly charged partisan atmosphere. But even in those highly divisive circumstances, men such as Acheson, Marshall, and Vandenberg saw an opportunity to forge a consensus about rebuilding Europe and forming NATO—a consensus that has lasted, largely intact, for a third of a century.

In one way or another, the above authors are wrestling with different aspects of one central question: could the beginning steps for any such consensus be possible, in today's climate, on strategic issues? If so, what should be its basic terms? If not, what are our prospects as a nation?

II

Ethical Issues

2

CHARLES KRAUTHAMMER

On Nuclear Morality

The contemporary antinuclear argument takes two forms. There is, first, the prudential argument that the nuclear balance is inherently unstable and unsustainable over time, doomed to breakdown and to taking us with it. The animating sentiment here is fear, a fear that the antinuclear campaign of the 1980s has fanned with great skill. One of the antinuclear movement's major innovations has been its insistence on a technique of graphic depiction, a kind of nuclear neorealism, as a way of mobilizing mass support for its aims. The graphics include slide shows of devastated Hiroshima and the concentrically circular maps showing where and when one will die in every hometown.

There are, however, limitations to this approach. The law of diminishing returns applies even to repeated presentations of the apocalypse. Ground Zero Day can be celebrated, as it were, once or perhaps twice, but it soon begins to lose its effectiveness. The numbing effect of detail, as well as the simple inability of any movement to sustain indefinitely a sense of high crisis and imminent calamity, have led to the current decline in popularity of the pragmatic antinuclear case.

Consequently there has been a subtle shift in emphasis to a second line of attack, from a concern about what nuclear weapons might do to our bodies to a concern about what they are doing to our souls. Medical lectures on "the last epidemic" have been replaced by a sharper, and more elevated, debate about the ethics of possessing, building, and threatening to use nuclear weapons. (The most recent and highly publicized document on the subject is the Pastoral Letter of the U.S. Bishops on War and Peace.[1] See also Michael Novak's response, "Moral Clarity in the Nuclear Age."[2])

The moral antinuclear argument is based on the view that deterrence, the central strategic doctrine of the nuclear age, is ethically impermissible. Yet two auxiliary issues, one a requirement of deterrence, the other an extension of it, have received the most public attention and become the focus for much of the fervor of the antinuclear crusade. The requirement is nuclear modernization, which is opposed under the slogan of "the freeze"; the extension is the American nuclear umbrella (the threat of nuclear retaliation against an attack, conventional or nuclear, on America's NATO allies), which is opposed under the slogan "no-first-use." In examining the different strands of the antinuclear argument, it is useful to start with the more fundamental challenge to deterrence itself.

The Argument against Deterrence

The doctrine of deterrence holds that a nuclear aggressor will not act if faced with a threat of retaliation in kind. It rests, therefore, on the willingness to use nuclear weapons in response to attack. The moral critique of deterrence holds that the actual use of such weapons, even in retaliation, is never justified. As the bishops put it, simply, one is morally obliged to "say no to nuclear war."[3] But the issues are not so simple. There are different kinds of retaliation, and different arguments (often advanced by different proponents) for the inadmissibility of each.

The popularly accepted notion of deterrence (often mistakenly assumed to be the only kind) is "countervalue" retaliation — an attack on industrial and population centers aimed at destroying the society of the aggressor. The threat to launch such retaliation is the basis of the doctrine of "mutual assured destruction," also known as MAD, massive retaliation, or the balance of terror. It is a balance constructed of paradox: weapons are built in order never to be used; purely defensive weapons, like antiballistic missile systems, are viewed as more threatening to peace than offensive weapons; weapons aimed at people are thought to lessen the risk of war while weapons aimed at weapons are thought to increase it. In Churchill's summary: "Safety will be the sturdy child of terror, and survival the twin brother of annihilation."[4]

The bishops—and others, including nonpacifists like Albert Wohlstetter,[5] who advocate "counterforce" deterrence—are neither reassured nor amused by such paradoxes; they are appalled by them. For them MAD is unequivocally bad. Deliberate attacks on "soft targets" grossly violate the just-war doctrine of discrimination. They are inadmissible under any circumstance because they make no distinction between combatants and noncombatants; indeed, they are aimed primarily at innocent bystanders.

The bishops, however, reject not just a countervalue strategy, but also a counterforce strategy of striking military targets. Since military targets are often interspersed with civilian population centers, such an attack would kill millions of innocents and thus violate the principle of proportionality, by which the suffering inflicted in a war must not outweigh the possible gains of conducting such a war. "It would be a perverted political policy or moral casuistry," write the bishops, "which tried to justify using a weapon which 'indirectly' or 'unintentionally' killed a million innocent people because they happened to live near a 'militarily significant target.' "[6] The bishops also reject, in a second sense, the idea that a counterforce war would be limited. They share the widespread conviction that limited nuclear war is a fiction—that counterforce attacks must inevitably degenerate into countervalue warfare, and thus bring us full circle back to the moral objections to MAD and all-out nuclear war.

That doesn't leave very much. If a countervalue strategy is rejected for violating the principle of discrimination, and a counterforce strategy is rejected for violating the principle of proportionality (and also for leading back to total war), one runs out of ways of targeting nuclear weapons. That suits the bishops: they make a point of insisting that their doctrine is "no-use-ever." The logic, and quite transparent objective, of such a position is to reject deterrence *in toto*.

However, the bishops suffer from one constraint: Vatican policy seems to contradict this position. Pope John Paul has declared that "in current conditions 'deterrence' based on balance, certainly not as an end in itself but as a step on the way toward a progressive disarmament, may still be judged morally acceptable."[7] What to do? The bishops settle for the unhappy compromise of opposing not deterrence in itself, but simply what it takes to make deterrence work. Accordingly, they do not in principle oppose the possession of nuclear weapons when its sole intention is to deter an adversary from using his; they oppose only any plan, intent, or strategy to use these weapons in the act of retaliation. You may keep the weapons, but you may not use them. In sum, the only moral nuclear policy is nuclear bluff.

It is a sorry compromise, neither coherent nor convincing. It is not coherent because it requires the bishops to support a policy—deterrence—that their entire argument is designed to undermine. And it is not convincing because the kind of deterrence they approve is no deterrence at all. Deterrence is not inherent in the weapons. It results from a combination of possession and the will to use them. If one side renounces, for moral or other reasons, the intent of ever actually using nuclear weapons, deterrence ceases to exist.

Pacifists unencumbered by papal pronouncements are able more openly to oppose deterrence. To take only the most celebrated recent example, in *The Fate of the Earth*[8] Jonathan Schell makes the case the bishops would like to make, stripped of any theological trappings. In its secular version the argument goes like this: biological existence is the ultimate value; all other values are conditional upon it; there can be neither liberty nor democracy nor any other value in defense of which Western nuclear weapons are deployed, if mankind itself is destroyed; and after nuclear war the earth will be "a republic of insects and grass." (Schell too rejects the possibility of limited nuclear war.) Therefore nothing can justify using nuclear weapons. Deterrence is more than a hoax; it is a crime.

Schell's argument enjoys a coherence that the bishops' case

lacks, but it is still unsatisfying. Judged on its own terms—of finding a policy that best serves the ultimate and overriding value of biological survival—it fails.

For one thing, it willfully ignores history. Deterrence has a track record. For the entire postwar period it has maintained the peace between the two superpowers, preventing not only nuclear but conventional war as well. Under the logic of deterrence, proxy and brushfire wars are permitted, but not wars between the major powers. As a result, Europe, the central confrontation line between the two superpowers, has enjoyed its longest period of uninterrupted peace in a century. And the United States and the Soviet Union, the two most powerful nations in history, locked in ideological antagonism and engaged in a global struggle as profound as any in history, have not exchanged so much as small-arms fire for a generation.

This is not to say that deterrence cannot in principle break down. It is easy to say that when a system that has kept the peace for a generation is to be rejected, one is morally obliged to come up with a better alternative. It makes no sense to reject deterrence simply because it may not be infallible; it makes sense to reject it only if it proves more dangerous than the alternatives. And a more plausible alternative has yet to be offered. Schell's recommended substitute is a call for a new world order in which all violence, nuclear and conventional, is renounced. Yet his 231-page brief against deterrence neglects to go into the details of exactly how this proposal is to be implemented. Of the job of remaking politics and man, he says, "I have left to others those awesome, urgent tasks."[9]

There is one logical alternative to deterrence, and it does not require remaking man or politics, though neither Schell nor the bishops are quite willing to embrace it: unilateral disarmament. (The bishops' position that one may possess but never use nuclear weapons, however, is unilateralist in all but name.) It has something of a track record, too. The only nuclear war ever fought was as one-sided as it was short. It ended when the nonnuclear power suffered the destruction of two cities (and then surrendered unconditionally). We have evidence also of a bacteriological war, the one going on today in Southeast Asia, where yellow rain falls on helpless tribesmen. The same Vietnamese forces in the same place a decade before never used these weapons against a far more formidable American enemy. The reason is obvious. The primitive Hmong, technologically disarmed, cannot retaliate; the Americans could. Similarly, there was our experience with chemical weapons in World War II, which were not used by either side even after the breakdown of peace because both sides were quite capable of retaliation.

Far from being a guarantor of survival, unilateralism is a threat to it. Thus whether one's ethical system calls its overriding value the sanctity of life or mere biological survival, unilateralism fails within its own terms, and with it fails the moral critique of deterrence. The breakdown of deterrence would lead to a catastrophic increase in the probability of precisely the inadmissible outcome its critics seek to avoid. The bishops unwittingly concede that point in a subsidiary argument against counterforce when they speak of such a strategy "making deterrence unstable in a crisis and war more likely."[10]

The critics argue that no ends can justify such disproportionate and nondiscriminatory means as the use of nuclear weapons. That would be true if the ends of such use were territory, domination, or victory. But they are not. The sole end is to prevent a war from coming into existence in the first place. That the threat of retaliation is the best available this-world guarantee against such a war is a paradox the bishops and other pacifists are unwilling to face. As Michael Novak writes, "The appropriate moral principle is not the relation of means to ends but the choice of a moral act which prevents greater evil. Clearly, it is a more moral choice and occasions lesser evil to hold a deterrent intention than it is to allow nuclear attack."[11] Or recklessly to increase the danger of such an attack.

Nevertheless, moral debate does not end with the acceptance of the necessity, and thus the morality, of deterrence. Not everything is then permitted. There is a major argument between proponents of countervalue and counterforce deterrence. The former claim that counterforce threats lower the nuclear threshold and make nuclear war more likely because it becomes "more thinkable." The latter argue that to retaliate against defenseless populations is not only disproportionate and nondiscriminatory but dangerous as well, since it is not credible and thus actually lowers the nuclear threshold. Note that the debate among nonpacifists is over the relative merits of different kinds of retaliation, and not, as is sometimes pretended, between a "party of deterrence" and a "war-fighting party." The latter distinction is empty: all deterrence rests on the threat of nuclear retaliation, i.e., "war fighting"; and all retaliatory (i.e., nonlunatic) war-fighting strategies from McNamara to today are designed to prevent attack in the first place, i.e., for deterrence. The distinction between these two "parties" has to do with candor, not strategy: the "war fighters" are willing to spell out the retaliatory steps that the "deterrers" rely on to prevent war but prefer not to discuss in public.

Whichever side of the intramural debate among deterrence advocates one takes, it seems to me that deterrence wins the debate with its opponents simply because it is a better means of achieving the ultimate moral aim of both sides—survival.

There is another argument in favor of deterrence, though in my view it carries less weight. It appeals not to survival but to other values. It holds that (1) there are values more important than survival, and (2) nuclear weapons are necessary to protect them. The second proposition is, of course, true. The West is the guarantor of such fragile historic achievements as democracy and political liberty; a whole constellation of ideals and values ultimately rests on its ability to deter those who reject these values and have a history of destroying them wherever they dominate. To reject deterrence unilaterally is to surrender these values in the name of survival.

The rub comes with the first proposition. Are there values more important than survival? Sidney Hook was surely right when he once said that when a person makes survival the highest value, he has declared that there is nothing he will not betray. But for a civilization, self-sacrifice is senseless, since there are no survivors to give meaning to the sacrificial act. For a civilization, survival may be worth betrayal. If indeed this highly abstract choice were the only one, it would be hard to meet Schell's point that since all values hinge on biological survival, to forfeit that is to forfeit everything. It is thus simply not enough to say (rightly) that nuclear weapons, given the world as it is today, keep us free; one must couple that statement with another, equally true: they keep us safe. A nuclear policy—like unilateralism—that forces us to choose between being dead or Red is morally dubious. A nuclear policy—like deterrence—that protects us from both calamities is morally compelling.

Although the attack on deterrence itself is the most fundamental assault on American nuclear doctrine, the case is difficult and complicated. It has, therefore, not seized the public imagination the way two other auxiliary issues have, issues that deal not with the basic assumptions of deterrence but with the weapons and some of the tactics that underpin it. These two campaigns have been conducted under the slogans of "the freeze" and "no-first-use."

The Nuclear Freeze

The moral attack on the weapons themselves takes two curiously contradictory approaches. The first, a mainstay of freeze proponents, is that beyond existing levels new weapons are simply redundant, that we are wasting billions of dollars on useless weapons that will do no more than make the rubble bounce, to borrow another memorable Churchian formulation. The moral crime, it is alleged, is that these monies are being taken away from human needs, like housing and health care and aid to poorer countries. This theme runs through much of the moral literature on armaments. It is featured, for example, in the Brandt North-South Report, which calculates that for every bomber one could instead build a given number of pharmacies in the Third World. The bishops also protest "the economic distortion of priorities— billions readily spent for destructive instruments while pitched battles are waged daily in our legislatures over much smaller amounts for the homeless, the hungry, and the helpless here and abroad."[12]

It is extraordinary that an argument so weak can enjoy such widespread currency. Compared to other types of weapons, strategic nuclear weapons are remarkably cheap. In the U.S. they account for less than 10 percent of the military budget, and for about 5 percent of the gross national product. The reasons are clear. Strategic nuclear weapons are not labor intensive. Once in place, they need a minimal amount of maintenance and fulfill their function simply by existing. Indeed, the argument turns against the antinuclearists. A shift away from strategic to conventional weapons would be extremely expensive. That is precisely why the West decided in the 1950s and 1960s to rely so heavily on nuclear weapons and to permit the current conventional imbalance in Europe. Rather than match the Soviet bloc tank for tank, plane for plane, the West decided to go nuclear because nuclear weapons offered, in John Foster Dulles's immortal phrase, "more bang for the buck." The decision to buy cheap nuclear defense permitted the West vastly to expand social spending. A decision to move *away* from nuclear to conventional defense would require a willingness to divert enormous resources from social to defense spending. Thus, if social priorities are to enter the moral calculus, as the nuclear critics demand, it is the antinuclear case that is undercut.

On the other hand, freeze advocates often argue that these weapons are not useless but dangerous, destabilizing, and likely to precipitate a nuclear war. The more weapons we build, the closer we come to nuclear war. The assumption is that high weapons levels *in themselves* increase the likelihood of war. That reverses cause and effect. Weapons are a result of tensions between nations and not their primary cause. It is true that distrust can be a dangerous by-product of an uncontrolled arms race. And yet arms control agreements like SALT can reduce the risk of war by building mutual confidence and trust, while at the same time permitting *higher* weapons levels. Historically, nuclear tension simply does not correlate well with weapons levels. The worst nuclear crisis took place in October 1962, when the level of nuclear arms was much lower than it is today. And nuclear tensions were probably at their lowest during the heyday of détente in the mid-1970s; at that time U.S.–Soviet relations were at their peak, while each side had by then vastly increased its capacity for multiple overkill.

There is an understandable built-in prejudice against new weapons. Even those willing grudgingly to grant the need for minimal deterrence recoil from building and deploying new weapons of mass destruction. "Enough is enough," they say. What is ignored in this critique of the weapons themselves is that deterrence has requirements, and one is survivability (the ability of one's weapons to sustain a first strike and still deliver a second strike). And survivability, in an era of technological innovation, requires modernization, often to counteract nonnuclear advances like those in antisubmarine or antiaircraft warfare (advances that a freeze would do nothing to curb). Thus, the new American bomber, whether it be the B-1 or the Stealth, will be better able to elude destruction on the ground and Soviet defenses in the air. It will not be any more destructive—or immoral—than the B-52. Similarly for the Trident submarines, which are quieter and (because they have longer-range missiles) can hide in larger areas of the ocean than Poseidons. In short, mainstream nonunilateralist freeze proponents are caught in the position of accepting the fundamental morality of deterrence but rejecting the addition of any new weapon for preserving it.

"No-First-Use"

The penchant for providing ends without means also characterizes the final flank attack on deterrence: the rejection of the doctrine of "extended deterrence," the threat to use nuclear weapons, if necessary, in response to an attack (even a conventional attack) by the Soviet Union on NATO. That policy, which derives ultimately from Western unwillingness to match Soviet conventional strength in Europe, has long troubled many Americans. But since the alternatives are massive conventional rearmament or abandonment of our European allies, it has had to serve through half a dozen administrations as the guarantor of the Western alliance.

The campaign waged against this policy has been spearheaded by four former high administration officials, all with interesting histories. Robert McNamara and McGeorge Bundy are the authors of "flexible response" (a euphemism for limited nuclear war); George Kennan, of "containment"; and Gerard Smith, of SALT I. In an influential 1982 article in *Foreign Affairs,*[13] they joined forces to call for adoption of a "no-first-use" policy on nuclear weapons.

This position has found an echo in many quarters, including, not surprisingly, the bishops' Pastoral Letter. It, too, doubts the possibility that limited nuclear war can remain limited, and resolutely opposes ever crossing the line separating conventional from nuclear war. Therefore any nuclear retaliation against any conventional attack is rejected in principle.

Leave aside the consideration that the impossibility of limited nuclear war is both historically unproven and by no means logically necessary. Assume that limited nuclear war is indeed a fiction. We are still faced with the central problem of the no-first-use approach. Its intent is to prevent any war from becoming nuclear, but its unintended consequence is to make that eventuality more likely. For thirty years war between the superpowers has been deterred at its origin: the prospect that even the slightest conventional conflict might escalate into a nuclear war has been so daunting that neither has been permitted to happen. Current policy sets the "fire break" at the line dividing war from peace; a no-first-use policy moves it to the line dividing conventional war from nuclear war. No-first-use advocates are prepared to risk an increased chance of conventional war (now less dangerous and more "thinkable") in return for a decreased chance of any such war going nuclear. But a no-first-use pledge is unenforceable. Who will guarantee that the loser in any war will stick to such a pledge? A conventional European war would raise the risk of nuclear war to a level infinitely higher than ever before. Thus, any policy, however pious its intent, that makes such a conventional war more thinkable makes nuclear war more likely.

And that is the fundamental flaw in both this argument and the general attack on deterrence. It examines current policy in the light of some ideal, and finds it wanting. It ignores the fact that rejecting these policies forces the adoption of more dangerous alternatives, and makes more likely the calamities we are trying to avoid. In the end these arguments defeat themselves.

Nuclear weapons are useful only to the extent that they are never used. But they are more likely to fulfill their purpose, and never be used, if one's adversary believes that one indeed has the will to use them in retaliation for attack. That will to use them is what the moralists find unacceptable. But it is precisely on that will to use them that the structure of deterrence rests. And it is on the structure of deterrence that rest not only the "secondary" values of Western civilization but also the primary value of survival in the nuclear age.

3

PATRICK GLYNN

The Moral Case for the Arms Buildup

That the Reagan administration has so far won most of the policy battles in the nuclear debate seems remarkable in light of the fact that it has lost virtually all the moral ones. Even as its defense programs have gradually gained approval in Congress, an enormous array of moral forces has mobilized against it. The press, the universities, even the hierarchy of the Roman Catholic Church — from nearly every institution vested with moral authority, powerful voices have been raised in opposition to its plans.

The ethical debate over nuclear arms has compassed a broad range of themes, but at its heart the moral case against the administration rests on two charges. First, and most important, is the claim that under Ronald Reagan American nuclear strategy has been moving from an essentially defensive posture to an essentially offensive one. It is this impression that has proved perhaps most dismaying to ordinary citizens. Occasionally the charge has shaded into the accusation that the administration actually "has come to plan," in the words of one antinuclear writer, "for waging and winning a nuclear war against the Soviet Union."[1] On the whole, however, few people seriously suspect the president of harboring the wish to launch a premeditated attack. What is more generally thought is that through a combination of factors—fervent anti-Communism, militarism, folly, incompetence—the administration, left to its own devices, could conceivably blunder into a nuclear confrontation with the Soviets.

The second charge, closely related to the first, is that the administration's program will inevitably spark a new round of the arms race. The arms race is deplored on the grounds both that it is wasteful, diverting resources that could be applied to more humane programs; and that it is provocative, increasing the risk of nuclear war.

Against these charges the administration has mounted only the most ineffectual defense, failing again and again to dispel the impression that it is significantly more willing than its predecessors actually to risk nuclear war. Even its active attempts to engage the opposition have tended to turn to its own disadvantage. Indeed, so badly has the administration generally put its case that it has often appeared to gain more from silence than from its maladroit efforts to persuade.

Yet in fairness to the administration, it must be acknowledged that the suspicions it has encountered do not spring solely from its policy formulations or even from its rhetorical ineptitude. The nuclear debate has been conducted in an atmosphere of deep distrust and mutual suspicion, and opposition to the administration's policies has come from two somewhat separate camps. The broad appeal of the antinuclear position has tended to obscure important differences between the moral perspectives of the two groups: while the grievances of one party might be said to find their root primarily in the "new" morality, the objections raised by the other party reach back to a much older moral consensus.

It is the first group that has formed the vanguard of the antinuclear campaign proper. Whatever concern nuclear weapons themselves may have provoked, the antinuclear movement has emerged partly as the product of a much broader sense of moral and political disillusionment. Critical to the movement's formation has been the experience of "demythologization" that touched so many lives in the 1960s and 1970s. For whole sectors of our culture, it should be recognized, moral thinking now finds its starting point in the *rejection* of received moral and political values. This loss of faith has had a profound effect on the perspective that many people bring to the problem of national defense. In particular, it has undermined in many minds the idea that the United States, at least as a political entity, is something basically good and worth preserving. Thus while protest is inevitably directed against the weapons, for many people it is the United States government that is the real object of distrust. At its roots, the contention of these people is not that the administration has a bad defense policy, but that in the end the United States, or at least the United States government, is hardly worth defending.

The strength of this view should not be underestimated, for among the young and the educated it enjoys extremely wide, if usually tacit, acceptance. Moreover, it has entered respectable discourse. Traces of this outlook can even be found in the Catholic bishops' pastoral letter on nuclear arms. "To pretend that as a nation we have lived up to our ideals," write the bishops, "would be patently dishonest."[2] Such moral judgments, whether warranted or not, cannot help but influence our thinking on the subject of our self-preservation. It would be no exaggeration to say that our sense of guilt has in recent years tended to prejudice us *against* the cause of our own political survival.

The Vision of "Assured Destruction"

Still, the most serious and powerful moral criticism of the Reagan administration's policies has come from people who believe strongly in our right to survive but who contend that the administration's policies far exceed any merely defensive requirement. The moral thinking behind this assertion is by no means new. The general conviction that Western nuclear strategy ought to remain defensive flows from a long-standing moral and strategic consensus, grounded in the doctrine of "containment" and forged in the wake of the Cuban missile crisis. This consensus has influenced both public feeling and government policy concerning nuclear weapons for upwards of twenty years. The most prestigious public figures who have risen in recent months to oppose the adminis-

tration—including a number of famous men from the Kennedy
administration—have done so largely in defense of this older
outlook.

The convictions that constitute this older consensus are now
very familiar: that nuclear war, once begun, will unleash a
catastrophe of unimaginable dimensions, resulting, effectively, in
the end of the world; that consequently nuclear weapons could
have no conceivable military use; that we already possess many
more times the weapons than we need utterly to annihilate the
Soviet Union and even to obliterate the world as a whole. To most
Americans these propositions have become nothing less than axiomatic. Indeed, so basic are these ideas to public understanding of
nuclear weapons that their origins in actual strategic theories
about nuclear war are now generally forgotten. It is widely
assumed that they spring from the simplest common sense. But in
fact the reigning public consensus on nuclear policy has its roots
in a very specific theory of nuclear strategy, first articulated by
the Defense Department under Robert S. McNamara in the early
1960s: the doctrine known as "assured destruction" or (as it eventually became) "mutual assured destruction." The public moral
consensus on nuclear armaments is in large measure a somewhat
simplified version of "MAD."

The outlines of this strategy are by now well known. In its original formulation, the theory of assured destruction stipulated that
a deliberate nuclear attack on the United States could be deterred
so long as the U.S. maintained the clear ability to inflict upon the
attacker an "unacceptable" retaliatory blow. Deterrence depended, in the words of two of McNamara's civilian strategists, on
"maintaining at all times a clear and unmistakable ability to inflict an unacceptable degree of damage upon any aggressor, or
combination of aggressors—even after absorbing a surprise first
strike."[3] "Stability" is the conflict between the nuclear superpowers would thus spring from the reciprocal vulnerability of
their two societies—meaning chiefly their cities—to devastating
nuclear attack. From these simple premises followed a number of
important consequences. First, the attainment by the Soviet
Union of a similar assured destruction capability was to be encouraged rather than opposed, since "deterrence" to be "stable"
must be "mutual." Second, the United States would gain nothing

from the attempt to acquire "superiority" in nuclear weapons, both because any effort to gain an advantage would be countered by the Soviet Union and because in the presence of assured destruction no real advantage can exist. Finally, defensive weapons such as an antiballistic missile system — especially when designed to protect civilian populations — were not to be sought but rather shunned as dangerous, for by threatening to rob one's adversary of an assured destruction capability they would "destabilize" the nuclear "balance."

From the standpoint of traditional military reasoning, these propositions have always appeared highly paradoxical, which may explain in part why over the years MAD has failed to find much support among the professional military. As Lawrence Freedman notes, it is among civilian strategists in the West that the doctrine of assured destruction has found its strongest adherents. Yet the challenge that MAD posed from the beginning to traditional military thought was made credible by the radically novel nature of the weapons at issue. Writing of nuclear weapons in 1959, Bernard Brodie expressed an idea that has since become commonplace: "The basic fact is that the soldier has been handed a problem that extends far beyond the *expertise* of his own profession."[4]

Moreover, whatever doubts may have been raised concerning its military validity, particularly in the past few years, MAD has persisted as a vision of imposing moral authority. This authority derives chiefly from two considerations: the inherent defensiveness of the doctrine, and its compatibility with the process of arms control. The strongest military argument against MAD—that it offers no guidance, in Benjamin Lambeth's phrase, "at the edge of war," that it is not in any operational sense a "strategy"—has tended to be the strongest moral argument in its favor. Precisely because it would be useless in war, the doctrine of assured destruction has seemed to many to strengthen the cause of peace. Even more important, MAD establishes a theoretical upper limit to forces necessary for deterrence and in doing so provides the strategic logic that permits arms control. It allows us to stop building even if the Soviets continue — so long, it would seem, as our assured destruction capability is indeed assured. MAD is valued in great measure because it seems to leave open a path to disarmament.

Beyond MAD

Nonetheless, it is fair to say that the doctrine of assured destruction has exerted a more enduring hold on public thinking concerning nuclear war than on government policy. Even in the
mid-1960s, when assured destruction was the official declaratory
policy of the U.S. government, actual military targeting priorities
remained at odds with MAD. Declaratory policy emphasized that
nuclear weapons would be used to make punishing strikes against
enemy civilian centers; but the Air Force continued to give
priority in its targeting to military sites.

From the mid-1970s onward, moreover, U.S. policy began gradually to move away from MAD. Contrary to the common conception, the Reagan administration is by no means the first to frame
its defense policy on premises at odds with assured destruction
thinking. In 1974, in response both to changes in missile technology and to new testing and deployments by the Soviet Union,
the Defense Department under Defense Secretary James Schlesinger moved from an assured destruction posture toward a policy
of "flexible response," or "flexible targeting." At issue were two
concerns: first, Schlesinger claimed that the threat that any
Soviet attack, however limited, would be met with retaliation on a
massive scale was losing credibility and no longer provided an adequate foundation for deterrence; second, he argued that it was
necessary to envision in more detail what might actually occur in
the event of Soviet nuclear aggression. Assured destruction
offered no guidance in the event that deterrence "failed." The so-
called "Schlesinger Doctrine" emphasized the need to develop
"sufficient options" between the "massive response" of assured
destruction and "doing nothing."[5] The goal was to limit escalation
in the event of a nuclear conflict by preparing to "hit meaningful
[i.e., military] targets with a sufficient accuracy-yield combination
to destroy only the intended target and to avoid widespread collateral damage."[6] This strategic evolution was continued under
the Carter administration with the issuance of Presidential Direc-
tive 59 (PD-59) under Defense Secretary Harold Brown, which
sought to further extend the emphasis on military targets and on
increasing possible options for responses in the event of nuclear
attack. Both the Schlesinger Doctrine and PD-59 were attacked as

departures from assured destruction; the latter policy statement aroused particularly vociferous opposition. In this sense, the current debate is merely a continuation of a dispute that originated in the mid-1970s.

Thinking Morally about Strategy

But while the basic issues of the debate have not altered, its shape has been critically affected by the emergence of the popular antinuclear campaign. A kind of fissure has opened between the moral and strategic issues in the conflict, with one side in the debate (the administration) resorting instinctively to strategic arguments, while the other side (the peace movement) resorts habitually to moral ones. In the process, the complicated relation between these two kinds of issues has been obscured.

The chief beneficiaries of this development have been the advocates of MAD, for the view of nuclear deterrence based on assured destruction has come to be understood by many as, in effect, the middle position of the conflict. There is irony in this development, since for most of the 1970s MAD was not the center but rather one side in the controversy over nuclear policy. Yet in comparison with the more extreme antinuclear activists, with their unilateralist sympathies, their suspicions of the United States, and their ambitious dreams of a utopian future, the adherents of MAD, once seen as the "doves" in the debate, have tended to appear more and more as hardened realists. After all, next to outright nuclear pacifism, any form of belief in deterrence tends to appear tough-minded. Thus over the past year numerous articles have appeared "in defense of deterrence"—by which is usually meant a view of deterrence based on MAD. It is this outlook that to many seems to combine best the moral concerns raised by the peace movement and the strategic concerns articulated by the administration. One writer expressing this view has tersely divided the debate into three camps: a "party of peace" (the antinuclear movement), a "party of war" (the administration), and, in the center, a "party of deterrence" (the advocates of MAD).[7]

Thus in the name of MAD the specter of unilateral disarmament has been vanquished again and again, but in the process the deeper relation between the moral and strategic issues has tended to be lost to view. The relation between these two concerns is not merely additive; a strategy that existed merely as an ill-conceived compromise between our strategic necessities and our moral ideals would hardly provide an adequate foundation for our defense. Moreover, what would be true of any other strategic doctrine is also true of MAD: its moral value depends entirely on its prior claim to practical, strategic validity. It may well be desirable to prevent the unstinted growth of nuclear arsenals and to avoid the costs and risks entailed by a U.S. military buildup. It may well be desirable to leave open a clear path to disarmament. But it is moral to attempt this *only if it can safely be done*—that is, only if by taking this course we do not embrace the greater risk of weakening deterrence to the point where a nuclear war becomes more likely as the result of our well-meaning efforts. Thus whether MAD offers intrinsically a more or less moral outlook on the nuclear problem depends on whether it is strategically valid; for any moral claim the doctrine may have rests in the first place on the assumption that it will work. Thus to answer the moral questions raised by the conflict between assured destruction and its alternatives, it is necessary to grasp with some precision the strategic realities at issue.

The Soviet Factor

Critical, above all, is the significance of the imposing military buildup undertaken by the Soviet Union over the past decade. That the Soviets have added massively to their military strength in the last ten years hardly any knowledgeable person will dispute. Indeed, the administration's strongest moral and strategic argument on its own behalf has been that its actions constitute nothing more than a necessary response to measures taken by the Soviet Union. Yet the force of this argument has been constantly undermined by the repeated denial on the part of prestigious figures in public debate that the Soviet buildup poses any real threat to the security of the United States—or at least a threat strong enough to merit the administration's response.

What is not widely understood is that this denial is based not on any factual dispute with the administration, but rather on a certain conceptual understanding of nuclear strategy: on the MAD hypothesis. Thus the whole moral argument hinges critically on this fundamental strategic assumption, and it is simply impossible to make an informed moral judgment on the debate until its merits and demerits are sorted out.

At the heart of MAD, in its initial formulation, was a promise of convergence—in technology, in strategic doctrine, in military behavior—between the two superpowers. It is this convergence that opponents of MAD, including the members of the Reagan administration, argue has entirely failed to come to pass. As envisioned by the framers of the doctrine, the rationale for convergence lay in the unprecedented nature of nuclear weapons. The weapons had only to exist, it was felt, for new laws of strategy to obtain—the laws of assured destruction. In the nuclear age, strategy and politics would be shaped ultimately by imperatives embodied in the technology. As one group of analysts wrote in the mid-1960s: "Technology seems to have a levelling effect which subsumes political, ideological, and social differences in various political systems."[8] Whether or not the rather radical changes these analysts predicted would come about, it was felt generally that nuclear weapons forced certain necessary choices on the leaders of countries that possessed them.

One of the critical difficulties that proponents of MAD confronted from the beginning was the overwhelming evidence that Soviet strategists had no such view of nuclear technology; on the contrary, the Soviets seemed to assume even a central nuclear war to be "winnable." This is not to be confused, as it occasionally has been, with the implausible claim that Soviet leaders or military men approach the prospect of nuclear war in a spirit of light-heartedness. The Soviets presumably recognize as well as anybody else the horrors that nuclear war would entail. But this has not prevented Soviet strategists from persisting in the conviction that in practice there would be a difference between "winners" and "losers" in such a war, and that this outcome would not necessarily be random but could be affected by the weapons, the defensive preparations, and the strategies of the two sides. While public statements of Soviet leaders were gradually adjusted to take account of Western thinking on nuclear war, behind this facade of apparent agreement Soviet military thinking remained extremely hostile to the prevailing Western notion that nuclear war would mean "the end of the world." "There is profound error and harm," in the words of Soviet strategist Gen. Maj. A. S. Milovidov, "in the disorienting claim of bourgeois ideologues that there could be no victor in a thermonuclear world war. The peoples of the world will put an end to imperialism, which is causing mankind incalculable suffering."[9] Whereas in the West the emergence of nuclear weapons led to the radical break with traditional military thinking defined by MAD, in the Soviet Union nuclear weapons were assimilated to the traditional military understanding of operations in war: the ordering concept was, and still is, that of "victory." As a result, Soviet strategy has retained two emphases that for some time dropped out of Western military doctrine and certainly from public understanding concerning nuclear war: the primacy of military (as opposed to civilian) targets, and the utility of civil defense. Thus even when discussing massive nuclear salvos, Soviet strategists envision the strikes aimed not at civilians but at military and economic facilities.[10] Civil defense is also seen to play an important role, as explained in this passage from a 1970 article in a Soviet military journal: "Obviously there will be a mass evacuation of the population from densely populated cities, major industrial and administrative centers."[11] Some preparations would be made in peacetime (for example, the Soviets currently possess hardened shelters to accommodate 110,000 key party and military personnel), but the most significant efforts would become visible during the period when, as Soviet strategy put it, events indicated that "war is coming."

The fact that Soviet strategic thinking diverged from that of the West was apparent even at the time that assured destruction was formulated, but it was not understood to present an insurmountable difficulty. For one thing, as Lawrence Freedman notes, Soviet doctrine had undergone some interesting revisions in the 1950s when it was altered to accommodate the existence of nuclear weapons and missiles. It was assumed that it could change again, and more radically.[12] For another, the Soviets lacked anything approaching the military capability to bring about what their strategy proposed. It is important to recognize that McNamara explicitly conceived the formulation of MAD partly as an educative effort to wean the Soviets away from what were understood to be "primitive" and tradition-bound military notions. The early posture statements setting forth assured destruction were written with great care, partly with the intent of instructing the Soviets, and McNamara expressed satisfaction at the number of statements purchased by the Soviet embassy in Washington.[13] This idea of "educating" the Soviet high command has remained a remarkably persistent theme among adherents to mutual assured destruction. As late as 1977, for example, Paul Warnke, head of the Arms Control and Disarmament Agency, referred in an interview to the "primitive" Soviet concept of victory: "Instead of talking in those terms, which would indulge what I regard as the primitive aspects of Soviet nuclear doctrine, we ought to be trying to educate them into the real world of strategic nuclear weapons, which is that nobody could possibly win."[14]

To judge from Warnke's comment, Soviet leaders have proved to be pupils of more than average recalcitrance, since it would seem that in 1977 the U.S. was still "trying to educate them" regarding ideas that had been first explained to them almost fifteen years before. Still, in measuring the success of this effort of education, both sides in the American debate have tended to agree that progress should be measured more by deeds than by words. Whatever the Soviets may say about "victory" in nuclear war, it is their actions that count. But even here controversy arises, for while there is broad agreement concerning the facts of the case, there is great variance in their interpretation. Readings of Soviet behavior seem to be materially affected depending upon whether one accepts or rejects the premises of MAD.

The Case of the ABM Treaty

Proponents and opponents of MAD tend to diverge markedly in their interpretations of even specific Soviet actions. Take, for example, the antiballistic missile (ABM) portion of the 1972 SALT I agreement. The ABM Treaty has frequently been praised as the most successful single arms control agreement concluded to date, since the treaty actually prevented the deployment of a wholly new weapons system that would potentially have transformed the strategic balance. The treaty has also been cited as concrete evidence of implicit Soviet acquiescence in at least the essential elements of MAD. Prohibitions on defensive measures seemed to run counter to the strong bias in Soviet military thinking toward the utility of measures designed to defend both military installations and economic centers. Soviet willingness to accept such provisions therefore was understood as a significant adjustment to the "realities" of the nuclear age. As Jerome H. Kahan put it in a 1975 article: "That the USSR has now accepted the inevitability, if not the desirability, of a mutual deterrence relationship with the United States is suggested strongly by Moscow's preference for stringent limits on area ABM deployments in the SALT treaty." Kahan acknowledged that Soviet doctrine had not shifted away from its explicit "war-fighting" orientation. Nonetheless, he insisted on the basis of the ABM Treaty that Soviet doctrine was "somewhat comparable to ours."[15]

Yet there was an alternative explanation for Soviet behavior regarding the ABM Treaty that successive events have rendered ever more persuasive. It is that, far from acquiescing in some new technological imperative of the nuclear age, or accepting MAD, the Soviets in negotiating limits on ABM systems were simply seeking unilateral military advantage in a very traditional sense. Notably, the Soviets actively pursued the development of defensive technologies throughout the 1960s. These efforts resulted in the creation of the so-called "Galosh" ABM system that is deployed to this day to protect Moscow and in fact much of the western Soviet Union.[16] (Under the treaty, each side was permitted two area systems, reduced to one in the July 1974 protocol; our response has been to dismantle our last remaining ABM sites.) During the 1960s the Soviets spurned all suggestions by the U.S. that such defensive deployments be limited by treaty. It was only when Richard Nixon had secured Senate approval for the technologically superior U.S. "Safeguard" ABM system that the Soviets became eager to discuss ABM limitations. In Henry Kissinger's account:

In 1967, before we had an ABM program, President Lyndon Johnson had suggested to Soviet Premier Alexei Kosygin at Glassboro that both sides renounce ABMs. Kosygin contemptuously dismissed the idea as one of the most ridiculous he had ever heard. By 1970, after the Nixon Administration had won its Congressional battle for ABM by one vote, Soviet SALT negotiators refused to discuss any other subject. Only by the most strenuous negotiating effort did we ensure that limits on offensive, as well as defensive, weapons were included.[17]

In short, once the full political context of Soviet actions is considered, the ABM provisions and even the SALT I agreement as a whole take on a new aspect. What one sees is not, as has been portrayed, the involuntary Soviet acquiescence in MAD but rather the effort of a traditional great power to secure by negotiation the military advantage that it could not attain by its own technology. In the United States, where the chief preoccupation in the strategic debate has tended to be the validity or invalidity of mutual assured destruction, the American Safeguard ABM system was seen as a threat to the logic of MAD. In Russia, one suspects, the U.S. ABM system was seen as a threat to the Soviet Union. The problem with the American Safeguard system, from the Soviet point of view, was not that it threatened to invalidate MAD, which the Soviets had never accepted in the first place, but that it threatened to neutralize the military and political value of Soviet rocket forces as a threat to the West. If this characterization seems harsh, it ought to be kept in mind that Soviet behavior in this regard would be consistent with the behavior of most powerful states through most of history. It is America that, in its preoccupation with the MAD hypothesis, turns out to be the odd bird.

Subsequent Soviet actions have tended to confirm this interpretation of the ABM episode. The effect of SALT I in the United States was to extinguish political interest in ballistic missile defense; consequently, funding for ABM research in the United States dropped precipitously. In the Soviet Union, by contrast, such research has continued apace. The Galosh system was modernized, and new phased-array radars of the sort used by ABM systems, and covered by the treaty, have been deployed in six sites. In recent months, testing and deployment has even skirted violations of the treaty. SAM-10 and SAM-12 anti-aircraft missiles have reportedly been tested in an ABM mode; and the recent detection of a new phased-array radar installation, deployed near a Siberian ballistic missile field in an area prohibited by the treaty, has prompted a debate within the Reagan administration concerning the wisdom—political and otherwise—of raising the issue of Soviet treaty violations.[18] Whether the administration will press its case is not clear at this writing. In this connection, however, the presence or absence of violations is less important

than the abundant confirmation that the Soviet Union is committed to a view of defensive measures totally at odds with MAD. The
main evidence for tacit Soviet acceptance of mutual assured
destruction would appear to have been misinterpreted.

The Apolitical Vision of MAD

It may be an overstatement to describe as "epistemological" the
differences that result in such divergent interpretations of Soviet
actions, but radical contrasts in perception are clearly at issue.
Critical is the role assigned to politics. Opponents of MAD have
tended to dwell more than their counterparts on the specific political character of the Soviet regime. MAD, by contrast, reflecting its
intellectual origins, offers a fundamentally nonpolitical account of
the conflict between the superpowers. Rooted in economic "game
theory," MAD arrives at its analysis by viewing strategic adversaries simply as rational actors abstractly understood. Presumably the logic of MAD would apply equally well to any two states
that found themselves in the circumstances of the United States
and the Soviet Union—i.e., to any two politically opposed states in
possession of nuclear weapons. While accepting political conflict
as a kind of axiom or condition, MAD abstracts from the content
of the political struggle, dwelling instead on the dimensions in
which the outlook and circumstances of the U.S. and the USSR are
rendered by virtue of nuclear technology "comparable."

Grand strategies, it has been observed, tend to reflect the
character of the regimes that devise them, and from the outset
there has been a close kinship between "assured destruction" and
the nature of the American polity. MAD stands as a kind of partial
reflection of the American ethos. In America, as in the MAD vision, technology is understood to be the decisive shaper of life, the
modern fact *par excellence,* the ultimate supplier and limiter of
human options. But even more important, the MAD doctrine is,
like so much of American political thinking, essentially apolitical
in orientation. In MAD as in American life generally, politics is
treated as a sort of afterthought, an epiphenomenon of a broader
"human" experience. The actors in MAD are essentially unaffected
by ideology or value: whatever their beliefs or other goals, they
respond predictably, almost automatically, to the imperatives em-

bodied in the technology. In this portrait of strategic actors there is something of America's genial, ethnocentric self—a confident projection of *homo economicus*: the assumption that, once the deal is spelled out, everybody is bound to agree on the basics with everybody else, to evaluate the costs and the benefits in the same way. In the context of American culture, the primacy that MAD assigns to technological influences and essentially economic calculations of advantage hardly seems surprising.[19]

There is now good reason to wish that in the nuclear era Americans had possessed more of what the poet John Keats called "negative capability"—the ability, simply speaking, to put oneself in another's shoes. Despite mountains of evidence to the contrary, the overwhelmingly prevalent assumption has been that, at least in the essential respects, Soviet views of nuclear strategy were "somewhat comparable" to ours. To most Americans and even to many American "experts," it has been inconceivable that the Soviets might approach nuclear weapons with different goals, different priorities, a different understanding of how the weapons might be used and what they could be used for. Nothing the Soviets themselves might say seemed capable of shaking this hypothesis.

Yet if the comfortable assumption of Soviet "comparability" has persisted for a long time, that is partly because for most of the nuclear era it has been, in the literal sense of the word, a "safe" assumption. That is to say, during much of the postwar period, Soviet military capabilities—especially nuclear—were so inferior to those of the United States that it hardly mattered what the Soviets thought about strategy at any level.

There is an irony in the history of MAD, for this doctrine of "mutual" vulnerability was formulated at a time when vulnerability was anything but mutual. As late as 1966, it should be remembered, the Soviets possessed only 350 land-based and only about 30 submarine-launched ballistic missiles as compared with an American total in the two categories of over 1,700.[20] Yet our doctrine was predicated on "parity." By a trick of memory it now tends to be assumed that it was "parity" of weapons that ensured our safety in the past. It was nothing of the sort. At the time of the Cuban missile crisis, the United States possessed overwhelming superiority in both conventional naval and nuclear armaments.

Those present at the crisis have since argued that it was not nuclear strength but in fact conventional force locally applied—in particular, the naval quarantine of Cuba—that brought successful resolution to the crisis. But as Peter Rodman has shown, this is not at all self-evident.[21] The fact is that the Soviet Union was aware of U.S. strength at all levels, and it is difficult to argue that nuclear superiority did not play a role. At all events, it was overall *strategic* superiority that gave the United States scope to act—and it is crucial to recognize that this strategic superiority, whether in nuclear or conventional arms, is now a thing of the past.

Technological and Political Imperatives

The whole dispute over the validity of MAD and the nature of Soviet intentions might have remained what it originally was— chiefly a theoretical argument—were it not for certain troubling developments. Yet changes in both technology and military deployments have forced these issues once again to the fore. Notably, technology has moved in a direction exactly opposite to that predicted by early proponents of MAD. Rather than force a convergence of doctrine and strategy upon the superpowers, it has helped to pull them, strategically speaking, further and further apart. The crucial factor has been the emergence of highly accurate nuclear warheads capable of destroying hardened military targets and even hardened missile silos. These so-called "counterforce" weapons endow "war-fighting" strategies of nuclear war— such as those articulated in Soviet military writings—with a physical plausibility that they never previously had. Thus technology has introduced into the military arsenals of superpowers a physical distinction corresponding to the strategic distinction between war-fighting and assured destruction doctrines. MAD envisions a punitive strike at the *society* of the enemy; counterforce weapons make it at least physically possible to destroy missiles in their silos and thus to strike at the enemy's *weapons*, the adversary's physical ability to wage nuclear war.

Yet even these technological developments might have been weathered by MAD had the Soviet Union not moved so decisively to take advantage of them. It is critical to recognize that the Soviet

Union responded to the emergence of counterforce technology in a manner fundamentally different from that of the United States, though in a fashion totally consistent with its own understanding of the function of nuclear arms. At this point in the nuclear era— if not before—there was a clear divergence in the behavior of the two superpowers. Throughout the 1970s the Soviet Union moved unstintingly to develop and deploy as large a number of counter- force warheads as was practical. Faced at the same moment with the possibility of developing such counterforce capability, the United States deliberately decided to forego its option, in the in- terest of preserving the relationship of mutual deterrence. From 1969 to 1974 the United States exercised deliberate restraint in the development of warhead accuracy so as not to threaten Soviet assured destruction capability. Thomas Wolfe summarized the U.S. action in a well-known study for the Rand Corporation:

From 1969 to 1979, it was U.S. declaratory policy, backed up by budget- ary controls, not to develop highly accurate weapons that might threaten hardened Soviet military targets. This policy was not universally ap- plauded on the U.S. side, as indicated by news accounts in August 1972 of Pentagon plans to accelerate the development of more accurate warheads but not to deploy them. Congress, however, rejected appropria- tions associated with these programs, illustrating continued congres- sional adherence to constraints upon improvement of U.S. counterforce capabilities. It was only during [James] Schlesinger's tenure as secretary of defense that the declaratory policy against accuracy improvements was formally stopped with congressional approval.[22]

In a pattern that was to be repeated again and again during the course of the decade, the Soviets failed to reciprocate the United States' gesture of unilateral restraint—its "self-denying ordinance."[23]

That Soviet leaders would move in such a direction is hardly surprising in light of Soviet strategic thinking; at the same time, the deployment of counterforce weapons on a massive scale gave new credibility to the Soviet strategic formulations that had been long dismissed in the West as absurd.

The Problem of U.S. Vulnerability

Thanks to massive Soviet deployments of counterforce weapons, it began to become apparent in the middle of the last decade that by the early 1980s the Soviet Union would have deployed a sufficient number of such warheads to destroy 90 to 95 percent of U.S. land-based missiles in their silos, using only a small portion of its own intercontinental ballistic missile (ICBM) force. Since the U.S. submarine-based missiles that would remain intact do not currently possess counterforce capability, it seemed that the president might be left with the sole option of retaliating against such an attack with a "countervalue" strike against Soviet society, only to face far worse countervalue retribution in return. Thus the Soviet buildup was operating to deprive us gradually of a credible retaliatory capacity. That we would have survivable missiles was not in doubt, but since the Soviets would possess an equal number and since the missiles could be targeted effectively only at civilian centers, there would be no possibility of U.S. retaliation short of mutual suicide. Even the Soviet first strike could produce casualties in the millions; but if retaliation meant 100 million more Americans dead, it was felt that the president's hand would likely be stayed.

The plausibility of this scenario was widely criticized. But what is important to recognize is that ten years earlier, even the hint that the Soviets might be allowed to achieve such an advantage would have been greeted with an outpouring of public concern. At the same time it should be stressed that the controversy over the so-called "window of vulnerability" had to do with the likelihood that the Soviets would launch such an attack. Among knowledgeable people the technical reality of U.S. ICBM vulnerability is no longer a matter for dispute. It has been confirmed not only by the Defense Department but by the bipartisan report of the Scowcroft Commission:

While Soviet operational missile performance in wartime may be somewhat less accurate than performance on the test range, the Soviets nevertheless now probably possess the necessary combination of ICBM numbers, reliability, accuracy, and warhead yield to destroy almost all of the 1,047 U.S. ICBM silos using only a portion of their own ICBM force. The U.S. ICBM force now deployed cannot inflict similar damage, even using the entire force.[24]

This passage is especially interesting in light of the popular conception that in the Scowcroft report the idea of a "window of vulnerability" was dismissed. It needs to be noted that the United

States does not possess a comparable capacity vis-a-vis the Soviet Union. Because of the smaller size and lesser accuracy of U.S. warheads, it is estimated at present that even a full-scale preemptive American attack against the Soviet rocket force would leave about 65 percent of Soviet ICBMs intact.[25]

It is important to recognize that the military and political significance of the Soviet Union's newly acquired preemptive capability does not rest on any foolish or simpleminded assumption that the Soviet leadership is somehow eager to make actual use of it. It has become customary in the nuclear debate to point out that the idea of a Soviet preemptive strike is preposterous and to assume that with this single stroke the argument is done. What is critical to grasp is that the missiles do not have to be fired to be of significant military and political weight. To the degree that relations between opposing states remain peaceful, they are based on the calculation, rather than the actual employment, of military power, and it is this calculation that the growth of Soviet strength decisively upsets.

Throughout the postwar period the security of the democracies has depended decisively on the U.S. "nuclear umbrella"; that is, the freedom of the West has been predicated on American strategic superiority, and American superiority in turn on superiority in nuclear arms. (There is reason to lament the degree to which the West has neglected conventional military strength in favor of less expensive nuclear deployments, but that is a topic for another time and place.) To say that the American nuclear advantage has been canceled by recent Soviet deployments understates the case. What people are pleased to call "parity," on the basis of a definition artfully grown vaguer and vaguer over the years and months, is, from the standpoint of any operational military calculation, Soviet superiority—growing clearer and clearer almost by the day. To the degree that these calculations describe physical possibilities that could be made to come about, they cannot be dismissed. It is not necessary to assume that the Soviets want to wage nuclear war; indeed, hardly anyone in or out of the administration does. It is only necessary to assume that the Soviets wish to banish from *our* minds any hope that if they chose to initiate such a struggle we would have a chance to survive.

What tends to be forgotten, moreover, is that the whole controversy over Soviet nuclear "parity" takes place in a strategic climate of overwhelming Soviet superiority in conventional forces. Numerically the Soviet Union far outdistances the West in nearly every category of conventional weaponry, and in many areas the technological gap that once worked to the advantage of Western forces has virtually closed. Even if the Soviets were to succeed in shifting the strategic conflict entirely to the conventional level, they would gain an enormous advantage.

For a long time it was possible to explain the Soviet buildup as an effort to gain "parity." And yet it is now obvious that the Soviet Union attained rough parity in nuclear armaments at least a decade ago and attained an assured destruction capability some time before that. (The 1972 SALT I agreement, it should be remembered, allowed the Soviet Union a quantitative advantage of 800 intercontinental missiles, to compensate for what was understood to be American technological superiority and for the existence of 162 nuclear missiles in the British and French arsenals.)[26] Even now, the Soviets continue to construct powerful, counterforce-capable ICBMs at the rate of nearly 200 a year. In the past decade, the Soviet Union has built a total of 2,000 ICBMs. (For comparison, it should be noted that the U.S. built 350 ICBMs during the same period; and even the controversial Scowcroft proposal concerning the MX envisions the construction of only 100 of these missiles.) In addition, 350 new, extremely accurate intermediate-range missiles have been deployed by the Soviets against Europe and Asia in the past six years. Even in areas where the Soviet advantage is absurdly overpowering, construction continues at a fantastic rate. Warsaw Pact forces now enjoy roughly a 5-to-1 advantage over NATO forces in tank power; yet in 1981, for example, the USSR and Pact countries built a total of 5,040 new battle tanks, as compared with a NATO and U.S. total for the same year of 760.[27] From 1969 to 1975, U.S. defense spending actually declined in real terms, while Soviet spending grew at roughly a 4 percent real rate. For much of the later 1970s, the Soviet Union was outspending the United States by as much as 50 percent, on a much poorer economic base. To this day, in the wake of Mr. Reagan's "massive buildup," Soviet military spending substantially exceeds that of the U.S.[28]

Denying the Danger

In a democratic nation alive to the requirements of its own survival, such a series of dark developments might be expected to arouse a sense of emergency and call forth a new consensus. Nothing of the sort has occurred. The absence of a sense of crisis, moreover, is self-reinforcing; for if, as the public mood suggests, there is no real emergency, then why worry? It is not MAD alone, of course, that has prevented acknowledgment of these new developments. Most of the really obvious changes have occurred in the past ten and many in the past five years — precisely the period during which American public opinion was occupied with the denouement of Vietnam and the crisis of Watergate. But critical in annulling any sense of emergency has been the vocal denial of extremely prestigious public figures — nearly all of them longtime partisans of MAD — that any real danger exists. Yet what is not widely understood is that this denial is not *factual* but *conceptual* in character. No responsible opponent of the current administration denies the veracity of its reports concerning Soviet military buildup; *what is denied is that it matters*. The basis for this denial lies in the MAD hypothesis: for if the U.S. continues to possess an assured destruction capability — and submarine warheads alone would seem to constitute such a force — then no Soviet actions, under the logic of MAD, could fundamentally threaten our security. Yet this conceptual denial of the importance of recent developments has tended to become confused in the public mind with a factual denial of their existence, just as opposition to the theory of MAD has sometimes been confused with the disposition to risk, "hawkishly," embarking on a nuclear war.

Yet it is worth asking whether the MAD hypothesis has not survived over the years simply by turning increasingly circular, tautological. In retrospect, the history of assured destruction thinking since its original conceptualization appears more and more a history of denial and rhetorical retreat: denial, first, of the importance of Soviet strategic thinking; denial, next, of the military utility of ABM; denial of the unceasing Soviet buildup, both in its early stages and even now when the supposed goal of "parity" has long since been surpassed; denial even of the military and political significance of a Soviet first-strike capability. At the same

time, there has been a steady tactical retreat from confident
assertions that the Soviets could be made to think and act toward
nuclear weapons the way we do; to the qualified claim that it
didn't matter what they thought so long as they acted properly
(the ABM Treaty); to the current rather implausible avowals that
nothing they think or do could ever make a difference. Thus, after
all the revelations of Soviet strategic thinking, after all the rever-
sals in American hopes for arms control, after all the discredited
predictions that the Soviets would stop building once they
achieved assured destruction or "parity," such a man as McGeorge
Bundy can still write, without humor, that "on the nature of
nuclear danger serious Soviet leaders and experts have repeatedly
shown an understanding not essentially different from that which
moved the [American Catholic] bishops."[29] In Bundy's new formulation, mutual assured destruction has been transformed into
something called "existential deterrence"—merely the latest
name for the twenty-year-old idea of MAD.[30]

In short, events and realities that to less committed observers
might seem to have clear and definite implications for our
strategic circumstances have successively been gainsayed or explained away in the service of the single hypothesis that assured
destruction is enough. "The more of doubt," says one of Robert
Browning's characters, "the stronger faith, I say/If faith o'er-
comes doubt." Against a cascade of doubts, MAD has proved a
marvelously resilient creed.

Yet so preponderant has become the need to discount or explain
away Soviet departures from MAD that the logic of the doctrine is
no longer applied in public debate with any consistency. MAD depends on what Glenn Snyder has termed "deterrence by pain"—
as opposed to "deterrence by denial."[31] MAD strategists argue, in
essence, that given the horrendous power of nuclear arms, the
threat of pain—i.e., the threat of retaliation against an enemy
society—should be sufficient to deter attack. War-fighting or
counterforce strategies, by contrast, emphasize the importance of
"denying" the enemy the military wherewithal to attain a decisive
advantage or "victory" at whatever price. From the standpoint of
deterrence by pain, the distinction between countervalue and
counterforce weapons hardly matters, because both are capable of
inflicting horrible punishment. For deterrence by denial, however,

the distinction could become extremely important, since the emphasis is on attacking the enemy's *means* of doing battle.

On this basis one could argue, perversely perhaps but still consistently, that if as MAD suggests the threat of pain should be sufficient to deter war, then a buildup of U.S. forces should not prove inherently dangerous to deterrence. That is because whatever additional armaments we may deploy the Soviets will always possess the ability to inflict horrible pain in retaliation. Even the possession of U.S. first-strike capability would leave the Soviet Union with upwards of 2,000 submarine-based warheads with which to retaliate—an assured destruction capability if ever there was one. One could oppose a buildup on grounds that it was costly or wasteful, but not on the grounds that it would lead to war. In other words, for the same reason that we are counseled not to feel threatened by the Soviet buildup, the Soviets should not feel threatened by ours. If the logic of deterrence by pain is in fact valid, war should not be made more likely simply by a buildup on one side or another.

But conversely, if the mere belief by American leaders (however fallacious) that nuclear war were in some sense "winnable" would make war more likely—and this is the gravamen of the charge against the administration—then it follows that a similar belief by Soviet leaders (however fallacious) would have the same result. Our ability to inflict pain in retaliation—i.e., our "assured destruction capability"—would not in the final analysis be sufficient to deter. Moreover, if, as is also often argued, moral suasion is insufficient to wean American leaders from this belief—if they must be denied the physical capability to accomplish what they would set out to do—then it follows that Soviet leaders also must be denied this capability. In America, we can place political pressure on the administration not to build the requisite weapons. But in the Soviet case such pressure on our part is futile. Indeed, the Soviets have already acquired the basic elements of a war-fighting capability and continue to acquire at a fantastic rate weapons whose only purpose is manifestly not to inflict pain but rather to circumscribe or if possible deny our ability to retaliate short of mutual suicide. Moreover, it is well established that Soviet strategy envisions even central nuclear war to be winnable (a fact borne out by the nature of Soviet deployments). Our only option is thus to take the measures to render the hope of victory not just *humanly* but *militarily* implausible. This means, in the end, acquiring a capacity to inflict equivalent military damage and doing what we can to ensure the invulnerability of our retaliatory capability. In short, once one steps out of the logic of deterrence by pain or MAD pure and simple, it becomes essential to think about the operational capabilities of weapons that one never intends to use. The capacity to deter war — to prevent war defensively from occurring — becomes logically indistinguishable from the ability to fight one. The recommendation to meet the Soviet buildup with a buildup of our own, therefore, comes not from belligerence or "imperial ambitions" on the part of American leaders, but simply from the straightforward necessity of securing our safety.

Self-Deterrence

The logic of MAD, in other words, has been applied in recent years more and more one-sidedly — to deter us from acquiring weapons to match and counter the Soviet buildup. Thus well-intentioned people have endeavored to stop the "arms race"; but the arms race is not war, and in stopping the arms race we are taking measures that logic and history suggest are making war more likely by making it more "thinkable" — for Soviet leaders.

The thinking embodied in MAD and arms control has tended to skew our discussions of these matters, so that we have come to debate the decision to acquire new weapons as though we were debating a decision to use them — as though adding to our arsenal, even for avowedly defensive purposes, were equivalent to launching an attack. The peculiarity of this position needs to be appreciated. At a time when the Soviet Union is adding MIRVed ICBMs to its arsenal at the rate of 175 to 200 per year, building hundreds of new aircraft, scores of new naval vessels, and thousands of new tanks, public figures in the United States rail against the procurement of the MX missile — the first new U.S. ICBM to be contemplated in over a decade — as though it were a heinous crime. Indeed, the metaphors that we employ in political discourse routinely treat the mere procurement of weapons as an action equivalent to murder. Writing of the administration's plans for a buildup, Theodore Draper has commented that deterrence "may yet equal liberty for the number of crimes committed in its name."[32] But an important distinction is being overlooked here. The "sins" committed in the name of liberty involved the actual killing of human beings; what Draper is discussing is merely a U.S. buildup undertaken to counter Soviet deployments and to deter aggression — i.e., precisely to prevent such weapons from being used. Yet he speaks as if the mere procurement of a weapon constituted an atrocity. Even the Catholic bishops have contributed to this moral perspective, describing the "arms race" as an "act of aggression" against "the poor."[33] It may be that if defense spending were less throughout the world, there would be more spending for the poor. But the United States is arming with the intention of defending itself, and not of persecuting its less fortunate citizens. So remote has public discussion in the West grown from the life-and-death realities of politics that we seem at times to have lost the capacity to differentiate between maintenance of peacetime defenses and the actual waging of war.

Little wonder that, in this looking-glass moral universe where arming for self-defense tends to be counted as equivalent to murder, an American administration has difficulty making a persuasive ethical case for its defense policies. But it must be understood that the moral objections to the administration's stance arise chiefly because the proponents of MAD succeed again and again in explaining away the rather simple and obvious *strategic* justification for the administration's actions. As a result, the debate must be conducted on the basis of premises so remote from the military realities with which policymakers must cope that even the modest successes achieved by the administration in the public forum seem surprising. Our whole discourse about nuclear weapons is dominated by a moral vision rooted in discredited strategic assumptions — assumptions at best appropriate to the strategic reality of 1965 or 1972 and in any case wholly irrelevant to the vastly changed circumstances of the present. Yielding to the temptation to play to this pervasive "moral" outlook, the administration has ended up more often than not with a lame, self-contradictory compromise between its own straightforward strategic logic and the prevailing nuclear orthodoxies.

But what of the more common worry that the existence of a stronger American arsenal might conceivably tempt American leaders toward adventuresomeness or a dangerous confrontation, or the more serious charge that elements in the current administration would be willing, under certain circumstances, to initiate a nuclear war? The latter charge, in particular, is rendered simply incredible by the actual state of the American arsenal when compared with that of the Soviet Union. No nation would be contemplating war in such a state of military disarray. The United States has nothing like the superiority of forces that would allow it to envision attacking the Soviet Union, whether by nuclear or by conventional means. Moreover, as the current administration is well aware, nothing in its defense programs envisions such superiority or even, for that matter, "parity," if "parity" is very strictly defined. It is worth remembering that every major new strategic system advocated by Mr. Reagan—the MX missile, the B-1 bomber, the Trident submarine—was originally proposed by previous administrations.

The Shibboleth of Warmongering

Indeed, the notion that the Reagan administration is contemplating war, for all its recent popular currency, is in fact little less than ludicrous. Much is made of the administration's supposedly fervent anti-Communism. But a government that cannot even bring itself to declare default on loans to Communist Poland or to withhold sales of wheat from the Soviet bloc to gain political and military leverage is hardly in a position to make the enormous economic sacrifices that would attend upon the actual waging of war. Besides, whatever various U.S. economic interest groups may gain from the "arms race," the West has nothing economically to gain from a war with the East. (For the East, of course, the situation is quite the opposite; much of the Soviet buildup has been designed to gain economic access to the West, preferably by political threats based on military power rather than the direct use of military means.) Our historical interest is not in conquest, but rather in securing trading partners—so much so that we can hardly restrain our commercial men from trading with our chief adversary even when such trade helps to build the Soviet military machine. There is simply nothing in the makeup of the Western commercial democracies to lead them to want war with the Soviet

Union. That this needs to be said at all is a measure of how far we have fallen from basic self-understanding. What is ironic is that Soviet officials, for all their disingenuous protestations to the contrary, are more aware of these realities than many of our own citizens.

At the same time, there is a point at which refusal to confront amounts to open retreat, and it is here that we must face up to the implications of possessing nuclear weapons. The world is still a dangerous place, and the political freedom of the West rests in the final analysis on the strength of the American arsenal. The vast economic power of America and Western Europe avails nothing if at the critical moment this economic power could not be translated into military force. Yet we seem at once too craven and too greedy to be willing to pay for our own defense.

Many in Europe and America appear to have convinced themselves that totalitarian rule would be tolerable. For these it is useful to remember that the combined casualties of this century's two world wars did not yet equal the number who died under Communist rule in Russia and East Europe before, during, and after World War II. Nazi Germany was responsible for the extermination of six million people; Communist Russia, by moderate estimates, for the murder of *ten times* that many.[34] To this day some two million people suffer in concentration camps in the Soviet Union. Hundreds are committed to psychiatric hospitals for "political" offenses.[35] And the worst horrors of the Great Purge are being reenacted today in Afghanistan, where thousands have been subject to summary executions and the most appalling tortures — to which the Western democracies, as is their wont, turn a deaf ear.[36] These — and not the "arms race" — are the real horrors of our time.

Yet there is one important step in addition to upgrading our nuclear forces that can be taken toward reducing the chances of nuclear war: it is to deploy conventional forces in sufficient numbers to deter aggression from Europe and other areas of "vital interest" — which is only to say where the Soviet Union may threaten the West itself or the very basis of the West's long-term survival. There is very broad support, in principle, for such a proposal. But unfortunately, many who have campaigned most vociferously against nuclear arms have also worked to close off this critical alternative. The American Catholic Bishops offer an emphatic critique of the "first use" of nuclear weapons in Europe, but are considerably less clear regarding the only viable alternative—namely, a buildup of conventional forces. Many senators and congressmen who campaign against the MX also consistently vote against increases in the defense budget that would expand conventional procurement. At a time when the conventional forces of the Soviet Union and Warsaw Pact nations outnumber those of the Western Alliance by several times, our legislators have set off on a crusade against "waste" in the Pentagon, whose inevitable effect is to erode already shaky public support for defense spending generally.

Moral Myopia

All this is done in the service of what are understood to be moral goals. Yet throughout this debate we have been tending to treat as "moral choices" what, in light of accumulated facts, barely appear to be "choices" at all, let alone choices in which ethical considerations could be held paramount. It is not merely that Soviet forces are gaining on the United States; it is that by every measure that could be counted meaningful, the Soviets have overtaken us. We talk as though the decision facing us were between maintaining parity and acquiring some kind of strategic "superiority," when the choice is in fact between bare parity and an inferiority in both nuclear and conventional armaments that increases by the month. We talk of "threatening" the Soviet Union, as though we had the comparative force to make that any more a real option. Given our history, it is only natural that we would conduct these discussions in an atmosphere of confidence, assuming that we had the ability to choose among a plethora of options. Through most of our postwar history such discussions have occurred in a climate of American freedom and strategic superiority. What Americans fail to understand are the implications of this era's having come to an end.

It has now become almost axiomatic in public debate that an adequate ethical response to the problems posed by nuclear weapons requires a heightened moral awareness. Yet so plain are the horrors of nuclear war and so inescapable are the problems facing us, that it is hardly clear that anything more than ordinary decency is required to form an adequate moral response. The fundamental moral imperatives of our time would seem both simple and clear: to prevent nuclear war, and to prevent at least the existing democracies from falling under totalitarian rule. One need not be a saint or a visionary or a moral philosopher to understand and embrace these goals. Indeed, it can be argued that from the beginning of the nuclear era, decent people in the democracies have never wanted anything else. In this debate the really critical questions facing us are not in the strict sense moral but rather political and strategic. It is on a clearer understanding of these latter issues that our survival now urgently depends.

4

MICHAEL QUINLAN

Thinking Deterrence Through

The concept of deterrence itself is a pretty old one; in one form or another it goes back to the Romans, and beyond. But it is only since 1945 that the word "deterrence" has become a part of our standard vocabulary. None of us needs any long reminder of why this is so. On two days in August 1945 there was proof, in the most direct way possible, that the ability to destroy in war, which had been progressively growing throughout the history of at least recent centuries, had suddenly made an abrupt and terrible leap upwards.

That leap meant, as was very quickly realized, that war to the maximum of mankind's power could never again be viewed as just an inferior and unpleasant way of managing international affairs; it ceased to be a way of managing international affairs at all. The

---

This paper was delivered as an address given by Mr. Quinlan to a conference of civil defense planners at York, England, in July 1981. It has been edited only to make its style compatible with that of an article.

53

idea of preventing war — at least all-out war between top-level powers — acquired an immediate and absolute cogency, a compulsion, that it had never had before. And in turn, because governments have been able to find no surer practical method of prevention than deterrence, deterrence has become the centerpiece of security policy.

So deterrence today is above all about the prevention of nuclear war. But that is not *all* that it is about. It does seem to me very important to recognize that the ghastly events of August 1945 did not mean that war suddenly became nasty after having been nice. It had not previously been nice. The carnage of the trenches in World War I is not to be easily forgotten; and World War II took the lives, in one way or another, of something like fifty million people before most of us had ever heard of a place called Hiroshima. We are, I suspect, sometimes lulled by the jargon we use — we talk of nonnuclear weapons as being "conventional," with a flavor of acceptability, almost of coziness. But nonnuclear war was appalling in World War II, and the weapons available for it are far more powerful now than they were then.

Nonnuclear war is not just appalling in itself; it is also the likeliest possible route to nuclear war. The notion of nuclear war coming out of the blue is farfetched; scenarios of the holocaust being launched just because some computer goes on the blink are plain rubbish. The risk of nuclear war would be most real in a situation in which bitter conflict had already broken out at a lower level; so we have an added reason for making sure that it does not break out at all.

The object therefore has to be prevention of all war, not only nuclear war, between the two great power blocs. Does the requirement for a policy of deterrence follow immediately from that? Well, not quite.

Another way of avoiding nuclear war would be to decide consciously on a policy of nonresistance — a policy, that is, of surrender if necessary. But the governments of the West have consistently taken a different view. They have judged, first, that they could not rule out the possibility that our way of life, our freedom, might be threatened by external force; and, secondly, that our way of life, for all its imperfections, is so much preferable to the main alternative as to be worth a great deal of effort to preserve. Now you can find people, in good faith, who will contest one or other or both those propositions. I'm not going to argue them here; I note simply that governments of both parties in office in Britain have essentially accepted them as the premises of their security policy. And when you accept those propositions and set them alongside our earlier aim, then you are led, inexorably, to a policy of deterrence. Put another way, deterrence is the policy you must have if you believe in the possibility of grave threat and yet want to continue in both peace and freedom—neither Red nor dead. I might note in passing that under the main alternative political system, in its various forms from Lenin and Stalin to Pol Pot, many millions of people were not given even that choice. But our aim is never to have to face it at all; and deterrence is a key element of the policies on which our governments have consistently relied for ensuring that. It does not, of course, assume a constant and implacable hostile desire to attack us. It simply judges, in the light of history, that we cannot prudently assume we would never be attacked even if attack on us were a soft option.

Deterrence as Message

Let me now turn to what deterrence means and how it works in the world as it exists now. In essence, deterrence means transmitting a basically simple message. It says, "To whom it may concern: if you attack me, I will resist; I will go on resisting until you stop or until my strength fails; and if it is the latter, my strength will not fail before I have inflicted on you damage so heavy that you will be much worse off at the end than if you had never started; so do not start." We seek, essentially, to get that message across.

Communicating that simple-sounding message in the real world is a pretty complex affair, and it needs hard and clear thinking— even uncomfortable thinking. In one sense, that thinking is more difficult because we have little fact and experience to go on. The data on nuclear war are scanty, thank God; just two isolated uses, half a lifetime ago, by someone who had those weapons against someone who hadn't. Beyond that we are working in theory and inference and hypothesis. That's not to say we're dealing in hot air and guesswork. That would be very dangerous to suppose, since the penalties for failure to think things through might one day be appalling. We can't afford to polish our deterrence theory by experiment, by trial and error; one failure will be one too many. So however convoluted or abstract, or even repugnant, we may find the outpourings of the strategic theorists, it is not a mark of wisdom impatiently to brush them all aside. The penalty for overelaboration and overinsurance may perhaps be some waste of time and money; but the penalty for skimping our thinking, and for underinsurance, may be almost infinite.

Thinking deterrence through is quite a tough intellectual discipline, and scholars have filled libraries with books about it. We have to reflect on hypothetical sequences of events, thinking many moves ahead, so that no sequence could leave a potential adversary with a window, a risk-free track. We have to consider not just how our own leaders would feel able to act (though that obviously matters) but also how an adversary would react from a background of very different attitudes and standards; and how he might react not just now, but in future circumstances that may be very different — perhaps much more awkward, for us or for him — from today's. We need deterrence that will work not only in easy circumstances, in calm, but also under pressure. We have to work in abstract concepts and metaphors — thresholds and escalation ladders and signaling and so on — that can mislead us if we get careless about their meaning, if we mistake them for the reality for which they are shorthand.

Without leading you through all the intricacies of NATO's deterrence theory, I want now to pick out a few themes that current debate tends to misunderstand.

Links between conventional and nuclear forces. My first point concerns the relationship between nuclear and conventional forces in deterrence. One can legitimately argue about the right proportions between the two, either for individual countries or collectively. But people sometimes talk as though they were alternative methods of deterrence. They are not. NATO's deterrence, in today's world, needs them both, and neither can work without the other. No amount of nuclear power will be credible if we have no effective lesser response available for minor attacks; and no amount of conventional power can be sure of keeping us safe if there is one-sided nuclear power ranged against us. East-West deterrence cannot operate in separate nuclear and conventional boxes, or with either of them alone, because East-West war itself could not be guaranteed to operate in separate boxes, especially when we faced a potential adversary with the particular strengths of the Warsaw Pact. However we may decide to share out particular tasks within NATO, the Alliance as a whole must have both kinds of forces, interacting and interdependent in deterrence; and we all must accept a collective burden of responsibility for that.

It is worth noting, incidentally, that conventional forces are far more expensive than nuclear ones, so that people who want both more reliance on conventional forces and also lower defense expenditure are riding horses in somewhat divergent directions. Indeed, the vast bulk of military expenditure worldwide goes on conventional forces; if there is an arms race that needs to be stopped or slowed in order to release resources for, say, the Third World, that race is sharpest and costliest in the conventional field, not the nuclear.

"War fighting" and credibility. Confusion about "war fighting" seems to me at present the single most prevalent misconception about deterrence. The argument runs, briefly, that Western thinking about nuclear war is in the course of making a most dangerous shift: away from the concept of deterrence and—with the introduction of more accurate and more limited weapons, together with more conscious and systematic planning for nuclear contingencies short of instant, all-out holocaust—toward plans for really fighting nuclear wars. This worry is often sincerely felt, but it really is a total fallacy, resting on a complete misconception. The fact is that the deterrent effect of weapons and plans is not something separate from and independent of their capability for actual use; deterrence operates precisely *through* capability for actual use. Weapons that cannot realistically be used cannot deter; the more difficult they are to use in any rational way the less credible they are, and accordingly the less likely to deter. Moreover, if an adversary thinks we have no meaningful plans for use, he will think we have no serious will to resist. Like it or not, a kind of paradox lies inescapably at the heart of deterrence. The more likely it is that you will use your capability if you need to, the less likely it is that you will ever be faced with the need. And the converse is equally true. So people who recoil from more accurate weapons and less widespread targeting plans are in fact proposing less credible deterrence and therefore more risk of war.

Let it be clear, though, that what I am saying is that we must have weapons capable of credible use, and plans to match. I am not saying that use should be, or even could be, for winning victories in the classical sense. I simply do not believe in such a notion, nor does NATO, nor did the U.S. secretary of defense when he explained the updated American planning concepts that aroused so much comment in 1980. At least in the West, governments clearly accept that ideas of actually winning wars with nuclear weapons have no reality. When both sides possess almost infinite destructive power, the idea of wearing down the other side's power to the point of exhaustion simply becomes obsolete. Indeed, the only thing our nuclear weapons can really do for us — but it is a vital thing — is to place that basic truth plainly before the eyes of anyone contemplating aggression against us. But those weapons cannot make that truth plain, nor even keep it true, if they do not exist, or if they are not capable of use in ways an aggressor could find believable. Deterrence and a capability for war fighting — not war winning, but meaningful resistance — are two sides of a single coin.

Limited war and escalation. NATO does not believe that nuclear wars can be won in anything like the traditional sense. Still less, accordingly, does NATO believe in the idea of winning limited nuclear wars, of using nuclear weapons to help bring military operations to a successful and decisive conclusion in the classical sense. The destruction in even a so-called limited war — for example, across the territory of Western Europe — could be appalling. But even more fundamentally, the size of East-West nuclear armories and the means available to deliver them are such that whatever the course of any limited engagement with nuclear weapons, the side temporarily coming off worst would always have a powerful alternative to accepting defeat: it could escalate the fighting, raising the stakes.

Now we need to think particularly carefully about what lessons that has for our policies and our plans. You will find people who say that it proves that the possession of tactical or theater nuclear weapons is pointless, or that escalation is a certainty. It does not in fact prove either of those things. Escalation is not an inexorable scientific process; it is a matter of human decision, to be taken moreover in circumstances of which we have fortunately no fully comparable past experience. We do not know, and I hope we never find out, precisely how statesmen—or soldiers, for that matter—will react if these fearful weapons ever start to fly about. Anyone, however eminent, who tells us that escalation is a certainty, or who purports to put a tidy figure of percentage probability upon it, is talking through his hat. The reality is surely this: no aggressor could afford to bring down thousands of nuclear weapons on his homeland. If he attacks, therefore, it must be on a calculation that the defender lacks the resolve to use the weapons. There must be at least some possibility that when met by a nuclear response, even on a comparatively modest scale, he may reassess his earlier calculation and prefer to back off rather than take the risks of going on. NATO's policy in the field of theater nuclear weapons is based on maximizing that possibility, be it large or small. It is entirely sensible—indeed necessary—to be ready to exploit that possibility, while at the same time continuing to recognize that whatever we do, it will remain no more than a possibility. Furthermore, because it is precarious and the risks are appalling, the central aim must remain outright prevention—that is, preventing the whole process of East-West war from ever starting.

Preparedness and war prevention. Expressed another way, my argument is that we must aim at outright prevention, but that we must also do whatever we can, imperfect though it is bound to be, to leave ourselves practical courses of action if outright prevention fails. Preparedness is plain common sense, but it has a double value in the deterrent context. The more evident it is to an aggressor that we have options for effective resistance if war comes, the less likely it is that he will reckon war—with all its dangers for him—to be worth his while; so outright prevention is itself reinforced.

There is a line of argument heard nowadays from time to time that civil defense is a cruel deception, because tens of millions will die anyway if there is an all-out nuclear war. Of course, the effect of nuclear war could never be less than ghastly. But this argument implies, in logic, that if the effects of a disaster cannot be reduced to zero, preparations that could limit their scale are a cruel deception. It says, if you like, that we should not wear seat belts because they will not abolish all road casualties. The second strand of the argument is that civil defense preparation means we are expecting a nuclear war. That seems to me to say that people who wear seat belts are expecting to have more crashes than people who do not. And the third is that civil defense preparation means that one is actually disposed towards nuclear war. It is worth asking, if that were logical, what inference we should draw from the enormous Russian effort in civil defense, and what lessons might then follow for our own defense policies. But of course the argument isn't logical; it says, in effect, that people who wear seat belts tend to be more dangerous drivers than people who do not, which is observably untrue.

The fact is, for deterrence, that if you take no precautions at all you transmit to an adversary the message that you are simply not prepared to think about the consequences if he does attack and you then resist. That message does not underpin deterrence—it undermines it. There is here another of those hard paradoxes. To say that you are not prepared to contemplate the failure of deterrence is actually to make that failure more likely.

Let me make clear that I am not suggesting that in order to support civil defense it is necessary to believe in the standard NATO view of deterrence. That is plainly not so. The case for civil defense is valid also for those who take other views, including the outright pacifist view. But I do say that a civil defense effort is perfectly compatible with, and indeed helpful to, support for and confidence in deterrence.

Increasing stability. A lot of people, including some of great distinction, talk as though the whole system of deterrence were desperately precarious and perhaps becoming increasingly so. With all respect to those who deserve it, I believe this is mistaken. We must not be complacent, of course; the price of stability is continuing vigilance. And technical competition in many areas goes on unremittingly, save for a few where arms control agreements (of which I wish there were more) have slowed it or sealed it off. The precise military balance is not static. But that does not mean that the overall system is unstable. There are many reasons to the contrary. There is, for example, the very size of the armories and the knowledge of what they can do. No one who lives with the facts and has to think about them can ever be trigger-happy or other than enormously cautious. I venture to speak as someone who has worked with these matters on and off for over twenty years, and who has not, I hope, grown insensitive to the realities—I keep pictures of Hiroshima and Nagasaki in view from my office desk as a stark reminder. Five-figure numbers of these awful weapons on each side are far too many, and I wish the Russians had accepted the Carter proposals for deep cuts. But at least these vast numbers do mean that no one can suppose that he could somehow ride the punch on tolerable terms.

Despite ups and downs, communication, understanding, and agreement between the two sides is far more extensive than it was, say, in the 1960s. The SALT I and SALT II agreements are in practice being kept, even though the first has theoretically expired and the second has not been ratified. There is a Standing Consultative Commission meeting regularly to monitor the agreements reached. Antiballistic missile deployments, which in the 1960s appeared to be a real threat to stability, are now closely constrained by treaty. There are hotlines, regularly exercised. There are practical agreements to avoid encounters at sea, to explain accidents, to notify in advance missile launch tests whose purpose might be misunderstood, to consult together about dangerous international situations. Intelligence, especially through satellite photography, means that each side knows far more surely than before what the other is doing. The delivery systems themselves are far less vulnerable to preemptive strike than they used to be, so there is far less incentive to launch first and ask questions afterwards. Mobile cruise missiles will be much less vulnerable on the ground than the present F-111s and Vulcans; and it is perhaps worth remembering that in the mid-1960s Britain's own strategic force relied on V-bombers held on runway alert and needing to get off the ground within two or three minutes, whereas our force now rests on submarines hidden at sea. And at the political level I believe that even the passing years themselves, and the successive crises surmounted, deepen the inbuilt habit and understanding on both sides that nuclear weapons must not be used, and that whatever the disagreements, the two great power blocs therefore simply must not come to blows. I do not claim certainty here; certainty is not to be had. But I do believe that claims of perilous instability, of a world teetering on the brink, are neither well founded nor helpful to peace.

Flawed, but Working

I do not like the system of deterrence centered on nuclear weapons; it is an unlikeable thing, even an ugly one. I wish we had a better system, and I hope discussion and challenge in the search for a better system will continue. Meanwhile, I hope we can continue to improve the present system, making it still safer and if possible less expensive. It cannot solve everything. It is not a recipe for universal peace; it does not claim to prevent the Third World conflicts in which "conventional" wars have killed something like ten million people over the last thirty-five years (while nuclear wars haven't happened at all). But within its context, the context of NATO and the Warsaw Pact, our deterrence has worked; it still works; I believe it can go on working, and working safely, *provided* we stay clearheaded in identifying what it requires and resolute in doing what it requires. Deterrence is, in essence, a system for helping to cope with a hard world in which we have to reconcile two realities — that sources of deep conflict exist; and that alongside those sources there also exist the means of conducting conflict in intolerably destructive ways. I see no safer system than this now within our reach; and until I do, I would not choose to gamble by discarding this one.

III

Strategic Considerations

5

BRENT SCOWCROFT

Understanding the U.S. Strategic Arsenal

It is not possible to put into proper perspective the present and possible future force structures and strategies for employment of strategic nuclear forces without some understanding of the evolution of thought regarding what has come in the nuclear age to be called "strategic conflict." This specialized use of the term "strategic" really began with the development of the airplane as a weapon of war. It happened because the airplane appeared to offer for the first time the prospect of subjugating an opponent without first defeating his forces in the field or starving him into submission through blockade.

Douhet and Strategic Bombing

An early and influential apostle of this revolutionary approach to warfare was Italian General Guilio Douhet. Writing just after the close of World War I, he drew on many contemporary currents of thought evaluating the appearance of the airplane and its impact on warfare and wove them into a comprehensive strategy.[1] Douhet asserted, first, that World War I demonstrated the permanent ascendancy of the defense in land warfare. Proceeding from this assumption, he developed a strategy designed to avoid the protracted slaughter that characterized that war. Rapid victory could be achieved, he claimed, through the device of all-out air attack on the enemy, especially including the civilian population. The overall objective in this strategy was to break quickly the enemy's will to resist; it was for this reason that the civilian population became a main focus of the attack. While unrestricted aerial bombardment of civilians ran counter to generally accepted notions of morality and the rules of warfare, Douhet argued that it was actually more humane. The attack would be focused on those least able to resist it and the end would come quickly, thus avoiding the seemingly endless carnage of World War I.

It was all very simple and neat. Victory would go, after a brief but intense struggle, to the side that struck first with the greater strength. War had to be total, victory depending on the smashing of the material and moral resources of the enemy through unrestrained aerial bombardment.

As it turned out, Douhet grossly overestimated the destructive potential of the small conventionally armed airplanes of that era. Nonetheless, his theories received enthusiastic endorsement within military circles in a number of countries and, as we shall see, have endured as a principal philosophic tenet of modern strategic warfare. Indeed, it has been the nuclear weapon that, if anything, has seemed to vindicate Douhet's thesis.

There was no doubt about the influence of Douhet on the strategic bombing campaigns of World War II. Supporters of heavy emphasis on strategic bombing argued that it could make a potentially decisive contribution to early victory if sufficient resources were allocated to it. Controversy over the relative weight to be given to strategic bombing, however, continued to the end of the war. While U.S. targeting was basically a mixture of critical industrial targets and area bombardment, British bombing operations were heavily oriented against large urban areas, in the best Douhet tradition.

In terms of Douhet's fundamental thesis, the bombing campaigns of World War II were a failure. The tonnage of bombs dropped exceeded by vast amounts anything Douhet had envisioned. It is apparent that the bombing of industrial "bottlenecks"—i.e., production sites of critical materials such as ball bearings—had a significant effect on the German war effort; for example, many German fighter aircraft could not be employed because of a shortage of fuel resulting from aerial bombing attacks. Had such bombing begun sooner, or had the war continued longer, it is conceivable that strategic bombardment might have had a decisive effect. But the results actually obtained were achieved only over an extended period of time and in conjunction with heavy ground fighting that consumed resources at a tremendous rate. With regard to population bombing, there is little evidence that the direct targeting of cities and civilian populations devastated German morale or greatly affected the war effort.[2] However important the effects of the bombing may have been, therefore, they hardly vindicated Douhet's thesis.

Massive Retaliation

It was the advent of the nuclear weapon that gave new life to the Douhetan outlook. The ability of the nuclear weapon, in very small numbers, to wreak unbelievable havoc on an opponent seemed to constitute the quick destructive capability necessary to validate Douhet's arguments. The doctrine of "massive retaliation," announced by Secretary of State Dulles in 1954, appeared to embody the quintessence of Douhet in a manner Douhet could not have imagined. Not only had the United States acquired the ability to devastate the Soviet Union quickly and with relatively modest forces, but that country had virtually no reciprocal capability against the United States.

The strategy of massive retaliation marked the triumph of the Douhet philosophy. It came as a logical outgrowth both of the development of nuclear weapons and of the political and strategic circumstances of the time. The United States had only recently concluded the Korean War. That conflict was widely believed at the time to have been the wrong war against the wrong enemy. The U.S. had become "bogged down" in an "old-fashioned" ground conflict in which the relative advantage lay with its militarily unsophisticated opponent. Moreover, in 1952 NATO had postulated a force in excess of ninety divisions as being required to cope with a Soviet attack on Western Europe.

Given these circumstances and the strategic (nuclear) balance between the United States and the Soviet Union, massive retaliation made considerable military sense. It appeared to be an effective and cheap way of dealing with Soviet aggression utilizing massive conventional forces. Rather than combat Soviet forces on their own terms and in areas of Soviet choosing, the United States could threaten to escalate any conflict to the strategic or intercontinental nuclear level where it was absolutely dominant. Possible or probable conflict outcomes at any lower levels of hostility could be reversed by elevating that conflict to the strategic nuclear level, where the United States had unquestioned strategic superiority, even supremacy. The Soviet Union understood this well and would therefore be deterred from any aggression. The obvious implication of this strategy was that the United States would initiate the use of nuclear weapons. This threat to respond to Soviet military moves with a Douhetan strategy—conceived, however, as a means of *preventing* rather than winning a conflict —ushered in the contemporary concept of "deterrence."

The principal problem with massive retaliation was not its military utility, for in fact it promised to permit great savings in conventional land, sea, and air forces while still protecting U.S. interests worldwide. Its chief liability was its questionable political credibility. That the United States would actually employ nuclear weapons against Moscow for anything but the gravest of provocations was at least questionable. As a consequence of the doubts about its political credibility, massive retaliation was not seriously applied outside Europe. Within NATO, however, much of the military history since 1954 has consisted of efforts by the United States to improve the credibility of massive retaliation, by such means as deploying tactical nuclear weapons, strengthening conventional forces, and switching to a strategy of "flexible response."

Development of the Triad

As the Soviet Union proceeded to develop its own nuclear weapons, with the intercontinental ballistic missile (ICBM) as the primary means of their delivery, concern naturally developed about the possible vulnerability of the U.S. bomber force. The result of this—together with other factors such as questions over the continued ability of the bombers to penetrate increasingly elaborate Soviet air defenses, and interservice rivalry—was the development of a multiforce strategic nuclear delivery capability consisting of bombers, ICBMs, and submarine-launched ballistic missiles (SLBMs).

The diversity of these elements came to be a very valuable characteristic of the overall force, for each element has its unique strengths and weaknesses. The bomber force has great flexibility in targeting and accuracy, can visibly demonstrate increased readiness, and is the only force that can be recalled. Bombers are very vulnerable to attack while at their bases, however, and must rely for survival on warning of attack, permitting them to escape before incoming missiles arrive. The bomber force is expensive to operate, has low alert rates, takes several hours to reach its targets, and must itself, or at present the cruise missiles it may be carrying, penetrate heavy Soviet air defenses.

The ICBM force possesses great accuracy, the most reliable communications, immediate responsiveness, a very high alert rate, and very low operating expenses. Until recently, the ICBM force did not require warning, in that Soviet missiles were not sufficiently accurate to destroy ICBM silos. This situation is changing, however, and the issue of ICBM vulnerability is one of the most acute strategic problems facing the United States at the present time.

The SLBM force, when deployed at sea, is the most survivable, with the shortest flight time to target. However, accuracies are not sufficient to permit the attack of hardened targets (this should no longer be the case after deployment of the D-5 missile near the end of the decade) and communications are less assured; it is also expensive to operate and has low alert rates (compared to the ICBM).

This multipartite force greatly complicates Soviet strategic planning and force requirements, both offensive and defensive. It provides as well a substantial hedge against the possibility of catastrophic failure of one or more elements of the strategic force or of a Soviet technological or operational breakthrough jeopardizing survivability of any portion of the force.

The Emergence of "Assured Destruction"

Nonetheless, the continued growth of Soviet strategic forces in size and diversity generated a debate in the United States regarding the targeting philosophy for the employment of U.S. strategic weapons. When Soviet strategic forces were small, they could easily be included in a grand Douhetan-type attack. By the early 1960s, however, it was apparent that this would not continue to be true much longer. In view of these changing conditions, the question arose: should U.S. forces continue to rely on a massive retaliation type of attack or should they be gradually increased to whatever level necessary to cover expanding Soviet forces? The new but in many ways very traditional argument was that the employment strategy of strategic forces should be oriented on enemy forces (counterforce), not on urban areas; the aim would be to aid in the prevention, through the destruction of those forces, of a devastating nuclear attack on the United States (damage limitation).

Positions in this debate ranged from those who argued that the United States should maintain a full capability to destroy all Soviet strategic forces (credible first strike) to those who believed that nuclear war could be deterred by the possession of only a few nuclear weapons sufficiently survivable that they could be reliably delivered on Soviet cities even after the worst possible Soviet attack (minimum deterrence).[3]

The massive retaliation philosophy prevailed. The targeting doctrine finally adopted during the Kennedy administration was that of "assured destruction." The concept of assured destruction was based on the assumption that a Soviet attack on the United States could be deterred by the possession of a capability to destroy a certain percentage of industrial floor space and a certain percentage of the Soviet population, even after absorbing a Soviet attack on U.S. strategic forces. The percentages required to constitute such a deterrence were argued at length, but the principle became the basis on which, for many years, U.S. strategic forces were developed.

Assured destruction, as it was designed, was more a device to bound the size of U.S. strategic forces than a way to specify precisely what Soviet targets should be attacked. Indeed, U.S. targeting continued to include a wide range of Soviet military forces. But despite the original intent, the concept itself—a Douhetan approach oriented toward the prevention of strategic conflict rather than toward the attainment of victory—tended to become the dominant thesis governing U.S. attitudes toward strategic nuclear forces.

As the size and sophistication of Soviet forces grew, they inevitably fulfilled the requirements themselves of an assured destruction force. Thus dawned the era of mutual assured destruction, with its all-too-apt acronym, "MAD." Since an assured destruction capability is relatively insensitive to comparative force size, it was widely assumed, after the United States adopted the policy of assured destruction, that the Soviet Union would build its own forces until it acquired a similar capability but would stop well short of the point of equality of numbers with U.S. forces. When, despite that assumption, the Soviets continued building past the point at which they appeared to have a capability for assured destruction, their failure to stop was rationalized on the grounds that the Soviet goal was still only an assured destruction capability but that the Soviets' psychological sense of inferiority required equality with the United States. The failure of the Soviet Union to stop even after reaching or surpassing most measures of equality, however, has profound implications for the strategic assumptions that have provided the basis from which the United States has proceeded for many years (see figure 1).

Soviet Strategic Thought

An analysis of what we know of Soviet strategic thinking, force deployment, and force employment reveals little reason to believe that the Soviet Union shares many of the U.S. attitudes regarding strategic nuclear war. The fundamental premise of Douhet has seemingly been widely accepted in the United States, although ap-

Figure 1

USSR Fourth Generation ICBMs

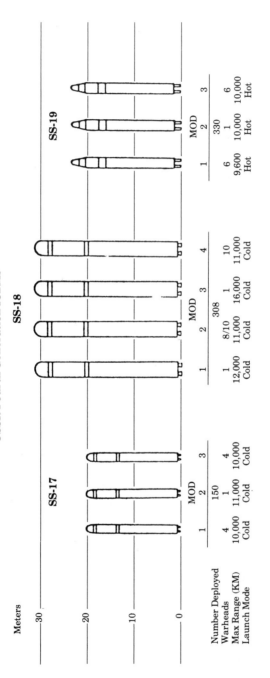

	SS-17			SS-18				SS-19		
MOD	1	2	3	1	2	3	4	1	2	3
Number Deployed		150			308				330	
Warheads	4	1	4	1	8/10	1	10	6	1	6
Max Range (KM)	10,000	11,000	10,000	12,000	11,000	16,000	11,000	9,600	10,000	10,000
Launch Mode	Cold	Cold	Cold	Cold	Cold	Cold	Cold	Hot	Hot	Hot

U.S. ICBMs

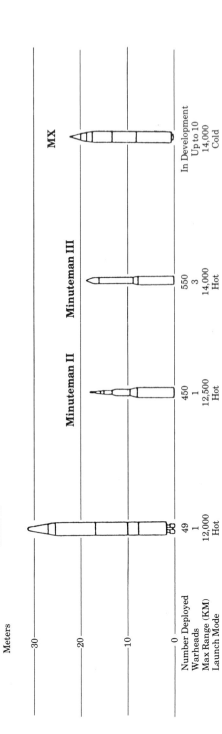

Source: U.S. Department of Defense, *Soviet Military Power 1983* (Washington, D.C.: U.S. Government Printing Office, 1983), p. 20.

plied not to the strategy for fighting a war but to the requirement for deterring war. That is, it has been widely assumed that nuclear war would be such a catastrophe that it could not happen or be allowed to happen. In contrast to Douhet's approach, however, these notions tended to reject outright the concept that there could be a "winner" in any meaningful sense as a result of substantial nuclear exchange.

Soviet premises appear to be different. First, the Douhetan idea of inflicting pain on the population as the quickest route to victory apparently did not really take root in the Soviet Union in the interwar period.[4] Military air forces, including bombers, by and large remained an adjunct to army and naval forces, in at least implicit rejection of the notion of victory through the application solely of aerial bombardment. Thus nuclear weapons have apparently been incorporated into Soviet strategic thought as a part of a combined arms concept, rather than as a distinct revolution overturning traditional concepts and objectives of warfare. In addition, the Soviets, as a result both of their history and of their ideological assumption of inevitable conflict between social systems and therefore of a hostile world, may be more inclined to accept the idea that, despite the awesome destructive power of nuclear weapons, war can still occur.

In light of apparent Soviet assumptions about the conceivability of nuclear war, and the "traditional" manner in which the Soviets have integrated nuclear weapons into their military concepts and doctrine, their military planning would logically be based on the notion of fighting a nuclear war successfully, however they may define that term. Given all these circumstances, it is hardly surprising that the USSR has never indicated any acceptance of the validity of the concept of assured destruction. It seems to run counter to all their developed and inherited attitudes about warfare.

The Soviets may be wrong. The very concept of victory may, as we tend to believe, have no possible meaning in the context of strategic nuclear warfare. With respect to deterrence of such a conflict, however, the question of who is right and who is wrong is not relevant. The only operative factor is what the Soviets believe. In the terminology of deterrence, the difference between these two attitudes can be defined in terms of the contrast between deter-

rence through pain and deterrence through denial. Under the latter form of deterrence, the Soviets would perceive that the United
States has both the military ability and the will to deny them attainment of their objectives. By contrast, deterrence through pain
means that the Soviets would believe that the United States has
the military ability and the will to inflict so much destruction
(pain) on the Soviet Union that attainment of their objectives
would not be worth those costs. While most Americans seem to
think more or less automatically in terms of deterrence through
pain, a fully prudent policy of deterrence, especially in light of apparent Soviet attitudes, would seem to require operating on the
basis of deterrence through denial.

The implications of that distinction for our strategic forces are
substantial. They impinge on most major strategic weapon decisions. They are at the heart of the assumptions of those who
charge that the United States already has strategic weapon "over-

Figure 2

**US and Soviet ICBM Launcher and Reentry
Vehicle (RV) Deployment, 1968–1983**

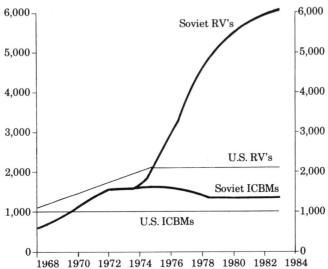

Source: U.S. Department of Defense, *Soviet Military Power 1983* (Washington, D.C.: U.S.
Government Printing Office, 1983), p. 19.

kill" and conversely of those who seek to regain strategic superiority or a "margin of safety" with respect to Soviet forces.

The development of multiple, independently targetable reentry vehicles (MIRVs) has also had a major impact on strategic force structure and policy (see figure 2). MIRVs were originally conceived as a means of overcoming an antiballistic missile (ABM) defense system, by saturating the defense with more targets than could be managed by the radar and fire control systems. With the negotiation of the ABM Treaty, completed in 1972, that need for multiple warheads disappeared, but their deployment continued, stimulated in part by two related factors. The first of these was economic efficiency. It is considerably more "cost-effective"—cheaper—to put a number of warheads on one launcher than it is to provide a launcher and associated equipment for each warhead. Another factor, surprisingly enough, was arms control. The unit of weapon limitation negotiated in the SALT I agreement was the missile launcher, not the missile itself or its warhead or warheads. There were compelling reasons for this at the time. Verification of compliance with the treaty was to be provided through "national technical means." That is, each side was to ensure, through its own intelligence systems, compliance with the restrictions of the treaty. Missile silos, submarines, and bombers were relatively easy to count and to monitor. Missiles and warheads, however, were at that time considered to be beyond national capability to verify. The practical effect of this "counting rule" was to provide an incentive to both sides to multiply the number of individual weapons, or warheads, to be installed in each launcher or silo.

The deployment of MIRVed systems, however, has a tendency to produce instability, especially in a crisis. This results from the fact that a MIRVed missile is a valuable target. If an attacker can destroy several warheads with one, as is the case when attacking MIRVed missiles, he will be relatively better off after such an attack than he was before. There is thus a temptation to plan to attack first should it appear that war is inevitable.

That same situation exists with bomber forces, each bomber having several individual weapons aboard, and it is compounded in the case of submarines. A single Trident submarine could carry around 200 warheads, making its value to an attacker enormous. Unlike the ICBM, however, the bomber and the SLBM submarine are difficult to locate except when at their bases. This difficulty of bringing them under attack has thus far more than compensated for the high-value targets that they represent.

U.S. ICBM Vulnerability

U.S. ICBMs were once themselves relatively invulnerable. While their location has always been known, the hardness of their silos has provided effective protection against attacks by warheads with only limited accuracy. The increasing accuracy of Soviet warheads, however, together with growth in their number and size, has now raised the possibility of the virtual elimination of the U.S. ICBM force by only a small fraction of the Soviet ICBM force. This increasing vulnerability is a serious strategic problem for the United States. Should it be followed by some Soviet technical development that could result in the comparable vulnerability of one or both of the remaining elements of our strategic forces, U.S. security would be placed in serious jeopardy.

The immediate problem, however, is not really the possibility of a deliberate Soviet attack designed to take advantage of U.S. ICBM vulnerability. Soviet leadership has a record of cautious behavior, influenced both by Russian national character and by ideology. To the extent that ideology still influences Soviet behavior, it teaches that historical forces operate on the side of socialism, that the task of the Soviet system is not to create history but to be the midwife of history, lending a helping hand on the inexorable march to ultimate victory. There is, therefore, no incentive to risk everything on a single roll of the dice.

The problem is really quite different. Any scenario for strategic nuclear war has a strong air of unreality about it, and those involving deliberate, calculated surprise attack have the additional artificiality that they run counter to the philosophical makeup of the Soviet system. Nonetheless, U.S. and Soviet views of the world, society, and man's place in it are fundamentally antithetical. This circumstance—coupled with the fact that the two superpowers impinge on each other with conflicting interests around the world, and that Soviet leaders are inclined at least to assist groups creating instability and having the potential of moving the world in a "socialist" direction—dictates almost necessarily that the two systems will be in competition and sometimes confrontation for as far into the future as one can usefully project.

It is in the course of this competition and these possible confrontations that critical dangers can arise. It is at these times that Soviet calculations of the "correlation of forces"—together with assumptions about the nature of nuclear conflict and the character of the forces and military doctrine constructed in reflection of these attitudes—assume critical importance. A confident Soviet assessment, for example, that in light of these factors the United States will obviously have to concede first in a crisis, could create the conditions from which conflict is very likely to arise. Put another way, in analyzing the circumstances out of which a strategic nuclear conflict between the superpowers could emerge, the immediate antecedents of World War I are much more illuminating than are those of World War II.

The task of the United States is to procure and maintain a structure of military forces, and a willingness to employ them, such that, regardless of the nature of circumstances of a confrontation when U.S. vital interests are involved, the Soviet Union can never logically make the evaluation outlined above. In calculating such a force posture, it is also important to consider that the force necessary to deter a "bolt from the blue" surprise attack may not be sufficient to deter in the circumstances of the tension and chaos of a crisis, especially if the political extinction of the leaders or regime may appear to be at stake.

"Overinsurance" vs. "Underinsurance"

Would such a strategic force be "excessive"? How much insurance against the failure of deterrence is warranted? One of the most troublesome aspects of deterrence is not only that it is inherently ambiguous, but that it can be tested only in its failure. If such a force is in excess of the essential requirements of deterrence, then procuring it will result in the waste of tens of billions of dollars. If in reality it is not excessive, however, and we do not procure it, we may in fact be encouraging the nuclear conflict we all seek to avoid. Given the stakes involved, overinsurance seems clearly preferable to underinsurance.

The United States is at the present time moving in the direction of the acquisition of such a force capability. It should be recognized that there are alternative ways to achieve the goal. One route is to rely solely on an arms buildup; another is to rely on arms control measures that would adjust the comparative force postures to achieve a comparable result. An obvious third course is to combine the first two, with the ratio between them dependent on the degree of success of negotiations with the Soviet Union. Yet with respect to negotiations, there should be no such thing as a weapon system designed and developed to be a "bargaining chip" in arms control negotiations. "Bargaining chip" weapons can be defined as weapons that are not developed for their contribution to the deterrent posture just described but are designed solely to be used as a "quid" to trade for a Soviet "quo." Such systems are not likely long to survive the U.S. budget process, nor are they likely to be taken very seriously by Soviet planners. While there are, or should be, no "bargaining chips," weapon systems designed to contribute to the essential requirements of our national security can be given up or traded away if arms control can offer an alternative way to achieve a comparable result.

The MX missile, for example, is not designed to be a "bargaining chip" in the usual sense of the term. It is important to the U.S. force structure for a number of reasons. Among these is a need to restore at least in part a balance in the capability for prompt, highly accurate attack. The present Soviet advantage in this regard contributes to instability. In addition, the MX is an important inducement for the Soviets toward serious arms control negotiations and toward a modification of ICBM forces (on both sides) that could enhance strategic stability. If these objectives can be obtained without full, or even partial, deployment of the proposed numbers of missiles, the MX will have made its contribution to the U.S. national security. It is enhanced national security that should be our goal, not the specific deployment of any strategic system as an end in itself.

At the present time there are either plans or programs for the modernization of all elements of U.S. strategic forces, designed to ameliorate their weaknesses and capitalize on their strengths. For example, the principal problems of the bomber force are destruction before launch or safe escape from the vicinity of the airfield, and penetration through Soviet defenses to the target. The latter problem is being dealt with in two ways. First, the aging B-52 is being equipped with cruise missiles that will permit it to launch its weapons from outside Soviet defensive networks and avoid the necessity to engage those defenses. Second, the B-1 and its successor, the Stealth aircraft, are being developed to improve our ability to penetrate the ever-improving Soviet defensive systems.

Protection against pre-launch destruction of the bomber force is difficult. The bomber is a very "soft" or easily destroyed target, and airfields are not difficult to render inoperable, at least temporarily. The B-1 will be able to escape to a safe distance in less time than is currently required for the B-52, and basing the bomber fleet at interior airfields obviously maximizes the time available for escape. But there seems no way short of continuous airborne alert to avoid the requirement for tactical warning if the bomber fleet is to survive. The Triad itself, however, provides an additional measure of protection in a different sense. While bombers are vulnerable to sabotage and at least some airfields to attack by close-to-shore Soviet SLBMs, the fact of that attack would alert the ICBM force in time to prevent its destruction in its silos.

Conversely, an ICBM attack on the U.S. ICBM force would alert the bomber force and allow sufficient time for safe escape of that portion on alert. The survivability that the bomber and ICBM forces thus lend to each other will endure until the USSR improves the accuracy of its SLBM force sufficiently to permit it to destroy ICBM silos.

The SLBM force suffers from the same kind of vulnerability as the bomber at its home base. At sea, however, the submarine is at present largely invulnerable and its weapons, under the protection of the ABM Treaty, have no significant problems of penetration. Modernization programs under way enhance submarine invulnerability by extending their operating areas and making the vessels more quiet. Programs under way for SLBM improvement will give the sea-based leg of the Triad sufficient accuracy to allow attack of hardened targets.

The submarine force has two handicaps, one actual and one theoretical. The current weakness relates to flexibility of communications. While communications to the submarine force have been greatly improved and further progress continues to be made, retargeting instructions or other communications during the course of a conflict, after at least some communication terminals could be expected to have been destroyed, could become complicated.

For years there have been gloomy prophesies predicting a breakthrough in antisubmarine warfare that would make submarines "visible" and thus susceptible to attack. It has not yet happened and perhaps never will. However remote that possibility, however, it is not zero and, as noted earlier, the high value of the submarine as a target provides enormous incentive to the Soviets to invest heavily in an attempt to achieve a breakthrough in detection. Even should that happen, of course, countermeasures could be expected to be developed and, as a consequence, submarine invulnerability may degrade only gradually. As a hedge against such an eventuality, and as a measure to improve force stability, it might be prudent to consider successor submarines that would be considerably smaller. This would reduce target value for the Soviets and permit deployment of more systems, thus enhancing stability and magnifying Soviet attack problems.

The principal problem of the Triad at the present time is that of ICBM vulnerability. The Soviets have capitalized on their big missile boosters to add large numbers of warheads and have succeeded in developing for those warheads sufficient accuracy to destroy U.S. ICBM silos. This development alone should provide an indication of a lack of dedication on the part of the Soviets to concepts of assured destruction. Whatever the motive, the vulnerability is growing and carries with it psychological, if not military, liabilities. In addition, this development is but the foreshadowing of a new era, an era of virtually infinite accuracy, when any undefended fixed target that can be located can be destroyed.

Coping with Improvements in Accuracy

What is the best means of coping with the threat that accuracy brings? There are several courses of action available. One is to abandon the ICBM in favor of reliance on the bomber and SLBM forces, but there are two principal drawbacks to this option. The first is that it would represent the abandonment of the synergistic effects of the Triad, both the disparate strengths and weaknesses of the different parts and the extent to which the Soviets must spread their resources to deal with a multiplicity of systems presenting a variety of offensive and defensive problems.

The other drawback is that the Triad is the chief hedge against technological breakthrough or catastrophic failure. Right now the ICBM force is threatened. If the United States had no other strategic forces, what is now a serious concern could become a disaster. Future technological threats against the bomber or the SLBM force cannot be excluded. Indeed, it would be advantageous if the United States could expand the Triad to a Quadrad or even a Pentad. Solving the vulnerability problem of the ICBM today could provide a critical hedge against a Soviet breakthrough in antisubmarine warfare (ASW), in air defense, or in ability to barrage the bomber force. The stakes are very high, and spreading the risk over a number of different systems is a prudent response.

Another possible response to the threat of increased accuracy is an antiballistic missile defense of the ICBM force. At least two problems have plagued ABM since the achievement of the technical ability to intercept an incoming missile warhead. The first of these is saturation of the defense. Proliferation of warheads, or decoys, poses immense problems for the ability of the defense to identify, track, and destroy each incoming vehicle. Unlike the requirement for perfection in a defense of population centers, however, a defense of ICBM silos can allow considerable "leakage," and technology is increasing the ability of the defense to cope with saturation attacks. Also contributing to the capability of the defense would be ICBM basing that permitted preferential defense or otherwise provided leverage to the defense forces.

Another ABM weakness is the vulnerability of the radar. By concentrating on the ABM radar or utilizing a precursor attack, the attacker can, if successful, blind the defense and render it virtually useless. Redundancy, mobility, and deception all can assist in reducing radar vulnerability.

Still another difficulty with utilization of ballistic missile defense (BMD) as a means of reducing the vulnerability of land-based missiles is the ABM Treaty between the United States and the USSR, in force since 1972. This treaty in effect prevents virtually all of at least the currently possible developments in BMD essential to its viability and effectiveness. The existence of the treaty has undoubtedly inhibited much research and development in the United States on improving the effectiveness of BMD, almost certainly to a much greater degree than has been the case in the Soviet Union.

There is little question of the theoretical potential for BMD to play a role in ICBM (and command-and-control) survivability. However, while there is an intense debate over the contribution that BMD could currently make, knowledgeable opinion seems to lean slightly to the view that potentially decisive benefits are still some time in the future, at least for ICBM systems in launching modes that offer substantial leverage, whether through the use of decoys or other similar measures.

The Role of Concealment and Mobility

Still other recourses against the growing threat of accuracy are mobility, deception or concealment, and reduction of the value of the target to the extent that an attack becomes militarily unremunerative. These measures can apply to all strategic systems, though the current critical problem is the ICBM force. Mobility and deception or concealment can be interdependent. For example, it is difficult to imagine, at least in the United States, deception or concealment being preserved indefinitely without mobility. On the other hand, mobility does not necessarily require deception as well, so long as the mobility is sufficiently rapid to move the target outside of the lethal radius of an attacking weapon in a period shorter than the intelligence cycle of the attacker.*

Providing mobility for an ICBM on the public transportation network of the United States would create serious problems of public interface. Restricting deployment of the missile system to U.S. military reservations could invite their destruction not by an attack directed at individual weapons, but instead by an area or barrage attack designed to put an "overpressure" over the entire area of deployment sufficient to destroy or render unusable all systems within the area. A barrage attack can be thwarted by taking steps that make it, in terms of numbers and size of warheads

---

* "Intelligence cycle" refers to the time required to locate a target, convey the location to attacking weapons, retarget those weapons on the new target, and place them on that target.

expended to create the required overpressure, too expensive in comparison with the weapons that would be destroyed. This can be done through a combination of the size of the deployment area utilized and the hardness (resistance to destruction) of the individual missile and transporter. The larger the deployment area and the more resistant the weapon system to nuclear effects, the more weapons would be required to disable the target missiles through barrage attack.

Finally, there is the expedient of reducing the value of the target, making its destruction more expensive than is warranted by the capability of the target weapon. There are two principal ways to do this—either through deception or by reducing to a minimum the value of the target itself.

Deception (and mobility) have already been discussed. One specific scheme to take advantage of deception to reduce the value of the target (or, conversely, to increase the cost of destroying it) was the multiple protective shelter (MPS) deployment system proposed by the Carter administration for the MX missile. Each missile was to be rotated deceptively among twenty-three shelters. With the Soviets not knowing which shelter housed the missile, they would be required to attack all twenty-three shelters, thus expending twenty-three warheads, or more probably forty-six, in order to destroy ten.[5] As long as deception was maintained, therefore, the MPS system would have been the functional equivalent of placing less than half a warhead in each shelter.

Another way to achieve similar results would be to remove all but one warhead from each launcher, thus de-MIRVing the ICBM force. The result would be that it would take more than one warhead to destroy one (given two-on-one targeting for reliability), an unattractive exchange ratio. The ratio can be made even worse by deploying single-warhead missiles in deceptive basing such as MPS.

Greatest stability can probably be obtained through adoption of a single-warhead missile. Unlike the use of deception to render the exchange ratio unfavorable, it does not depend on maintenance of that deception to prevent catastrophic failure of the system or on the very elaborate and costly devices that provide mobility for a very large MIRVed missile. As noted above, to the inherently stable qualities of the single-warhead missile can also be added deception, mobility, and defense, creating a system against which an attack would be singularly unattractive.

Were the United States and the Soviet Union to concur in developing their ICBM forces in the direction of a small missile, a new strategic situation could eventually emerge. Since it would make little sense to attack the ICBM forces, redoubled efforts would perhaps be directed toward attacks on command-and-control and communications (C³), in an attempt to separate the political leadership from management of the strategic forces. Additional efforts might also go into ASW, given the extremely high value of each ballistic missile submarine, and perhaps as well into defense against bomber/cruise missile attack.

Ballistic missile defense may or may not receive emphasis. As discussed above, it could be of value in protecting bombers, C³ sites, or even ballistic missile submarines. However, as a means of defending area targets such as cities, ABM defense is a much more dubious prospect. The fact that a single nuclear warhead is so devastatingly destructive against population centers means that no "leakage" by the defensive system can be permitted. The prospect of creating such a perfect military system, even through the use of such exotic devices as directed energy beams, is a daunting one. If it could be done, it could alter in a most fundamental way our circumstances in the nuclear age. Both sides can be expected to pursue vigorously research and development programs on advanced ABM systems. Even if such devices, together with their associated acquisition and aiming equipment, should prove practical, effective countermeasures could also be expected to be developed. Finally, if all these problems were to be successfully surmounted, such a system would have to be deployed either cooperatively or in such a manner that the prospect of its being successful did not prove to be so destabilizing as to make an attack before it was fully in place a serious possibility.

Space is also likely to receive greater attention, especially in terms of its value for C³ and intelligence platforms. Space as a full-fledged medium for strategic warfare is likely to develop slowly, if at all, even in the absence of arms control. Space objects are expensive, cannot be concealed, and are not easily defended. In addition, space is likely to remain for some time a means to an end rather than a military objective in its own right. For the next several decades, therefore, space conflict may remain an ancillary activity rather than an objective in itself.

Conventional forces may also increasingly be the object of strategic attack. Indeed, if one can assume that any strategic nuclear conflict between the United States and the Soviet Union would most probably arise from confrontation or aggression at lower levels, conventional forces should already be a high priority for attack.

There is one possible outgrowth of enhanced stability for ICBM forces that could be less than beneficial. It could, in fact, bring us back full circle to the old Douhet notion of warfare. If the strategic military systems on both sides were to become, by and large, impervious to attack, might not any conflict then become, once again, the exchange of pain? It is to be profoundly hoped that, instead, the effect would be simply to reduce the chances of nuclear war to the lowest possible level given the existence of nuclear weapons. More than that, perhaps, cannot be expected in an international system of competitive states. Despite the idealistic dreams of many, nuclear weapons cannot be "dis-invented." In any world that can be foreseen at the moment, therefore, our goal should be that stability which reduces to the lowest possible degree the chances that nuclear warfare will occur.

6

WILLIAM J. PERRY

Technological Prospects for U.S. Strategic Forces

Four distinct characteristics of strategic forces have a direct effect on their capabilities:

1. *Lethality*—the ability of forces to destroy an assigned target even if the target is hardened; lethality is determined by the accuracy with which the nuclear warheads can be delivered and the number and yield of those warheads;

2. *Survivability*—the ability of delivery systems to survive a surprise attack while they are still at or near their bases;

3. *Penetrativity*—the ability of missiles and aircraft to defeat or evade an active defense while carrying out their strike mission;

This is a modified and updated version of the author's "Technological Prospects," ch. 6 of *Rethinking the U.S. Strategic Posture,* ed. Barry M. Blechman (Cambridge, Mass.: Ballinger, 1982). Copyright 1982, the Aspen Institute for Humanistic Studies. Reprinted with permission from Ballinger Publishing Company.

4. *Connectivity*—the ability of national command authorities to determine the status of, and transmit commands to, the various elements of strategic forces in the presence of a variety of disrupting factors, including nuclear detonations and countermeasures.

Current U.S. strategic forces were conceived in the 1950s and for the most part developed in the 1960s. The technologies of that era allowed the development of strategic forces that could survive any attack then considered plausible and could penetrate known active defenses with a residual force whose lethality was more than adequate to execute their deterrence mission. During the 1970s, there were dramatic changes in the technologies that affect these four fundamental characteristics of strategic forces and that continue unabated in this decade. These changes necessitate a review of the assumptions that originally defined U.S. strategic forces in order to determine how to maintain viability throughout the rest of this century.

Lethality

Well-advanced technical developments in the U.S., which lag about five years in the Soviet Union, are converging toward "infinite" lethality for nuclear weapons. Because of improvements in guidance technology, reentry technology, and propulsion technology, we are developing weapons that approach perfect accuracy and that have ever-increasing numbers of warheads.

Accuracy. The inertial guidance systems already on our operational weapons have accuracies that give them some probability of destroying even very hard targets, such as missile silos. In the course of the next decade, improvements will be made in inertial systems that will reduce delivery error to about one-half what it is now. Given the lethal radius of nuclear warheads, this approaches what could be called "zero circular error probable" (CEP), since it assures destruction of each target that is engaged.

In a sense, this is the nuclear equivalent of the precision-guided munitions now being deployed with conventional forces. Nearly equivalent accuracies will be achievable for submarine missiles in the near future, using the same inertial components combined with a stellar (star-seeking) system to compensate for the inaccuracies that come from the uncertainty of the submarine position at launch.

Even better accuracies could be achieved by employing a terminal guidance system. The cruise missile employs a form of terminal guidance called TERCOM, which has accuracies several times better than those derived from the inertial systems on land-based intercontinental ballistic missiles (ICBMs). A similar scene-matching guidance system is used with the Pershing II missile and could be adapted to ICBMs or submarine-launched ballistic missiles (SLBMs). Another form of very accurate guidance system positions itself by reference to new navigation satellites (NAVSTAR). Six of those satellites are already in orbit, and the program calls for eighteen to be in orbit by the late 1980s. With the appropriate radio receiver and computer, any vehicle can locate itself at any time and any point to very fine accuracies. NAVSTAR is intended for navigational purposes for ships, airplanes, ground vehicles, and Trident submarines. Also, during the test program of the Trident missile, it is being used as an instrumentation system to check on the accuracy of the missile's stellar-inertial guidance system. Had it been decided to "close the loop," NAVSTAR could have been converted into a very accurate guidance system for either submarine-launched missiles or for ICBMs. Richard Garwin has proposed a variation of this scheme called "inverted" NAVSTAR. This system envisions beacons like those in the satellites but deployed on the ground in quantities of hundreds to allow a guidance input to SLBMs or ICBMs from any position within line-of-sight of those ground beacons. ICBM accuracies better than those based on advanced all-inertial systems could be achieved with such a system. In sum, a variety of different technical paths to extremely high accuracies for either ICBMs or SLBMs will be available by the end of the decade.

Reentry technology and propulsion technology. Coupled to improvements in accuracy will be further developments in the technology of multiple, independently targetable reentry vehicles (MIRVs). The MX missile will be able to carry from ten to fourteen warheads the size of the current Minuteman warhead (Mk 12A). It could be designed to carry up to twenty warheads of the size of the Trident warhead. The latter option would be technically attractive with guidance system accuracies on the order of 100 meters. The Soviets would have considerable potential for increasing the number of RVs on their SS-18 and SS-19 missiles if they made improvements in the efficiency of their warhead designs or if they accepted a lower-yield warhead as they improved guidance accuracies. Both the SS-18 and SS-19 could accommodate at least twice as many Minuteman-size warheads as they now carry and three times as many Trident-size warheads.

The effect of improvements in reentry technology will be to allow the United States (and the Soviets) to put more warheads in a given payload. At the same time, propulsion efficiency is improving significantly, which allows a greater payload to be put on a missile of a given size. These two factors taken together indicate that, for a missile of a given size, the number of warheads and the amount of destructive power are going to increase manyfold in the next decade. The United States, for example, could develop the capability to carry twenty to thirty warheads on a single ICBM. Already, twenty cruise missiles are being placed on one B-52 bomber, and that number could increase to thirty with propulsion improvements in current cruise missiles. An alternative way of using these technologies would be to go to a missile with one warhead and build it very small; for example, one could build a 30,000 pound missile capable of delivering a single warhead to ICBM ranges. Thus, technology might lead in either of two directions: it could result in large quantities of small, low-cost missiles with single warheads, or it could lead to a multiplication of warheads using the same number and same size of missiles as are deployed today.

Summary of lethality improvements. The net effect of advances in guidance, warhead, and reentry technology will be to make ballistic missiles into even more fearsome weapons than they are today. Each ballistic missile will be able to carry twenty to forty warheads, and each warhead will be directed to its target with "zero-CEP"; that is, it will bring the target within its lethal radius virtually 100 percent of the time, even if the target is very hard. At an even earlier date than these ballistic missile improvements are available, cruise missiles will be entering U.S. strategic

forces with equivalent lethality. These improvements will not require technical breakthroughs but only a continuation of the guidance technology, MIRV technology, and propulsion technology
that already are well advanced.

An ironic consequence of these improvements in ICBM capability is a dramatic increase in ICBM vulnerability. That is, ICBMs
could be used in a counterforce mode to attack other ICBMs, and
no amount of silo hardening would offer adequate protection. Hardening only increases the requirement for accuracy—therefore it
could delay the date (but not by long) by which a given missile is
vulnerable and increase the cost to the attacker. This emerging
vulnerability of ICBMs to surprise attack could be extremely
destabilizing. They will therefore evolve from a highly stabilizing
component of strategic forces, which they were in the 1960s and
1970s, to a dangerously unstable component in the 1980s and
1990s unless substantial reductions in their vulnerability to
surprise attack can be negotiated. We are led, then, to seeking
ways of enhancing the survivability of ICBMs—by increasing the
ICBMs' ability to ride out a surprise attack or by actively defending them against such an attack.

Survivability

It is a matter of overriding importance to devise ways of reducing
the vulnerability of U.S. strategic forces—that is, improving their
survivability, which we define as the ability of a system to avoid
being destroyed at or near its base.

Launch under (or before) an attack (LUA). For years, U.S.
strategic planning has accepted that those bombers and submarines still at their bases during a nuclear attack would be
destroyed. When we talk about the survivability of submarines
and bombers, we mean only those submarines and bombers that
are no longer at their bases. This means further that high operating costs to maintain a high percentage of submarines and bombers on operational alert are accepted. More than 60 percent of
U.S. strategic submarines are at sea at any one time and are thus
invulnerable to surprise attack. Of U.S. bomber forces (depending
on the level of strategic alert), 30 to 60 percent are on strip alert

and could be airborne in a matter of minutes if an attack were detected.

Likewise, if the ICBMs were not at their bases when attacked, they would not be vulnerable either. However, a very significant difference with ICBMs is that once they leave their bases they cannot be recalled; the bombers and submarines can be, of course. In a presumed counterforce attack — ICBM against ICBM — the president would have only minutes to decide whether to move either bombers or ICBMs from their bases. While, in the past, ambiguous warnings have been sufficient to order removal of bombers from their bases, no president has ever decided on the basis of any alert to move ICBMs from their bases, for that is an irrevocable action.

Launching ICBMs under attack has been proposed as a viable way of dealing with the vulnerability problem. It would be an extremely destabilizing and dangerous situation, however, to have the president believe that the country's security depended on his decision to launch ICBMs on the basis of a computerized assessment of a possible attack. This would make the United States vulnerable to the unlikely, but not impossible, risk of a computer malfunction. Consequently, U.S. planners are seeking to restore the previous situation in which ICBMs could "ride out" an attack.

Survivability of ICBMs. For two decades, ICBMs have achieved their survivability through hardened basing (silos). The guidance accuracy already demonstrated by U.S. and Soviet ICBMs allows them to destroy missiles in these hardened silos with a single shot/kill probability greater than 50 percent. Improvements in accuracies that could be achieved during this decade would increase that to nearly 100 percent. Further hardening can be achieved with confidence; some advanced designs may be able to give ten- to twentyfold increases in hardness. But even the hardest conceivable silo could be overwhelmed by improvements in accuracy that would place the silo within the warhead's fireball. And such improvements in accuracy could be achieved in the same time frame as the proposed improvements in hardening. Thus, while further hardening can raise the cost of attacking silos, it is no longer a viable means of insuring the survivability of the ICBM force.

An obvious alternative to hardening is stealth — that is, basing the missile so that its location is unknown and thus could not be targeted effectively, even with a zero-CEP weapon. Submarine-launched ballistic missiles already use a combination of mobility and stealth to achieve survivability. Indeed, if their locations were known, they would be substantially more vulnerable than land-based missiles because of their concentration of relatively large numbers of missiles on one relatively soft launching platform. A number of alternatives have been considered for giving land-based missiles this same combination of mobility and stealth. Air mobility presents no significant technological problems. The issues are security and cost. Security could be compromised if over-the-horizon tracking systems to track airplanes were developed, and life-cycle costs for air mobile systems could be higher than for ground mobile systems — substantially higher if some fraction of the force were required to maintain a continuous air-borne alert. Mobility on roads would be a relatively inexpensive option if conventional transport vehicles were used, but because of the softness of these vehicles, this deployment would require continuous movement of nuclear missiles on public highways to provide a target area broad enough to withstand a barrage attack. This poses a small but probably intolerable risk of nuclear accidents occurring in populated areas. Designs have been proposed for missile transporters sufficiently hardened (up to 30 psi) so that a barrage attack would not be feasible even if the deployment were limited to military bases. These designs, while not yet proven, appear to be feasible at least for smaller ICBMs but much more expensive than conventional transporters. A third variation is a road transportable system where the missile is based in hardened shelters to avoid a barrage attack and moved deceptively to present many more targets than missiles. This is the so-called multiple protective shelter (MPS) system approved by the Carter administration. This system would be effective but expensive, both in dollars and political costs, and could require a supplemental ballistic missile defense system if the Soviets escalated their counterforce threat. The option of defending ICBM sites with an antiballistic missile (ABM) system is discussed in the section on penetrativity.

All of these methods of achieving ICBM survivability are

difficult and expensive because the pace of technology (especially guidance improvements) makes it *possible* to target ICBMs and the increase in ICBM value brought about by MIRVing makes it *attractive* to target them. An indirect but effective way of dealing with the ICBM vulnerability problem is to decrease the value of the ICBM as a target. A single-warhead ICBM is not an attractive target because the attacker requires at least one warhead (more likely two warheads) to destroy it; thus an attack would always result in an unfavorable exchange ratio for the attacker. A single-warhead ICBM, besides having this fundamental advantage, also is small enough to lend itself well to mobile deployment. In particular, a hardened transporter is feasible and could be used on existing roads.

If none of these survivable basing modes seems attractive, we could give up trying to preserve the ICBM as an *independently* survivable component of the strategic forces and instead depend on the other components of our strategic forces — submarines, cruise missiles, and bombers — to provide a "shield" for the ICBM forces. These different components would force the Soviets, if they were to contemplate an all-out attack, to make choices that would lead them to reduce significantly their effectiveness against one component in order to attack another. For example, if Soviet war planners should decide to attack our bomber and submarine bases and our ICBM silos with simultaneous detonations — by delaying missile launches from close-in submarines so that such missiles would *arrive* at our bomber bases at the same time the Soviet ICBM warheads (with their longer time of flight) would arrive at our ICBM silos — then a very high proportion of our alert bombers would have escaped before their bases were struck. This is because we would have been able to, and would have, ordered our bombers to take off from their bases within moments after the launch of the first Soviet ICBMs. If the Soviets, on the other hand, chose rather to *launch* their ICBM and SLBM attacks at the same moment (hoping to destroy a higher proportion of our bombers with SLBMs, which have a short time of flight), there would be a period of over a quarter of an hour after nuclear detonations had occurred on U.S. bomber bases but before our ICBMs had been struck. In such a case the Soviets could have no confidence that we would refrain from launching our ICBMs during that interval after we had been hit. It is important to appreciate that this would not be a "launch-on-warning," or even a "launch-under-attack," but rather a launch-*after*-attack — after massive nuclear detonations had already occurred on U.S. soil.

Thus our bombers and ICBMs are more survivable together against Soviet attack than either would be alone. This illustrates that the different components of our strategic forces should be assessed collectively and not in isolation. It also suggests that whereas it is highly desirable that a component of the strategic forces be survivable when it is viewed separately, it makes a major contribution to deterrence even if its survivability depends in substantial measure on the existence of one of the other components of the force.

Survivability of bombers. If the U.S. does not try to achieve *independent* ICBM survivability, clearly a heavy burden will be placed on bomber and submarine survivability. In the case of bombers, only a certain percentage would safely escape their bases in a surprise attack optimized against bombers — 30 to 60 percent, depending on the stage of strategic alert that may exist. Of those that make it into the air, what chance would an opposing force have of destroying them while airborne?

The airplanes operational today have a fairly wide radius of vulnerability to a nuclear airburst. A nuclear bomb fired at them doesn't have to hit them. It has to come only within a few miles of the aircraft to destroy it in flight. The aircraft could therefore be subjected to a barrage attack. If an attacker devoted a dozen or two warheads to attacking a single airplane, then he would have to know the location of the airplane only to within a radius of several tens of miles to be effective. That means, then, that the bombers would have to be widely dispersed, that they would have to get away from their individual dispersal points quickly, and that they should not be detectable in flight.

We therefore are interested in the long-range techniques for detecting airplanes in flight. Two systems in development today are relevant to this problem. One is called an over-the-horizon (OTH) radar; the United States could have by the late 1980s an operational over-the-horizon radar that could detect at several thousands of miles airplanes flying at any altitude. This radar could locate an aircraft within a circle of perhaps a ten-mile radius; while that is a crude location, it is good enough for a barrage attack. The second kind of system—a spaceborne infrared detector—could be operational by the early part of the next decade. These detectors are sophisticated heat measurement devices in satellites that look down at the earth and measure small changes in temperature, thereby detecting the presence of airplanes, particularly those flying at high altitudes.

These two technologies could be used to detect and locate airplanes while they are on their way to targets. Neither country has that capability today, but either could have operational OTH radars by the late 1980s and infrared satellites by the early 1990s. In the face of such detection systems, maintaining the survivability of aircraft while in flight would require the development of countermeasures that could degrade the range and accuracy of those detection systems.

Survivability of submarines. Attacking missiles while they are still in a submarine requires locating the submarine and mounting an attack on it. It is a mistake to think of this problem in terms of tactical antisubmarine warfare (ASW), where a submarine detects another submarine and fires a torpedo at it. The greatest threat to strategic submarines would arise from a global ocean detection system that could locate submarines in open ocean areas and then direct a missile attack at them. In a barrage attack on submarines, much as in the case of the bombers, twenty or thirty warheads could barrage a large area of the ocean. If a submarine could be localized to twenty or thirty miles, barrage attacks would become feasible. The goal in submarine survivability is to prevent the Soviets from locating to accuracies of twenty or thirty miles our submarines on patrol in broad ocean areas.

The Soviets cannot do this at present nor will they be able to, I believe, for a good many years in the future. A crucial question, however, is the extent to which technological improvements over the next two decades could change this assessment.

A prominent form of technology used in tactical submarine detection is sonar—transmitting a sound wave that bounces off a submarine and comes back. No existing sonar system is useful for the detection of strategic submarines, nor is one likely to be useful in the foreseeable future. A closely related technology, which might be called "passive sonar," uses acoustic receivers to monitor the acoustic energy unintentionally emitted by a submarine, including noise from the screw, the main engine, and auxiliary engines. These sounds are propagated at very long ranges in open ocean areas and can be received by sensitive acoustic sensors. Acoustic technology has advanced sufficiently so that a global network of acoustic sensors could be deployed to monitor the location of submarines in broad ocean areas. Such a system would take advantage of submarines that generate high levels of noise. U.S. submarine designers pay a great deal of attention to suppressing noise, so that U.S. submarines presently have a low vulnerability to this kind of noise detection.

Even if a submarine is noisy, performing successful detection requires very sophisticated sensor devices — very long acoustic arrays and super computer-processing systems — technologies in which the United States has a preeminent position. In short, the situation in acoustic detection is asymmetrical. The United States has a very significant capability today, which could be extended and improved in the future. The Soviets do not. As in the case of other technologies, the Soviets might eventually catch up with U.S. detection technology. One element of the equation, however — the noise characteristics of our submarines — is under U.S. control. As long as the United States continues to emphasize quiet submarines, it can probably avoid open ocean detection by acoustic means.

Another technology of potential significance in submarine detection involves the internal waves made by a submarine. As a submarine moves through the water, it pushes the water aside, causing waves below the surface. Eventually, these waves reach the surface, causing visible disturbance. A very sophisticated system might be able to discriminate that disturbance from the disturbances already present on the surface of the water — the natural waves. Although that sort of detection system can be conceived, its realization is exceedingly difficult and would require a very powerful computing system. While the United States is performing research and development on these techniques, I do not anticipate broad ocean-search systems to become operational in the foreseeable future.

A third technique, known as blue-green laser detection, uses a laser in a radar mode to detect a submarine. Radar waves at radio frequencies bounce off the water without penetrating to submarine depths, but a laser of the wavelength corresponding to blue-green light can penetrate the water down to submarine depths and reflect energy back to the surface. (Clear water appears blue-green because it is transparent to the blue-green component of sunlight but opaque to other components.) To realize this capability would require deployment of a satellite sensor system not yet developed. Moreover, even the light of a wavelength best able to penetrate could not make a round trip to submarines cruising below a certain depth, and this limitation could not be improved by increases in laser intensities beyond those now contemplated. In short, development of blue-green ASW lasers would require the solution of many technical problems, including development of high-power laser sources. Of course, such laser detection systems would be sensitive to the turbidity of the ocean; under conditions of high turbidity, no laser could penetrate very far. Even in clear water, the submarine might avoid laser detection by cruising at great depths.

Finally, the probability of submarine detection is always threatened with a breakthrough or discovery that might come next year or next decade but that is not now predictable. Even if a system were developed that were capable of detecting submarines in the ocean, it would still face the threat of countermeasures that might be deployed against it. If it were acoustic, for example, it would be susceptible to acoustic decoys; if it were a blue-green laser, greater depth and other countermeasures could be used to degrade or defeat it. Both the United States and the USSR are pursuing intensive efforts in submarine detection research and development. During this decade, we likely will have a high degree of technical progress in various techniques now under development, but the operational systems resulting from such technological progress do not necessarily pose a threat to our strategic forces. Even if they did pose a threat, we probably could devise effective countermeasures for such a threat. In this field, the offense will continue to have the advantage over the defense; that is, strategic submarines should be able to maintain their high degree of invulnerability.

It is likely that by the 1990s, however, strategic submarines will no longer have a "free ride"; that is, it may become necessary to develop operational countermeasures in order to maintain the relative invulnerability of submarines to detection in open ocean areas.

Penetrativity

"Penetrativity" is the ability of strategic forces to survive an attack by active defense systems at or near the target area; that is, it is the ability to penetrate active defenses. A discussion of penetrativity need consider only two categories of strategic forces: bombers and cruise missiles may be lumped together since they both must penetrate the Soviet air defense systems; submarine missiles and ICBMs both have to penetrate any Soviet ABM defenses.

Penetrativity of bombers and cruise missiles. The ability of U.S. bombers to penetrate Soviet strategic air defenses today is very good. It is achieved by flying low, which masks bombers in the ground clutter returns of Soviet radars and prevents the Soviets from extracting the bomber targets with sufficient signal strength to track them. More than ten years ago, the United States developed radars capable of extracting airplane targets out of that kind of ground clutter. The simplest way is to employ the Doppler radar, which is able to detect signals from moving targets and reject signals from stationary targets. Since ground clutter is stationary, a Doppler radar can be used as a means of separating airplanes from ground clutter. Such radars are now operational on our airborne warning and control (AWACs) systems, as well as F-14, F-15, and F-18 fighter aircraft, and are used to detect and track low-flying airplanes in the presence of ground clutter.

The Soviets have not had such a radar, allowing the United States the same kind of "free ride" in bombers that it gets in submarines. But the free ride for U.S. bombers is almost over. In the last five years, the Soviets have developed and are beginning to deploy such a "look-down, shoot-down" radar and associated missile. When that system becomes operational in quantity in about the mid-1980s, the tactic of flying low will no longer be sufficient as a way of evading Soviet strategic air defenses. At that time, the effectiveness of the U.S. B-52 force as penetrators will be greatly reduced.

Any solution to that problem must involve defeating those radars or avoiding the use of penetrating aircraft. Two techniques are in hand for defeating the radars: stealth and electronic countermeasures. The cruise missile system is already operational, with a sufficient degree of stealth to defeat existing Soviet air defenses. Additionally, cruise missiles can degrade the effectiveness of the new generation of Soviet look-down radars, since none of the look-down radars can extract perfectly a moving target from the background; some background clutter remains, which can obscure small targets. The first generation of American look-down radars and the present Soviet version can extract medium to large aircraft from background noise but not aircraft with small radar cross sections. In particular, current U.S. cruise missiles are small enough to substantially degrade first-generation look-down radars, but U.S. second-generation look-down radars, already operational, are capable of detecting cruise missiles of significant ranges. It is only a matter of time, therefore, before the Soviets develop that same capability and then will be able to track effectively first-generation U.S. cruise missiles.

When that happens, the continued effectiveness of these forces will depend on revolutionary but feasible improvements in electronic countermeasures and stealth technology. Stealth technology will be applied to some degree in all of our future tactical airplanes and missiles. Technology also is rapidly changing in microelectronics, which will allow dramatic improvements in electronic countermeasure (ECM) systems. Little more than a decade ago, ten transistors were put on a single chip; today more than ten thousand transistors can be put on a chip, and these large-scale integrated circuits will be used in ever-increasing quantities in military equipment in the years to come. Even more important is the revolution in very large-scale integrated circuits (VLSI) that is about to begin. VLSI technology will reduce element spacings on chips from 4–5 microns, which was the state of the art at the beginning of this decade, to 0.5 microns by the end of the decade. This 10-to-1 compression in linear dimensions will result in a 100-to-1 increase in the number of transistors on a chip, a

100-to-1 improvement in processing speed and, in time, a 100-to-1 reduction in cost per transistor. That will provide the basis for truly revolutionary changes in ECM systems. It is obvious that we will be able to make these systems smaller and lighter, and more cheaply. We also will see substantial increases in computer power, which will lead to significant improvements in the effectiveness of our ECM systems.

I have discussed stealth systems and ECM systems as two separate technologies, each of which will have a revolutionary impact on our ability to penetrate Soviet defenses. Perhaps most interesting of all is the synergism between the two. For example, reducing the cross section of an airplane tenfold is not enough to make it immune to an air defense system, but it does reduce the requirement for power on the ECM system defending the vehicle. ECM systems with ten watts of output power would provide the same protection that a hundred-watt ECM system could do with a larger-cross-section vehicle. The introduction of stealth technology would therefore allow the use of low-power ECM systems, which will permit designers to put the entire system on a few microchips.

In sum, the advantage will continue to be with the offense; that is, we will continue to build missiles and bombers capable of defeating any conceivable Soviet air defense system. It will be difficult and expensive, but technology will permit the United States to stay ahead of improvements in Soviet defenses at a significantly lower cost than what the Soviets spend on their air defense system.

Penetrativity of ballistic missiles. There was an intense debate in this country in the 1960s over whether antiballistic missiles should be used to defend the country against an ICBM attack. For a variety of reasons, they were vetoed. This decision reflected a doubt that ABMs would be effective. It is therefore important to examine the new technological developments that have occurred since the 1960s that might make this decision worth reconsidering.

In the last 15 years or so, both ABM radars and interceptors have improved in evolutionary ways. There are no dramatic differences, but technological advances have permitted improvements that make the current generation of ABM experimental systems more efficient at shooting down ballistic missiles. The radar, however, is still vulnerable to a saturation attack by large numbers of reentry vehicles. Therefore, the parallel development in the Soviet Union of MIRVed offensive missiles, with large numbers of MIRVed delivery vehicles, more than offsets the improvements made to U.S. radars and interceptors. It is still a reasonable projection that ballistic missiles would achieve a high percentage of penetration against even these improved ABM systems.

On the other hand, newly developed exoatmospheric technologies are a revolutionary departure from the technologies developed during the 1960s. Optical detection systems, the same technology used in tactical precision-guided munitions, provide extremely accurate guidance that allows an interceptor warhead to make a direct hit on a reentry vehicle, thereby destroying it by the kinetic energy of the collision and without using a warhead. The intercept vehicle could thus be quite small, allowing the ABM interceptor to be MIRVed. Twenty or thirty interceptor warheads could be placed on a single ABM, in effect deMIRVing the offensive force — that is, canceling the penetration advantage of MIRV systems deployed on ICBMs by matching them with a MIRV capability on ABMs.

However, as it is conceived today this system would still be vulnerable to penetration tactics. In particular, it would be vulnerable to decoys, such as balloons. A balloon could be built that when blown up is the size and shape of a reentry vehicle. It could be very light and have a thin coat of metal to look like a reentry vehicle to either an optical system or a radar. Instead of releasing ten reentry vehicles, for example, the ICBM could release nine reentry vehicles and hundreds of balloons. Currently available experimental data suggest that it would be very difficult for even advanced detection systems to discriminate between balloons and warheads outside of the atmosphere, so there is no reason to be optimistic about our ability to deal with the decoy problem. Even though we may be able to deMIRV the ICBM attacking force and remove the threat of RV saturation, we still would face a saturation threat from effective decoys.

The advantage, therefore, still lies with the offense. The offense will continue to be able to penetrate more readily than the defense will be able to figure out ways of dealing with each kind of penetration, resulting in unacceptable leakage through the defenses. It is worth pointing out that an ABM system 90 percent effective in defending the United States against an ICBM attack would still allow 10 percent of a few thousand reentry vehicles— that is, a few hundred one-megaton warheads—to strike the United States. Technological developments presently identified would not provide a high-confidence defense of the United States against a determined ICBM attack that included several thousand reentry vehicles and huge quantities of sophisticated decoys.

Space-based ABMs. One other revolutionary change in the ABM field is still in the early stages of development. Directed-energy weapons, high-energy lasers in particular, theoretically could be placed on space vehicles and attack an ICBM during its launch phase by burning a hole through the booster while the missile was still under powered flight. The ICBM might thus be destroyed, not only before it reached its target but before it even had a chance to release its warheads. To put adequate levels of energy on an ICBM target would require deploying the laser on a low-altitude satellite that must be located over the launch area when it fires its laser beam. This means that not one but a whole constellation of satellites—about twenty—would be necessary to be able to shoot down any particular ICBM at any given time that it were launched. A few seconds would be required to detect, track, lock on, and dwell on the target long enough to burn a hole through it. Therefore, any given laser is tied up for a few seconds in this operation, which has to occur during the few minutes the ICBM is in powered flight. The twenty satellites required for continuous coverage of the launch area could attack in sequence perhaps a few tens of ICBMs that were launched simultaneously, but they could not handle a mass attack of a few hundred or one thousand ICBMs. Therefore, the base number of twenty satellites would have to be multiplied by five or ten to deal with a mass attack. In other words, one to two hundred satellites continuously orbiting the world would be needed to maintain enough laser beams to deal with a mass attack against the United States.

Assuming it were feasible to orbit one hundred or more of these space stations, there is still the question of the feasibility of developing the necessary laser weapons. Space-based ABM lasers would require a pointing and tracking accuracy of a few inches at a range of a few hundred miles; that is, better than one part in a million accuracy. This accuracy is significantly better than has been demonstrated in space-based systems. A feasible but difficult and expensive development program would be required to achieve a pointing and tracking system of sufficient accuracy and stability. With the beam properly pointed, it must have sufficient energy to burn a hole in the missile skin; this would require about a tenfold increase in power over what has already been demonstrated for high-energy lasers. Finally, the reflecting mirror for this whole system would need to be larger than any that has been built. These very substantial engineering developments would have to be demonstrated before we could begin to build an operational weapon system.

If a laser system were developed with these capabilities, it would be too large to be launched from the space shuttle. Four or five shuttle launches would be required to place the components of one of these space stations in orbit, which would then be assembled in space. Thus, four or five launches on a shuttle would be necessary for each of 100 or 200 battle stations. The most optimistic view is that such a program would cost well in excess of $100 billion in today's dollars and could perhaps reach a beginning operational status by the end of the century. Estimates of lower costs or more rapid availability are, in my view, unrealistically optimistic.

If the United States embarked on such a program and, in fact, achieved the developmental objectives that have been cited, it would still have to worry about the countermeasures that might be adopted, some of which are straightforward. The most obvious would be to use infrared decoys to simulate the heat sources of missile launchers. Another obvious one would be to coat the ICBM skin with the same kind of heat-absorbent material used on reentry vehicles so that higher levels of energy would be required to burn through the skin, requiring increases in laser power or in the mirror size of the laser weapon. Direct countermeasures against the space stations also might be possible. For example, space mines would have to be reckoned with. The space-based laser would be most vulnerable, ironically, to ground-based lasers.

Other exotic concepts for space-based ABM systems have been proposed, one of which uses particle beams instead of lasers as the kill mechanism, another of which involves a novel use of nuclear energy. While these may be more effective than the high-energy laser, their technology is less well-developed and understood. Moreover, they still are susceptible to operational difficulties, including countermeasures.

Silo defense by ABMs. Even if ABM systems do not have the potential of providing a high-confidence defense of the United States against an ICBM attack, ABMs might be employed to defend ICBMs from an attack by opposing ICBMs. A 50 percent leakage rate could be tolerated in an ABM system defending hardened ICBM silos, whereas a 10 percent leakage rate is unacceptable for population defense. The United States has under development a system called LOADS (low-altitude defense system), which is designed to provide a "bloody-nosed" defense of fixed, hardened sites. This type of ABM system is deployed at the site and fired at the incoming RV at the end of its trajectory to allow the atmosphere to separate out the decoys from the real missiles. Once this separation has occurred and the ABM system has decided which target is a real missile, it has only tens of seconds left to operate, so it requires a missile with very high acceleration, which is feasible with current solid fuel technology. It also requires a nuclear warhead to be sure that the incoming warhead is destroyed.

A LOADS or similar defense system should provide a high probability of defending a silo against a single RV attack. However, its effectiveness against additional RVs would become doubtful because of the self-interference effects of nuclear weapons. A silo defense system could therefore raise the cost of an attack by a factor of three or four, but it could not provide a total defense.

Past arguments used against ABMs are not applicable to a silo defense ABM system. A decade ago it was argued that the ABM did not have any hopes of performing its mission. The defense of the United States seemed then and today still seems beyond our ability to achieve, but it is not out of the question to provide a level of defense for a silo. In fact, the only application for which ABMs will be seriously considered in the next decade or two is defense against a counterforce attack. Although there are substantial engineering, economic, and arms control problems with such a

system, the one glaring technical weakness of all ABM systems —
their vulnerability to leakage — is not a disqualifying factor for
silo defense.

Connectivity

The system controlling U.S. strategic forces comprises three components:

1. Sensors that monitor activity in the Soviet Union and at sea
   and assess whether an attack is under way;

2. The national command authority (NCA), which receives this
   and other information and decides what action to take;

3. The operational commands that execute decisions made by the
   NCA by deploying weapons as appropriate.

Each of these components consists of a variety of units in widely
different locations. So that each component can perform its function
in a timely manner, its scattered units are interconnected by
a communications network. Additionally, each of the three components
is interconnected by redundant communications links.

We say that strategic forces have connectivity whenever each of
the three components is functioning and when they are able to
communicate with each other. The loss of connectivity of strategic
forces can be as detrimental to their mission as losing the weapons;
if it were to occur for even twenty minutes at a critical time, it
could cause the loss of a major part of the force to a counterforce
strike.

The present system could carry out its mission if the operating
environment were sufficiently benign, but the system is fragile;
that is, it is susceptible to interruptions or malfunctions. The most
serious generic problems for the system prior to a nuclear attack
are the following:

- Susceptibility to interruption because of equipment failure;

- Susceptibility to false alarms because of equipment malfunction;

- Susceptibility to sabotage of ground stations;

- Susceptibility to a nonnuclear attack on warning satellites;

- Susceptibility to interference (jamming or natural) with radio links.

During or after a nuclear attack, the system would face all of these problems plus the very real possibility that command-and-control centers and communications satellites would themselves be targeted. Even if they were not, the communications systems' connectivity would suffer some degradation by the disturbances to radio propagation that would follow a nuclear detonation.

In recognition of these problems, a degree of redundancy and fail-soft circuits have been built into the system that give it a reasonably good immunity to radio failure or computer malfunctions, but it would be difficult and expensive to render the system invulnerable to a precursor attack. If the Soviet Union were to launch a deliberate preemptive attack on U.S. strategic forces, however, they might attempt a covert precursor attack against the brain and nervous system that might otherwise command the targeted weapons to leave their bases before the strike arrived. In the event of a surprise attack, our system should be capable of alerting the NCA in time to deploy recallable and alert forces, but there would not be sufficient time to deploy forces not on alert. Additionally, it is quite possible that U.S. leaders might not have sufficient confidence in their assessment to launch the ICBM force, which could not be recalled.

It is even more difficult to render the system resistant to nuclear bombardment, which could occur simultaneously with or shortly after a nuclear attack on U.S. strategic forces. By its very nature, command, control, communication, and intelligence (C³I) equipment is scattered over the globe and in space, usually in inherently exposed positions. Many sensor systems must have line-of-sight to the Soviet Union—which means that weapons in the Soviet Union also would have line-of-sight to them. The ground stations are at fixed locations, the satellites are in known orbits, and all antennas necessarily must have a degree of exposure to function efficiently. After a nuclear attack in which the command structure were not targeted, we could quickly recover virtually complete capability to communicate because the propagation disturbance effects would be relatively short-lived at microwave frequencies. However, if the command structure were targeted extensively, very little would survive beyond those forces airborne or moving on the ground at the time of the attack. Reconstituting the command structure and restoring its connectivity would be a long, difficult undertaking with uncertain results.

A major effort is planned to improve this situation for the 1980s. It will involve changes in operational procedures and changes in equipment, both of which are necessary.

Sensors in the warning system could be improved in both sensitivity and jam resistance. Missile launch detection systems currently use a scanning infrared sensor. Their performance could be substantially improved by shifting to an array of infrared detectors with hundreds of simultaneous beams staring at the target area (this is called a mosaic sensor). These new sensors would have substantially more sensitivity than present sensors, so that smaller targets (including high-altitude aircraft and cruise missiles) could be detected; they would provide more refined tracking data to improve attack assessment characteristics and would be much more resistant to laser jamming. To further improve jam resistance, they could be multicolor; that is, they could operate at several different frequencies in the infrared band.

Ground detection systems could be similarly improved by upgrading the ballistic missile early warning system (BMEWS) to include phased array radars, such as those used in the Pave Paws SLBM detection system. Additionally, a redundant ground radar system based on over-the-horizon techniques could be installed. An OTH radar operates in the 3 to 30 MHz band, at which frequencies the ionosphere bends the radio waves back to earth instead of allowing them to pass into space. It therefore could be used to detect targets inside the ionosphere that are considerably beyond the line-of-sight limitation of ordinary radars. In particular, OTH radars could be installed in the northern United States to look at ICBMs during their boost phase over the Soviet Union. These systems would not have the same reliability as microwave radars because of their inherent susceptibility to interference — both manmade (jamming) and natural. In particular, since such a radar would be looking approximately over the North Pole, it would have substantial interference from the aurora borealis, which could render it inoperable at unpredictable times. However, as a redundant system with independent failure modes, compared to microwave radars or infrared satellites, OTH radars are well worth considering.

It is also possible to put radars and infrared detection systems on aircraft. To maintain such a system on continuous airborne alert would involve very substantial procurement and operating costs. Illustratively, a fleet of fifty or so aircraft would be needed and ten or so would need to be airborne at any one time in order to provide geographic coverage of the most obvious attack corridors. The system would be of only doubtful effectiveness against an ICBM attack but could provide warning of a bomber attack. On balance, however, it does not seem likely that the life-cycle costs would be justified by the value of the information, since it is unlikely that the Soviets would launch a bomber attack on the United States prior to an ICBM attack.

Finally, it is important to consider combinations of these sensor systems. Because of the susceptibilities described—to physical attack, to jamming, to natural interference, to equipment malfunction—it is desirable to have redundant sensors that fail in different ways and under different conditions. We should have both ground and satellite sensors; the satellite sensors should be multicolor and the ground sensors should include both microwave and over-the-horizon systems.

Survivability of communication links also could be improved by multicolor modes (called "frequency diversity" in communication systems) and by having redundant paths—ground, airborne, and satellite—for connecting stations. A fair amount of redundancy is already built into the system, but more is desirable and would be relatively inexpensive. Additionally, there are three other features that should be built into some of the communications links coming into operation in the 1980s—hardness, stealth, and fail-soft. Communication antennas do not lend themselves to high levels of hardness when functioning. In some ground systems the antennas can be stored in a hardened shelter when not in use, much like a missile, but some antennas in the warning system must be exposed to allow the system to be alerted to a surprise attack. Moderate hardness could be achieved on such antennas— low-frequency antennas may be buried to depths of a few feet; microwave antennas may be embedded in plastic radomes; electronics may be shielded to protect them from electromagnetic pulse (EMP) effects. None of these provisions, however, would protect the system from a direct attack; they would only increase its probability of surviving an attack on a nearby target. Since ground and satellite links are fixed or predictable targets, only airborne links have high confidence of surviving a direct attack and then only if the location of the aircraft is unknown to the attacker. Today, this is true of any aircraft flying outside the coverage of Soviet air defense radars. As the Soviets develop more sophisticated aircraft detection systems (OTH or satellite-borne), it may be desirable to incorporate stealth features in our communication relay aircraft. This may not be feasible because the aircraft would have to be hardened as well as stealthy, since the Soviets could barrage a large operating area with relatively few warheads if the airplanes were as vulnerable to nuclear effects as commercial transport aircraft are. Future military communication satellites also could be designed to make attacks against them very difficult. This would require a combination of redundancy, stealth, and hardening. If such a system were designed and deployed, it could have greater endurance than the airborne links.

Since redundancy of links is a key to survivability, it is important that a viable communications network be able to be reconstituted after a number of its links have been destroyed. This fail-soft feature can be accomplished most effectively with a new technology known as "packet switching." A message on a packet radio is digitized and segmented into a number of packets that are transmitted sequentially over the packet network. At each junction of the net, a microprocessor assesses the best route to the destination. Depending on traffic density or link outages, each group may go to its destination by a different route, but they are then reconstituted into the original message at the destination point. A packet system can therefore give good performance in the face of overloaded circuits, jamming, or a physical attack on part of the network. A reasonable strategy for a survivable system is to connect hundreds of stations by packet switching. Even if each station were soft, the network might still be able to carry a message to its destination.

Today the attack assessment system is effective when the data it handles are not "noisy," but in an operational environment where we can expect jamming, loss of stations, and propagation disturbance the data would be noisy and difficult to interpret. One solution to this problem is lowering the threshold; that is, assessing that an attack is under way even if the confidence level is not high because of noisy data. This, of course, raises its vulnerability to false alarms, which if acted on by the NCA could lead to tragic results. It is imperative that we insist on a high threshold in our assessment system, even in the face of noisy data. Current computer software technology permits major improvements in this respect. Error-correcting codes could be employed in computer software that virtually eliminate any probability of computer false alarms on noise. Similarly, much more sophisticated algorithms could be introduced for attack assessment calculations—which compare the data being received with a variety of stored models— so that data that violated certain physical or operational constraints would be rejected. These algorithms also would protect against false alarms on noise. Both error-correcting codes and the comparison algorithms are costly in terms of computer memory and computer speed and are not compatible with the relatively old computers presently in the attack assessment system. Modern computer designs could easily accommodate these software improvements with even less computer time than is presently used and could provide higher hardware reliability as well.

In sum, the present C^3I system works, but it is susceptible to countermeasures, physical attack, and accidents. It is useful for alerting the NCA to a surprise attack in time to deploy alert and recallable forces. It is of questionable reliability for deploying nonrecallable forces like ICBMs, however, and it would have little endurance after a nuclear attack.

Technology permits us to make substantial improvements in the survivability and endurance of this system. These include new infrared mosaic sensors, new OTH ground radars, new hardened command aircraft, and a new computer system with state-of-the-art hardware and error-correcting software. It is very important to pursue these improvements; if we do not, we allow an instability to develop that could even be an incentive for a surprise attack.

Technology, however, no matter how diligently applied, cannot provide complete security. There will always be a finite possibility of a computer false alarm, especially in a high-stress environment. That is why we continue to prefer that nonrecallable forces like ICBMs be capable of riding out an attack. Technology cannot give us high confidence that we will be able to control our forces days or

weeks after a nuclear war has started: these links have a basic
vulnerability to a nuclear attack, and a host of unpredictable
effects would attend any mass nuclear attack. Above all, there is a
very real question of how those humans in the command structure
who survived a massive attack would perform under those
unpredictable and unimaginable conditions.

Conclusions

Both the United States and the Soviet Union are pursuing strategic technologies at the highest level of national priority. As a
result, they will continue to advance at a rapid pace during the
next decade. This inexorable application of technology to strategic
weapons will create a dynamic new environment that will pose
new problems for arms control but that also will present new
opportunities.

The technologies that are leading to infinite lethality for
strategic weapons probably cannot be limited meaningfully by
arms control agreements. They already have advanced too far in
systems that are either deployed or in an advanced stage of
development. They also make obsolete the previous controls on
launchers, since one launcher in the coming decade could have the
destructive capability of twenty or thirty launchers as envisioned
at the signing of SALT I. But these new technologies also present
an opportunity: because of the increased efficiency they give to
strategic weapons, it is possible for both the United States and the
Soviet Union to make major reductions in the numbers of weapons
they deploy and still have an equivalent deterrence level.

New weapons also will have greatly increased levels of mobility
because new guidance and MIRV technologies (on the other side)
make it necessary, and because new guidance and propulsion
technologies (on our side) make it possible. This presents an opportunity for new arms control agreements on theater nuclear
forces because it reduces the military advantage (to both sides) of
forward basing and allows for an agreement for standoff basing of
SLBMs so that bombers are not threatened by a surprise attack
that destroys them at their base. This increased mobility also presents a new problem for arms control because it makes verification by national technical means much more difficult. While it is

true that these national technical means are also becoming more sophisticated and more effective, the problems posed by mobile systems, especially deceptively based mobile systems, still require some form of cooperation to supplement the national technical means.

New technology will allow ballistic missile defenses (BMD) to be designed during the 1980s that would be much more effective than those envisaged when BMD deployments were prohibited in 1972. On the other hand, the technology to penetrate BMD defenses has also advanced, so that neither side could have confidence in defending its country from ballistic missiles. Therefore, it remains to the advantage of both sides not to begin such a competition. However, if neither arms restraint nor mobility is seen to solve the ICBM vulnerability problem, it is possible that a BMD silo defense system would be invoked as one of several means of dealing with that problem.

The exotic new BMD system — a space-based directed-energy weapon — is in such early development stages in both countries that it could effectively be limited by arms control agreements if both countries decided that this would be in their best interest. While it would be very difficult to control research and development in this field, it would be easy to control deployments, since any effective deployment program would take many years to implement and would be highly visible.

New microelectronic and computer technology will lead to major improvements in warning and command systems, thereby improving our confidence in these links and reducing their vulnerability to false alarms. Bilateral agreements could also help, whether or not these agreements were part of a formal arms control treaty. Agreements to improve communications operations are particularly important — continuation of and expansion of the hot line is an important example. Confidence-building measures such as prior announcements of maneuvers and missile test firings also could reduce the probability of false alarm, and an agreement that limited antisatellite weapons to their present low-altitude capability would reduce the vulnerability of communication satellites.

In sum, technology has created substantial improvements and efficiencies in strategic weapons this past decade that will con-

tinue to evolve at a rapid pace during the next decade. In aggregate, technology is creating strategic weapons that are incredibly
lethal. In spite of advances in defensive technologies, the advantage will remain with the offense for the foreseeable future. The
main threat to offensive weapons will be from other offensive
weapons; we therefore will be faced with the extremely destabilizing situation in which these highly lethal weapons are also highly
vulnerable to a surprise attack. In a partial attempt to deal with
this problem, we will make our weapons more mobile and improve
our warning system, but we will also try to reduce the danger by
arms control. In this pursuit of arms control, we will face both the
problems and the opportunities presented by technology. Our
challenge will be to seize the opportunities and overcome the
problems.

7

RICHARD BURT

The Strategic and Political Lessons of INF

The experience with intermediate range nuclear forces (INF) has been one of the most significant phases in the history of the Atlantic Alliance. In dealing with the problems posed by Soviet INF superiority, NATO has relearned many of the common values that sparked its beginnings; it has strengthened and reshaped its approach to the crucial question of nuclear arms control with the Soviet Union; and it has modernized its political and strategic concepts to ensure the enduring unity of the Alliance. The efforts that have gone into the "two tracks" of the Allied approach to the INF issue — arms control negotiations and deployments — will thus have several lasting positive effects on the shape of the Western security community.

First, and most obviously, we are now more than three years into the successful implementation of the dual-track decision of December 1979. The Alliance is providing a credible framework for response to the Soviet challenge, in both the arms control and the strategic areas. Contrary to most expectations, our unity and commitment have increased over the period, as a direct result of greater understanding of the issues and their consequences.

Second, from the INF experience there are now beginning to emerge important new lessons for Alliance security, political relations, and the conduct of arms control. INF will prove to have been not a temporary interlude in the course of arms control and strategic development, but a lasting factor that shaped assumptions in many areas.

The details of the December 1979 decision and the history that led to it are well known and need not be rehearsed here. Similarly, the steps that the Alliance has taken to implement that decision, including the establishment and conduct of the negotiations in Geneva and the preparation for deployment of U.S. Pershing II and ground-launched cruise missiles (GLCMs), have been extensively reported. Not only have these been open decisions openly arrived at, but their implementation has been a matter of the daily record for the past three-and-one-half years. It is clear to all that the Alliance is determined to implement both tracks of the decision, including initial deployments at the end of this year in the absence of an agreement in Geneva obviating such action.

What is important to consider in this article, therefore, is less the history and current development of the INF issue than some of its longer-term implications for the future of nuclear weapons arms control. In effect, the INF question has brought us to a new stage in arms control that differs significantly from the assumptions and frameworks of the 1960s and 1970s. At the same time, it has influenced our perceptions of security and Alliance relationships, revitalizing many of the concepts of collective security that had become stale with repetition over the years. If we are to think coherently about the shape of arms control for the rest of the decade, we need to begin by understanding the characteristics and potentialities of the stage to which INF has brought us.

The Refocusing of Arms Control

Some years ago, this writer argued that arms control was off course—that it was failing to deal with the central political and security issues; that it was not making a significant contribution to stability, peace, the reduction of tensions, or any other tangible outcome; and that its premises needed serious rethinking. One of the central problems not then being adequately addressed was, precisely, the INF.

The initial Western concern with the INF problem arose, not coincidentally, out of widespread dissatisfaction with the inadequacies of then-existing arms control frameworks in dealing with the broad political and security needs of the Atlantic Alliance. Indeed, it appeared that continued unthinking perpetuation of existing arms control frameworks risked deliberately distorting and prejudicing the very basis of Alliance trust and cooperation. Fortunately, the experience of INF offers concrete evidence that Western governments can design and carry out new and effective arms control approaches to deal with common political and security problems, even when these are complex and dynamic. And this ability, once successfully demonstrated, may have broader application.

By bringing the question of Alliance security to center stage in arms control, the INF negotiations reversed the situation that prevailed in SALT I and SALT II. Then the focus had been consciously restricted to the U.S.–Soviet bilateral relationship in terms of intercontinental nuclear weapons. While the U.S. strategic responsibility for the security of its allies was always implicit in the American approach to the SALT negotiations, the chosen negotiating focus was more limited. The specific Soviet threats to our allies were not on the table, whereas paradoxically some of our potential counters to that threat had been made subject to negotiation. In this framework, it was possible for some of our critics at the time to argue, as they did, that the U.S. and the Soviet Union were seeking to establish a pattern of "superpower hegemony" to the detriment of the security interests of other countries, or that the U.S. was simply insufficiently attentive to the real security requirements of its allies.

Now that an INF negotiation is under way, and the issues of

Alliance security hold equal place with those of the intercontinental balance, it is difficult to recall the way of thinking of a decade ago when these same issues were relegated to the periphery. The shift has evident strategic and arms control implications. But more immediately, it has moral and political implications.

Arms Control and the Moral Unity of the West

If the Western Alliance is to function as a community, sharing risks and responsibilities and sustaining a common defense, then it is clearly essential that the arms control policies pursued by the United States give a central place to the security requirements of all members of the Alliance. The security interests of the Western nations cannot be dealt with in separate, artificial compartments, some of which are subject to reductions and limitations and some of which are left to run free. That is a recipe for discord and failure, as Americans and Europeans found out in the course of the debate over SALT.

Moreover, as the participants at the Williamsburg economic summit meeting recalled in their statement on peace and security, the community of interests among the industrialized democracies is today truly global. That fact, too, may have been implicit in our earlier arms control approaches. But it has been only through the INF experience that it has achieved such explicit and conscious recognition. In this sense, the INF arms control process has played a genuinely path-breaking role in strengthening and broadening the Western sense of community.

It is instructive to recall, in this regard, that the policies of the Soviet Union in the Geneva negotiations and in its public propaganda are clearly designed to reopen the strategic and political divisions between the U.S. and its allies that the INF process has closed. The Soviet negotiating framework would return us to a period when the American-Soviet nuclear balance was calculated without specific regard for the interests of our allies in Europe and Asia. Such an anachronism would be even less acceptable now than it was earlier, in view of the massive increase in Soviet nuclear forces capable of attacking our friends and allies.

Indeed, INF negotiations have made explicit and visible the basis of Soviet global policy, which is to divide the other nations of the world and deal separately on a national or regional basis with each. Thus the Soviets have sought to create a specious difference in interest between the nuclear and nonnuclear states of Europe by focusing on the nuclear capacities of the United Kingdom and France. They have sought to weaken the U.S.–European strategic umbrella, and to undermine the basis of psychological and political trust on which it depends. And they have sought to generate differences between Western publics and their governments.

Maintaining Western unity by blocking divisive Soviet thrusts has been both a requirement and an accomplishment of the INF negotiation process. In this sense, the challenges we have confronted in the INF area are not dissimilar to those faced in numerous other areas of national and international policymaking, where the pressures against common solutions are rising.

The most dangerous trend in the world today is the drift to insularity. In economics this is represented by the rise of protectionist pressures in many countries—pressures that are perhaps understandable in a time of recession, but that are nonetheless extremely damaging to the long-term interests of individual states and the overall Western community. In politics, insularity comes to the surface in exaggerated nationalist rhetoric and suggestions that individual countries can or should set themselves apart from other members of the community. In the security area, the same dangers are present. The burdens of collective defense have not become lighter, and the temptation to seek panaceas in unilateral solutions is present on both sides of the Atlantic.

collective security

One of the principal services of the INF debate has been to remind everyone of the realities of our common security situation, and to underscore both the benefits of mutual cooperation and the futility of unilateral strategies. This is, in the highest sense, a moral accomplishment. Collective security, on which peace has depended for decades, is a moral engagement of nations and individuals. The willingness to work together, to share risks and responsibilities, and to provide jointly for the security of the community has always been the foundation for human progress.

Arms Control and Security: The Chicken and the Egg

The two-track INF strategy decided upon by the Allies in 1979 posed a number of significant questions for the future relationship of security and arms control policy. On the one hand, some people have seen the parallel introduction of arms control attempts and deployment decisions as a violation of a cardinal principle of arms control: that security should not be made hostage to Soviet good-will in a negotiation. They have been concerned that repetition of the experience could prove harmful to U.S. and Allied ability to maintain an effective deterrent.

On the other hand, some people have argued that the two tracks were unnecessary, and that NATO should have relied on arms control alone. While their primary focus has been on the specific INF issue, they could be expected to contend more broadly that arms control should be conceived of as an independent activity, unencumbered with preparations for defense. Some of these people, of course, take the position that no INF deployments or defense efforts should be undertaken, and that all faith should be placed in arms control negotiations — proving the fact that their very stance undercuts any possibility of achieving positive results in those negotiations. Others recognize the need for defense efforts, but tend to believe that these can be postponed while arms control is "given a chance." While certainly well-meant, as a practical suggestion such a course would in effect make it impossible to negotiate because it would leave the Soviets with every possible incentive to drag out the process and never reach a conclusion.

Finally, the defenders of the two-track strategy have regarded it as a realistic framework for dealing with the INF imbalance on two fronts at once, while at the same time serving as a powerful educational instrument, bringing home to governments and publics the interrelationships between arms control and security —which are all too often treated as though they existed in separate, self-contained compartments.

The INF double decision is a model that may not prove applicable in many future cases. The political and strategic circumstances that surrounded the decision were special and unlikely to be replicated in the same form. At the same time, the coupling of arms control efforts and deployments in the same decision has been proved to be the correct approach to the specific INF problem. It has provided a serious basis for negotiations with the Soviets, as well as a framework that has focused and maintained Allied unity despite the public controversy over deployments. Moreover, the dual nature of the decision has effectively made clear both to governments and to publics the interrelationship of arms control and security in a way that no number of academic articles and speeches could ever have done. This relationship, as has recently been seen in the American domestic discussion of strategic force modernization and the Strategic Arms Reduction Talks (START), is crucial for properly understanding any arms control question.

Critics of the two-track decision as an arms control model acknowledge that the Alliance did not actually grant the Soviets a *droit de regard* over deployments. These deployments were unambiguously decided upon in 1979, and the Alliance undertook to review only the scale of the deployments (with zero being one possible outcome), and then only if a concrete agreement were achieved that provided for levels beneath those set forth in the NATO plan.

The critics contend, however, that the double decision nevertheless permitted a situation where a Soviet political *droit de regard* emerged as a result of intense public attention. For some of these critics, the Alliance would have been better off to have simply proceeded with deployments, reestablishing the military balance and eliminating the Soviet monopoly in INF missiles, and only then to have turned to arms control from a position of confidence. Applying that logic to the future, they recommend that all U.S. and Alliance armaments decisions be made independently of arms control considerations.

It is certainly a valid principle that security policy and arms control cannot be made mutually hostage. To do so would guarantee both arms control stalemate and a progressive deterioration of security and stability. In practice, this principle was fully respected in the INF decision.

The Soviet Union, however, has made every effort to twist the rails and derail the Alliance effort to reestablish the nuclear balance and preserve trans-Atlantic coupling. The Soviets have done this by seeking to divide the elements of the two-track decision from each other, so that they can defeat each in detail rather than having to face their combined force. They have sought to nullify the deployment option through political pressure. And they have blocked the arms control option by a simple refusal to negotiate seriously in Geneva.

The combined result of these tactics would, if successful, eliminate the possibility of effective arms control and leave the Soviet Union in unrestricted possession of a politically and strategically dangerous monopoly of nuclear power vis-à-vis all the countries on its periphery. The weakness of the Soviet approach, however, is that it is an old story. The artificial distinction between arms control and security, on which it is based, was once a potent propaganda argument. But the increasing sophistication of public opinion, and the realization by governments of the pitfalls of such a simplistic division, have robbed this argument of its erstwhile drawing power.

INF and Western Strategy

The INF process has reemphasized the unity of the Alliance to a greater degree than at any point in recent history. It has also led to a healthy inspection of the premises of Alliance strategy, and of the requirements for making it credible in the present day, which has gone well beyond the specific concerns of INF. While everyone has readily agreed that the basic NATO doctrine of flexible response remains valid and indeed essential, the experience of INF arms control and modernization has sparked a very productive discussion on the means to enhance each of the elements of the NATO triad.

In the past this writer has been critical of a tendency of debates over arms control to freeze thinking on political and strategic subjects in order to provide a more convenient framework for achieving an agreement. This was certainly true in some instances, including SALT, where many people seemed to prefer to gloss over the implications of disturbing developments in technology and the shifts in Soviet forces, rather than change their strategic models to take account of them.

But in the case of INF, the framework of the arms control and modernization discussion, far from freezing thinking, has been dynamic. It has opened up new perspectives and highlighted new issues. It has led to new thinking not only on arms control questions but also on their relation to political dynamics, Alliance strategy, and the composition of the overall nuclear stockpile of NATO. The latter, for example, has been under study as a direct result of the December 1979 decision, which included—although that is often forgotten—the withdrawal of 1,000 U.S. nuclear warheads from Europe and the commitment to accomplish the INF modernization within the level of warheads remaining in Europe after that withdrawal. The Alliance has thus had to undertake an evaluation of the residual stockpile and the most appropriate composition of the short- and medium-range systems apart from INF. It is clear that the Alliance will want to continue to involve as many nations as possible in the nuclear deterrent so as to confront the Soviet Union with the broadest possible deterrent to aggression. At the same time, by consulting on the specific composition of the stockpile, the Alliance is seeking to develop a better understanding of the requirements of the deterrent for present circumstances—recognizing that much of the posture was installed a number of years ago.

It is also evident—although the effect has been less direct—that the debate on INF, by highlighting the interrelationship of all elements of the NATO triad of strategic, theater nuclear, and conventional forces, has revived thinking in Alliance governments and academic groups regarding the strengthening of conventional forces. There is a widespread understanding, which was expressed at the top governmental level at the Bonn NATO summit in the spring of 1982, that improvements in conventional defenses can be achieved by proper exploitation of new technologies and the development of effective tactics, and that such improvements can make an important contribution to a more balanced force posture, in which both conventional and nuclear forces have essential roles to play in deterring the Soviet Union.

Beyond stimulating work on the several legs of the NATO triad, the INF experience has generated greater introspection with regard to the meaning of the trans-Atlantic nuclear relationship. Over the decades, there has probably never been a point in Alliance history when there was a sufficiently broad public understanding of NATO nuclear doctrine, or of the political and strategic commitments between America and Europe that it represents. Understanding has been either too narrowly held among the experts, or too superficially disseminated among the general population. And this mix of narrowness and superficiality has made the Alliance vulnerable to violent swings of opinion on defense issues, particularly nuclear security issues. Not surprisingly, the terrain is littered with misconceptions and fear concerning the dangers of weapons systems and the risks of mutual commitments.

Many of those fears and misconceptions have of course been evident in the public reaction to the prospect of INF deployments. But at the same time, the debate over INF deployments and arms control has led many people to think more seriously about the strategic purposes of the Alliance and about the particular context in which the West finds itself today.

In the early years of NATO when the United States enjoyed strategic superiority, the question of deterrence and of the risks and moral responsibilities involved in its maintenance was assumed to be relatively simple. U.S. capability for "massive retaliation" was held to be an adequate deterrent to Soviet conventional attack. Questions of NATO conventional defense capabilities, or the linkage of the U.S. umbrella to Europe through theater nuclear capabilities, did not have to be confronted. The balance of the military, financial, and moral contributions of the two sides of the Atlantic to common security, while obviously important, did not seem to require rigorous scrutiny.

Later, as the Soviets moved toward strategic parity, the strategic and ultimately philosophical choices became more difficult for Americans and Europeans. The added complexity embodied in the doctrine of flexible response is only a pale reflection of the added complexity of Western strategic and political thinking brought on by the advance in Soviet nuclear capabilities.

One of the most evident innovations of flexible response was the introduction of a far more significant role for the European allies in the overall scheme of deterrence. This was true at the levels of doctrine, of policy coordination, and of force posture. Conventional forces acquired increased importance. Programs of cooperation provided nuclear weapons, under U.S. custodial control, to Allied forces. The issue of coupling between Europe and the American strategic deterrent became a central theme for debate. Symbolizing this shift was the creation of the Nuclear Planning Group, bringing U.S. and Allied defense ministers together to consider basic questions of strategy.

But even in this period, there remained artificial distinctions between strategic and theater questions. Although this doctrine of flexible response ordained a continuum in NATO systems and policy, in practice the compromises inherent in the doctrine and the lag in developing forces to implement it left gaps in both posture and policy.

These gaps became apparent with Soviet achievement of strategic parity, and the rapid Soviet expansion of its intermediate-range nuclear potential. The "gray area" thus created forced to the surface some hard questions that had been ignored in both American and Alliance thinking. Neither the United States nor the Allies had given much thought to intermediate-range missile systems since the early 1960s, when the U.S. Jupiter and Thor missiles had been withdrawn from Europe. Not only was it necessary to revisit the technical aspects of these systems, but more importantly it was necessary to rethink the political and strategic implications.

For some in Europe, uncomfortable questions were raised about the meaning of the standard NATO phraseology of "shared risks and responsibilities," which is the essential counterpart to collective security and the nuclear umbrella. If modernized deployments were necessary to ensure the effectiveness of the deterrent — or to bolster the chances of success in the arms control negotiations to remove the Soviet threat to the credibility of that umbrella — then countries would have to face the political realities of making such deployments.

It is a mark of the maturity and solidity of the Alliance that the decisions that have been made have been sustained through a period of questioning and pressure. Whenever questions have come up in the past three-and-one-half years, they have been resolved in favor of Alliance unity. Public and governmental choices have not gone in the direction of isolation in any of the countries scheduled to receive deployments of new U.S. missiles in the event negotiations do not obviate that requirement. This runs counter to the journalistic warnings that the issue was essentially divisive, not unifying. And it runs counter to the conventional wisdom that it is impossible to present difficult issues of nuclear security to the judgment of public opinion.

The INF experience will ultimately have been successful if NATO is able to restore the credibility of Alliance deterrence. This is a matter both of the hardware and of the theology of the nuclear umbrella, and of the subjective understanding on both sides of the Atlantic that the U.S.–European security relationship is an enduring one, and that, unlike in 1914 or 1939, the U.S. will not absent itself from a potential crisis in Europe.

The nuclear element will remain of particular importance in this trans-Atlantic connection. The role of the American conventional combat forces is obviously essential and—along with Allied forces—helps to give NATO a credible ability to meet a conventional attack. But the U.S. nuclear forces have a unique quality that cannot be replaced by conventional forces: they unambiguously tie the security of our two continents together and make clear to the Soviets that any aggression would pose a risk of direct engagement of American strategic power.

The INF experience has both sustained the U.S.–European nuclear relationship and altered perspectives on it. Because of the range of INF systems, they offer coverage of the Soviet Union, making clear that Soviet territory is not and cannot be a sanctuary. This will clearly have a deterrent effect on Soviet calculations. Moscow is far more concerned for its own security than for that of its Warsaw Pact allies. Its protest against the U.S. INF deployments is that they can reach Soviet territory; it has never made such a protest against weapons that can reach the territory of its Warsaw Pact allies, weapons NATO has long possessed. (Its attitude toward Eastern Europe is equivalent to its attitude toward Western Europe, where it fails to acknowledge the concerns caused by its SS-20 deployments.)

By providing an option for striking the Soviet Union, INF systems also serve to complete the spectrum of NATO nuclear forces, easing the dilemma caused by the concentration of the existing NATO stockpile on shorter-range systems. Such systems are designed to deter the Soviet Union from exploiting its conventional force superiority for an offensive armored thrust into the

West. It is obviously essential that the Alliance be able to deter such a threat. At the same time, it has always been a source of concern that too great a reliance on such shorter-range systems could become politically controversial—because the systems would for the most part have to be employed on NATO territory—and might not pose a sufficient risk to the Soviet Union to deter aggression. If it proves impossible to reach an agreement in Geneva eliminating the entire category of U.S. and Soviet nuclear weapons systems, INF deployments will enable NATO to confront the Soviets with a full spectrum of options, without excessive dependence on any particular one.

INF and the Future Shape of Arms Control

The INF issue is not going to be solved at the end of this year, contrary to the hopes of some and the fears of others. On the deployment side, the NATO program will stretch over five years. On the arms control side, although we have been talking since November of 1981, the Soviet Union has still not addressed the central issues. It may be, as some have predicted, that the Soviet Union will not negotiate seriously until it has evidence that the West is prepared to carry out INF deployments, and thus the negotiating process will have serious prospects only after December. We would hope to have that judgment proved wrong by a demonstration of serious Soviet willingness to negotiate even in advance of deployments. But if this is not to occur, then we will face the question of what course the INF arms control issue is likely to take after 1983.

In part, of course, this will depend on the Soviets and their objectives. Moscow has made numerous threats, ranging from additional missile deployments to breaking off negotiations and imposing political pressure. It is, however, pointless to speculate on the actual course the Soviets will follow. What is important is to design a Western approach that offers a realistic arms control framework that can be advanced systematically.

Clearly the United States and its Allies will retain a strong interest in controlling the level of nuclear weapons deployments, both strategic and intermediate-range. And, assuming for the moment that no agreement has been reached in 1983, the situation thereafter will be one in which the Soviets no longer enjoy their present INF monopoly. In negotiating terms, the chance of framing a constructive agreement should be enhanced once that monopoly has ceased to exist.

There has been a lot of speculation about the interrelationship of the strategic and intermediate-range issues, and of the specific START and INF processes. Some analysts have even speculated that the resolution of INF may be found in an integration of INF issues into START. However, while there is clearly a strong substantive relationship between the two, it does not seem productive to look for solutions to INF in terms of alternative negotiating frameworks before the major substantive questions have been addressed.

It is sometimes argued that geographic asymmetries make the INF problem insoluble in any arms control framework. There are a number of subissues here: the question of the Soviet focus on Europe vs. the U.S. global approach; the issue of British and French systems that the Soviets have insisted on including; and the basic definition of what is at issue—in effect, the Soviet refusal to accord legitimacy to the security interests of Western Europe.

Some well-meaning observers have argued that the Soviet insistence on these points is so strong and enduring that the only way an agreement can be achieved is by modifying the U.S. position to take account of these demands. However, apart from the political and strategic consequences of acceding to such one-sided demands, which would amount to acceptance of the Soviet INF monopoly and consequent political and military hegemony over Europe, the consequences for the future of arms control would also be devastating. The principle of equality, which has been established in a series of agreements, would be forfeited. The ability of the United States, or any other Western nation, to conduct a negotiation with the Soviets, and achieve a result that could be sustained politically in domestic debate, would be destroyed. Arms control would be thoroughly discredited as an element in interstate relations.

Substantively, there is no reason why the Soviet Union should have forces equal to the total of all other nuclear powers in the world. If it could achieve what it is asking for in the INF and START negotiations, the Soviet Union would be the acknowledged world hegemonical power, with forces equal to all others combined. As it is seeking to cover the U.K. and France in INF, so too it is seeking to cover China in START.

This would create a situation in which, through a bilateral negotiation with a single other power—the United States—the Soviet Union would have been granted superiority over the U.S. and over any other combination of forces in the world. The political and strategic consequences of this demand are obvious, not only for the nuclear powers but also for the nonnuclear states of the world, whose security depends in large measure on the maintenance of a stable nuclear balance.

A demonstration of the unacceptability of the Soviet demands from the point of view of the rest of the world does not, of course, ensure that Moscow will immediately moderate these demands. But it does establish a baseline from which the United States, in consultation with its Allies, can conduct serious negotiations. Moreover, it is evident that the Soviet demands are in fact excessive in terms of their own security requirements. The Soviet Union could, for example, maintain an effective deterrent against any conceivable quarter with forces that were, say, of the dimensions of the planned U.S. INF deployment—or some smaller number should they wish to pick one. It should be remembered that they would not only have this force, but would have, as they always have had, the availability of extremely large strategic nuclear forces, which have also been assigned theater as well as intercontinental roles. These forces, of course, vastly outnumber those of the states on the Soviet periphery, and would appear to be more than enough for any conceivable political or military purpose.

There is only one possible rationale for the Soviet desire to equal all other powers combined: the Soviet Union believes that for reasons of political prestige it must be seen as *primus inter pares*. This cannot be an acceptable basis for international stability and security.

Looking Ahead

The INF experience is not over. But it has already created a renewed understanding of the political and strategic fundamentals of the U.S.–European relationship. It has restored credibility to the arms control process, which had become increasingly irrelevant to the central concerns of the Atlantic Alliance. And it has stimulated new thinking about the defense and deterrence posture of the Alliance. The lessons that are being drawn from the process of INF modernization and arms control will affect development in all of these areas for the decade ahead.

IV

Arms Control and Politics

8

WALTER B. SLOCOMBE

Arms Control:
Prospects

There is perhaps more public interest in nuclear arms control now than there has been in the past twenty years during which it has been pursued. This concern is a product of three broad influences.

First, the Soviet Union has, over the 1970s, achieved numerical parity in strategic nuclear forces as a result of a sustained program begun after the Cuban missile crisis showed the impossibility of gaining strategic parity on the cheap. The advent of unquestioned parity has made clear to the general public that nothing the U.S. could do would avoid immense costs in a nuclear war, even if those costs fell short of the total destruction of human life and organized society. And parity coupled with the period of the worst Soviet–U.S. relations in many years has made many people believe that the risk of nuclear war is increasing.

Second, the nonratification of the SALT II treaty has aroused a public previously willing to leave the process of controlling nuclear arms to the experts, in confidence that things were somehow well in hand. That a treaty negotiated by three presidents over seven years was not ratified by the Senate made many Americans realize that the process of arms control, which had seemed to offer a source of assurance on the nuclear problem, might itself be threatened. The arguments of many on both the Right and the Left that the SALT process had in any case failed to come to grips with the reality of the arms race only exacerbated the public impression that this problem was anything but well in hand.

Finally, rhetoric of a policy of nuclear victory, of a belief that nuclear weapons can be expected to do more than deter and can actually be used as affirmative instruments of national policy to produce a costly but still tolerable and advantageous military result, has been heard more widely. Some of this rhetoric was no more than ill-advised or confused statements on a complicated issue, some expressed the wishes of unauthoritative spokesmen rather than official policy, some reflected sound reasoning but was expressed in a context or with a casualness that gave concern, and some was an effort to clarify the complex requirements of deterrence in the age of parity. But all of it scared people and made them more interested in arms control.

The principal public manifestation of this concern in the United States is, of course, the nuclear freeze movement. Poll data— confirming referendum results in the November 1982 elections— show broad support for the concept. Recent efforts in the House of Representatives to move from the freeze as a rallying cry of concern and commitment to a concrete legislative blueprint for negotiations have been less successful. Yet it is possible to have grave doubts about the utility, or even the relevance, of the freeze concept as a prescription for concrete arms control negotiating proposals, and still recognize—and for advocates of arms control, welcome—this mobilization of public support for controlling nuclear weapons. For it builds a political constituency previously lacking for weighing the risks of arms control agreements against reality, not against an idealized world of perfect security.

The public concern in the United States was presaged, and is being echoed even more strongly, in Western Europe. The 1979 decision to deploy American cruise missiles and Pershing IIs—a decision consistent with past NATO policy that was an initiative of the Europeans, not of the U.S.—has set off in Europe a controversy of unprecedented breadth over nuclear weapons. At a minimum, the debate over the deployment program and its parallel arms control track has dramatized the degree to which it is critical to public support for defense programs that Western governments, and especially the United States, be perceived as genuinely committed to arms control.

This public pressure for arms limitation and reduction—which may even be seen as an incipient disaffection from basic premises of deterrence—is, of course, a pressure only on Western governments. The Soviet Union eagerly exploits Western antinuclear feeling, just as it ruthlessly suppresses any glimmerings of such opinion at home. But the Soviet regime's ability to prevent public opinion from having any real impact on this, or any other, Soviet policy is unlikely to have suppressed the idea, even within the Soviet populace, that avoiding nuclear war by agreeing on limiting nuclear weapons should have a high priority. And indeed there are indications that the Soviet leadership, for reasons of its own, recognizes its interest in such agreements, quite apart from their political significance.

But if the public expectations for arms control are great, the obstacles are also immense. The purpose of this paper is to outline some of the background, problems, and possibilities for arms control in the next few years. The focus is on limits on strategic nuclear systems and the INF (intermediate-range nuclear forces) talks, although most of the observations apply equally to such other arms control fields as improved U.S.–Soviet crisis communication or the possible resumption of discussions on limiting nuclear tests or antisatellite systems. Not within this chapter's purview, however, is what may be the most important nuclear arms control issue of all—nonproliferation. There the Soviet Union and the United States are far from the dominant players, and lessons drawn from the history and foreseeable future of a strictly bilateral U.S.-Soviet enterprise have only the most limited applicability.

The Arms Control Record

First, we must consider the record of arms control. Despite its manifest failure to achieve all that was—and perhaps should have been—expected of it, arms control has proved to be a substantial technical and strategic success:

- The Limited Test Ban Treaty of 1962 stopped nuclear tests in the atmosphere and thereby eliminated a major environmental threat. Further, although each side has, underground, actively conducted tests at a higher rate since the treaty came into effect than before, information obtained from underground tests is less accurate and realistic than that which could be obtained by tests under more realistic conditions, thereby hampering precise prediction of nuclear effects. As a result, the treaty has probably had some inhibiting effect on confidence in first-strike attacks.

- The ABM Treaty of 1972 restricted each side to a token interceptor force. By these limits, each side foreswore further deployment of first-generation antiballistic missiles (ABMs). Such missiles, which both the U.S. and USSR were actively deploying when the treaty was signed, would have been expensive and would have produced only highly ineffective defenses. But those defenses would probably have been good enough to have had very substantial destabilizing effects, viewed from the other side's perspective. To a considerable degree also, by its limits on development and deployment of a variety of more advanced ABM concepts, the ABM Treaty inhibits the propensity of both sides to pursue fanciful defense schemes—although each side, particularly the Soviet Union, conducts a substantial ABM research and development program, to which President Reagan's "Star Wars" speech has given new attention, if not added feasibility.

- It is fashionable to denigrate the other part of SALT I, the 1972 Interim Agreement on offensive systems, but that agreement too has proved useful. It enforced a halt to the rapid increases in Soviet launcher levels that had been the principal feature of the Soviet buildup during the previous decade. Moreover, it required that old systems be dismantled as new ones were deployed. The SALT I agreement did not, and was explicitly not intended to, stop multiple, independently targetable reentry vehicles (MIRVs). As a result, in the decade since it was signed there has been a rapid increase in warhead levels, first on the

American and then on the Soviet side, while MIRVs were deployed. The agreement has been widely criticized on this score—not least by some of the same observers who warned in 1972 that impending Soviet ABM breakthroughs made a U.S. MIRV essential and that verification uncertainties made *both* a MIRV ban and ABM limitations quite risky. However, there is every reason to believe that the Soviets (and the United States) would have carried out their planned MIRV programs on at least as large a scale without the agreement. In the Soviet case it also seems likely that but for the SALT I agreement, the new generation of MIRVed missiles would have added to, rather than replaced, the prior generation. Moreover, the Soviets likely would have kept the several hundred older ICBMs and submarine missiles that have been retired as required by the SALT I Treaty as replacements were deployed, as they retained their older SS-4s and SS-5s while deploying the new SS-20, in conditions in which they were subject to no arms control constraints.

In addition, the ABM Treaty and SALT I agreement set up a structure of negotiations and of consultation on verification questions that has helped to set the framework for subsequent progress.

- SALT II, signed in 1979, may be unloved; it has been called fatally flawed. Its ratification was called into question by a host of political misadventures, most of all by concern over Soviet adventurism in the Third World, and the treaty was finally sabotaged by the Soviet invasion of Afghanistan. Its ratification seems now an immensely remote prospect. But on the merits, the Joint Chiefs of Staff assessment of the treaty as "modest but useful" remains valid (as does the observation that there is little enough in public life that is both). Once ratified, SALT II would have begun a process of reductions; and even in its present observed but unratified state, it puts a cap on the MIRV race and limits the increase in the number of missile warheads and the proliferation of improved types of intercontinental ballistic missiles (ICBMs). Perhaps the strongest testimony to the continued utility of SALT II is that the United States and the Soviet Union, for all the current vicissitudes of their relationship and for all the Reagan administration's proclaimed disdain for the "fatally flawed" treaty, have continued to keep it in effect for some four years now, pending the negotiation of further agreements.

In sum, the accomplishments of arms control over twenty years have been real, though limited when measured by the magnitude of the task. For all our problems, the world is a more stable place than it would be without these agreements. The chance of nuclear war has been reduced because of them; the size of the arsenals, excessive though they are, has been constrained; and certain dangerous technologies have been limited in useful ways. Moreover, a process has begun that is rightly taken by many as a symbol of the hope that mankind will find a way to control these terrible weapons.

We can reasonably expect more of arms control in the future, but the record so far has proved that far from being an impossible task, arms control produces positive and concrete results when measured against realistic expectations. In particular, the Soviets have proved willing to limit their forces to levels below those of which they were certainly capable and in some instances clearly below those they had planned on, to agree to steps that facilitate verification, and to make politically significant concessions as well, especially in connection with U.S.–Allied relations.

Arms control has not, of course, solved all of our problems, and it definitely does not remove the need for adequate U.S. programs to maintain deterrence and stability against Soviet threats that are not limited by the agreement. But all of our strategic problems of today would exist in essentially the same form if none of the existing arms control agreements were in effect. Furthermore, none of the responses to the challenges we face—dealing with ICBM vulnerability, improving command, control, communications, and intelligence (C^3I), maintaining the longer-term viability of the bomber and submarine elements of the Triad, counterbalancing Soviet intermediate-range nuclear force improvements, or developing a more flexible deterrence strategy—is limited or banned by any existing agreement. (The single exception is that the ABM Treaty stands as an obstacle to claims that we can find an easy way out of our problems by antiballistic missiles. So far such claims are so lacking in technical promise that their strategic desirability need hardly be debated, but even a technically work-able ABM plan would raise serious policy questions as to whether it would serve our interest to release constraints on Soviet missile defenses.) Rather, without the limitations on the scale and shape of the Soviet threat, we would almost certainly face substantial additional problems as well.

U.S. strategic programs of the past decade may have been inadequate (although even that proposition is fairly subject to debate). But the idea that arms control is to blame for whatever inadequacies there may have been in U.S. strategic programs is absurd. Far more blame properly attaches to the effect of the Vietnam War on discounting the degree to which military strength is essential for a strong U.S. international role, and perhaps even more serious, to the collapse in confidence of U.S. international leadership produced by Watergate and by two failed presidencies. In contemporary circumstances, it is clear that far from undermining domestic political support for needed defense (both conventional and nuclear), a credible and serious arms control effort, capped by some actual accomplishments and buttressed by observance of existing agreements, is virtually essential for the publics both in the United States and in Western Europe to be willing to spend adequate resources on military programs in difficult economic times.

Obstacles to Progress

But if the accomplishments are real, experience has also identified some very significant problems that will shape—and limit—the prospects for future agreements.

First, SALT is inevitably linked to U.S.–Soviet relations. The idea that the Soviets need arms control so badly (or that agreements are so little in our interest) that the U.S. can use arms negotiations as leverage on Soviet conduct in other contexts has proved itself an illusion. Indeed, given the vital importance of adequate nuclear deterrence, it is difficult to see how any Soviet political action, which almost by definition would be subject to change at any time, could make acceptable an agreement that would otherwise be too risky. Arms control cannot be, as Henry Kissinger may have seemed in the early days of détente to claim it could become, a way to cause improved Soviet behavior. Still more clearly, it is not in our interest to delay seeking arms control until we find some evidence of good Soviet behavior that we are anxious to reward.

Nonetheless, even recognizing that avoiding nuclear war—and doing so by agreed-upon limits on forces—is an almost unique area of U.S.–Soviet common interest, arms agreements do not exist in a political vacuum. There is some basic minimum of decent U.S.–Soviet relations that is necessary for progress on arms control. Still, to expect much more is to ignore our own interest in meaningful agreements.

The greatest difficulty SALT II faced in the ratification process was concern over the unsatisfactory state of overall U.S.–Soviet relations. Equally, the pressures on the Reagan administration for arms control agreements come in no small measure from growing (if not obviously justified) fear that its policies are increasing the risk of war with the USSR.

At bottom, arms control is an aspect of dealing with the unpleasant fact that the USSR will not disappear and is not likely to reform. It is clear that we must not fail to compete diplomatically and militarily, including by conventional defense adequate to the myriad of more likely immediate confrontations and by nuclear programs adequate to sustain a military balance in any event. However, it is also in our unilateral interest to deal with the Soviet Union in ways that will control the risk of nuclear war. In that process arms control is one—although far from the only—element. Ultimately the basis for the process—and for hopes of progress—is that the two sides, who disagree about practically everything else in international affairs, have begun to agree on that narrow range of issues in which they have a common interest based on their fear of a general nuclear war. This sense of mutual interest is reinforced as a stimulus to agreement by the fact that neither is fully eager to test the outcome of an unrestrained competition in the construction of strategic nuclear weapons, pitting U.S. technology and economic power against the Soviet capability to commandeer vast resources for the military without regard to economic weakness or popular opinion.

The second reality is that arms control is a process of trade-offs. The U.S. and the Soviet Union share an interest in avoiding nuclear war and, derivatively, in avoiding unrestrained weapons competition. They face broadly the same technological facts and the same military and strategic realities about the capabilities of nuclear weapons. But their policies, their military doctrines, their force structure, and their military missions — not to mention their fundamental values, their international political objectives, and their domestic political settings — differ sharply. This inevitably makes it difficult to find areas of agreement.

Indeed, the fact that one side genuinely wants a particular limitation almost always means that the other side has only the most limited incentive to agree, and may even see that element of an agreement as positively harmful. Agreements must therefore be composed of sets of limits, the individual elements of which may serve the two sides' interest to different degrees but compose a package that is acceptable to each on an overall basis. Nothing is easier than to conceive arms control agreements that will serve American (or Soviet) interests, or the cause of arms control, better than those that the two sides have actually negotiated. The difficulty is to attain agreement on such improvements. The fact that agreements must be negotiated—not imposed by fiat— means that the end result will almost always fall short of the maximum that is desirable from each side's unilateral point of view.

The fact that arms control is a process of compromise has implications for both ends of the U.S. spectrum on these issues. Both Left and Right in varying ways dislike recognizing that, in dealing with the Soviet Union, the U.S. cannot expect to get something for nothing. On the one hand, "liberal" arms control advocates often dislike recognizing that a serious U.S. strategic modernization program is essential to arms control success, not as a way of providing inherently expendable bargaining chips, but as a way of making clear to the Soviet Union that in the absence of an agreement the U.S. not only will maintain a balance but will also pose greater problems for the USSR, which arms control gives them a way to avoid and limit. And, to have an incentive to agree, the Soviet leaders must regard such U.S. progress as politically viable, not just technically feasible.

On the other hand, "conservative" advocates of a "tough"

posture in negotiations dislike acknowledging that we cannot realistically expect to produce fundamental changes in the Soviet force structure with minimal alterations in our own. This is equally true even if one quite sincerely believes that the Soviets would be better off if they agreed to our prescriptions for fundamental changes in their programs. Furthermore, they are too ready to discount the Soviet will and ability to prevent us from "winning" an unconstrained arms race.

Third, verification will remain an essential issue. The test of our ability to verify an agreement is whether the United States would be able to detect Soviet violations and take effective countermeasures soon enough to prevent the Soviets from obtaining a military or political advantage from cheating—not whether there is some theoretical chance of marginal, undetected violation. The Soviets would cheat not for the joy of getting away with illegality, but to secure an advantage. Ultimately we want to monitor compliance not in order to discover Soviet perfidy, but to protect our security.

Probably more can be verified by national technical means than most critics (and some advocates) of arms control choose to believe. The domestic political reality is that the inherent uncertainties (and the secrecy) of the intelligence process cause severe problems in the politically charged arms control context. However, verification is in an important sense merely a special application of general intelligence on Soviet strategic forces. We are, after all, equally interested in most facts that arms control requires us to collect about Soviet strategic forces whether or not an agreement exists, and we should be equally interested in timely detection of concealed Soviet efforts to gain an advantage. Because of that interest, which is independent of arms control, the U.S. has devised a complex, sophisticated, and on the whole quite successful system for learning about the Soviet strategic program. The intelligence system gives us information on the full range of Soviet strategic nuclear forces. With such systems—aided by plausibly negotiable cooperative measures—we should be able to detect violations of agreements limiting most aspects of the strategic competition.

However, an adequately verifiable treaty requires more than an ability to *detect* violations. The objective is not to enjoy the moral or emotional satisfaction of catching the Russians if they cheat, but to prevent them from attaining a meaningful gain by doing so. The United States must also have adequate research and development and other program hedges so that it can do something about such a discovery, i.e., take effective measures to prevent the Soviets from gaining some advantage from violation. Indeed, the knowledge that the United States could respond to detected violations in ways that would prevent any Soviet gain is at least as important a deterrent to Soviet cheating as the knowledge that the United States would detect the violation.

Past Soviet behavior is such that verification uncertainties will be a significant factor in negotiations for the indefinite future. Indeed, the recent Soviet record on arms control compliance casts a shadow over immediate prospects. Nothing in Soviet history indicates that we can rely on trusting their general fidelity to the sanctity of international law. In particular, the increasing evidence of Soviet-backed use of illegal chemical weapons in Southeast Asia, and perhaps in Afghanistan as well, and Soviet stonewalling on efforts to determine whether they have violated the Bacteriological Warfare Convention are cause for serious concern. Preliminary information about recent Soviet missile tests also raises potential problems, if only because their high degree of telemetry encryption obscures the events.

Nonetheless, with respect to the SALT agreements which, in contrast to the chemical warfare and bacteriological warfare treaties, include detailed verification-related provisions, there is so far—and despite many leaked charges over many years—no evidence of actual Soviet violations. So far, all instances have involved the Soviets' pressing at the margins of permitted conduct and exploiting uncertainties about what is permitted.

In these situations, the appropriate United States response to such Soviet probing of the limits of an agreement is neither to ignore it because we lack sufficient evidence to prove our case beyond a reasonable doubt to a skeptical jury, nor, at the other extreme, to pronounce arms control impossible because of Soviet perfidy. It is instead to make use of the established procedures, through the Standing Consultative Commission (SCC) and otherwise, to clarify obligations and stop Soviet conduct we find unacceptable before it attains a level of military significance. The record of SALT so far is that the SCC process, and U.S. readiness to challenge Soviet action far short of absolute proof, have provided means to resolve all problems satisfactorily, and to clarify what conduct is permitted in the future.

So far arms control has relied primarily on so-called national technical measures (NTM), an undefined but generally understood conglomeration of technical intelligence collection systems including photographic satellites, radars to observe tests, telemetry monitoring systems, and other devices. However, verification becomes inherently harder as arms control goes from relatively observable matters such as limiting the number of fixed ICBM silos and missile-carrying submarines to controlling reloadable mobile systems, weapons numbers, qualitative limits, or production constraints.

These added information requirements make arms control more difficult; they do not make it impossible. They do add to the negotiating agenda a new and complex technical issue, and one in which the United States almost invariably has the primary interest — additional agreed-upon methods for verification, beyond national technical means. NTM will always lie at the core of verification, if only because we will ultimately rely, in assessing what the Soviets are doing, far more on what we find out for ourselves than on anything they tell us. However, cooperative measures of a wide variety of kinds can make national technical means work better, remove uncertainties about what is or is not permitted on the agreement, and even make agreements possible in areas where NTM alone would not suffice. The Soviets have in earlier negotiations agreed to certain cooperative measures (including detailed substantive provisions, counting rules, and a limited data exchange) and an important determinant of how much further progress is possible will be how much more they are prepared to agree on.

The most promising focus of such cooperative measures is almost certainly *not* on-site inspection (OSI), if by on-site inspection is meant the occasional presence of a limited number of inspectors at a designated time and place, and not joint manning and operation of strategic systems. OSI would be of marginal utility for most areas of current arms control interest where verification is an obstacle. However, openness by the Soviet Union to observation that is less intrusive, but potentially more informative on relevant issues, could pay substantial dividends. Included in this category are agreements on counting rules, means of making tests more open to observation, declaration of production facilities and deployment locations, and enhanced exchange of data.

A fourth area of difficulty is that the negotiation of arms control agreements is necessarily a complex process. The basic concepts of arms control agreements may, and indeed should, be simple if only because simple concepts are more likely to win the necessary public support. But the negotiation of provisions necessary to implement even simple concepts will almost always be complex. For example, in SALT II the concept that each side could test and deploy only one new type of ICBM was simple enough, but months of negotiation and hundreds of words of treaty text were required to define what was permitted and what was prohibited.

As arms control moves into new, more controversial, and technically more difficult areas, these questions of detailed specification of the limitations will be even more important. In particular, if an agreement is to be both meaningful and verifiable it must define with clarity what is limited, and in particular what are the boundary conditions, i.e., what systems or activities just beyond those limited are not constrained. Further, it will usually be necessary to agree on verification arrangements, e.g., cooperative measures for data exchange or collection.

Negotiating all these elements is complicated by the fact that in almost every case a given particular aspect will have more impact on one side than on the other, so that agreement on that issue will be linked explicitly or implicitly to progress on the other side's issues. One important implication of the complexity of the process is the utility of incorporating concepts and rules from previous agreements wherever possible, in order to avoid renegotiating the basic framework from scratch.

The Prospects for Arms Control

In the past two years, the stock of arms control has shot up, perhaps unrealistically so. There is no shortage of ideas for proposals that are popular, promising, and/or innovative. And there is substantial ground for agreement going beyond past pacts. Yet the prospects for short-term agreement seem bleak.

SALT/START. The principal focus of U.S. public interest is the negotiations on SALT-limited systems, renamed START (Strategic Arms Reduction Talks) to symbolize the Reagan administration's determination to break new ground.

The current (July 1983) American proposal on strategic arms would impose a limit of 5,000 on the number of missile warheads and a sublimit of 2,500 on ICBM warheads, limit the number of missile launchers to 1,200, and require a cut in Soviet MIRVed missiles to a quarter of their current levels. Bomber forces by contrast could continue at essentially present levels, and there would be no special limits on cruise missiles, bomber weapons, or new missile types. (Nor would there have to be, in the initial phase, direct limits on missile throw-weight.)

Although generally described as a "deep reductions proposal," the outstanding feature of this proposal is not the scale of general reductions required on both sides. Rather, it is that the proposal calls for a fundamental restructuring of the Soviet ICBM force with minimal impact on U.S. plans: the Soviet ICBM force would have to be cut by more than half (from about 6,000 reentry vehicles to 2,500), while planned U.S. submarine and land-based missile forces would have to be reduced only modestly, given our discounting of Minuteman as nonsurvivable. U.S. bomber and cruise missile programs would be essentially unchanged.

Such drastic changes in the Soviet ICBM force would unquestionably be in our interest. However, the Soviets are entirely unlikely to agree to any such unilateral restructuring; so the issue is not the abstract desirability of the proposal but whether some less fundamental agreement would be in our interest. Changes in the U.S. posture that might allow for exploration of such agreement began to be debated within the administration in the spring of 1983. The initial changes in the U.S. position reflected an unwillingness to face up to the fact that the basic Reagan administration approach is totally nonnegotiable. Whether, under domestic electoral pressure, Allied influence, and the need to secure support for the MX, the administration will go further soon enough to reach agreement before the 1984 election remains to be seen.

The Soviet START position contains, predictably, even more catches than the American opening position. Its overall framework is in some respects more like that of prior SALT agreements. For while the U.S. position treats bombers separately from missiles, the Soviet proposal, like SALT II, would cover ICBMs, SLBMs (submarine-launched ballistic missiles), and bombers. The Soviets propose a reduction to 1,800 (from the 2,500 current Soviet level and the 2,250 limit of SALT II) in overall launcher numbers and corresponding—though smaller—cuts in the other SALT II sublimits. One innovation would be a limit, at an unstated but reduced level, on "charges"—a term the Soviets use to cover both missile warheads and bomber weapons.

These two aspects of the Soviet proposal offer a good deal of basis for discussion. But in other critical respects—which they stress as integral parts of their proposal—the Soviets call for unilateral U.S. concessions even more far-reaching than the U.S. proposals for the USSR. For example, in a blatant effort to stop virtually all U.S. modernization programs at virtually no cost to themselves, the Soviet proposal includes a general call for minimum modernization, though they have apparently dropped their earlier demands for a halt to construction of Trident submarines and a ban on cruise missiles of all types (implicitly repudiating the SALT II bargain whereby planned U.S. air-launched cruise missile (ALCM) programs were essentially unconstrained, given the lack of limits on Soviet air defenses). The proposal also continues to insist on a freeze on "forward based systems" (thereby resolving all the issues in the INF talks on Soviet terms). No limits evidently would be placed on Soviet theater nuclear forces (TNF), or on their new bomber or missile programs.

In short, the sides remain far apart. Many critical issues of detail—notably those related to verification—have been essentially unaddressed. Nonetheless, somewhere between these two positions it may be possible to work out a useful agreement.

One feature of the U.S. proposal, the 1,200 limit on missile launchers, is, even at its recently increased level, clearly not in the American interest and is inconsistent with the new emphasis of a single reentry vehicle ICBM.

If, however, the U.S. is to test whether the Soviets are willing to reach useful new SALT agreements, we will need to go beyond merely making the U.S. position compatible with our own newly reshaped ICBM program; we should also now be considering basically different approaches. One area that deserves attention is the establishment of an overall ceiling—at significantly below current levels (which stand at about 8,000 a side)—on all strategic nuclear weapons, including both missiles and bombers. Such a concept has, to be sure, some problems of its own. For example, a global ceiling counting every nuclear explosive carried in an ICBM, SLBM, or heavy bomber would equate very different weapons, with no recognition of their capabilities or the defense against them (a problem that also exists, at least so far as capabilities, in the current U.S. proposal for an overall missile warhead ceiling). Moreover, in seeking an overall quantitative weapon limit, there is a strong case for also seeking some qualitative constraint on the "destructive potential" of the two forces. Qualitative limits are always harder to negotiate than quantitative ones, but the prospects for limits on throw-weight would be far more promising if bomber payload as well as missile throw-weight were taken into account (if only because the current Soviet advantage would be greatly reduced). A system of sublimits, to prevent the mix of forces from changing in a destabilizing direction, could also be used to improve some qualitative controls.

A comprehensive weapons limit—however much reenforced by sublimits, special counting rules, and payload-related collateral limits—could, however, serve a number of arms control objectives. First, it would produce significant reductions, for which there is strong (and justified) public support. Second, it would avoid either side's attempting to impose major unilateral changes on the other's forces. Third, it would allow modifications in existing forces that would increase stability without perpetuating the impression of an endless increase in arms. This concept of an overall weapons ceiling could, for example, be meshed with proposals for an agreed-upon "build down." Finally, while it could include detailed special rules to promote and address qualitative stability issues, the agreement would be simple in concept, and could build on already established detailed provisions from earlier agreements. In short, such an approach would respond to much of the basis for the deeply felt, and entirely reasonable, reasons for the popular appeal of the "freeze" movement in the United States and the antinuclear movement in Western Europe, without falling afoul of all of the strategic, technical, and verification difficulties of attempting in a literal sense to prevent all changes in the nuclear forces of the two sides.

Intermediate-range nuclear forces. The administration's position in INF has recently been modified to take account of the Soviet refusal to accept the administration's initial "zero/zero" proposal. The new U.S. proposal for an "interim" agreement would impose an equal limit on INF missile warheads of the U.S. and USSR wherever the missiles are located. No specific number has yet been advanced, but it would presumably be well below planned NATO deployments. The time is fast approaching when, to give concreteness to the U.S. offer, a number should be specified.

The Soviet proposal would, by contrast, apply only in European theater, cover certain aircraft as well as missiles, ban Pershing and ground-launched cruise missiles (GLCMs), and count British and French forces. Politically, it would effectively negate an American role in long-range nuclear deterrence in Europe, while strategically it would establish a legal permanence to existing Soviet force advantages.

The administration's rejection of the Soviet plan, and its current position (like its earlier one), is firmly based on the three fundamental principles of an acceptable agreement in this area:

First, the agreement should be *global* in scope and not permit the Soviets simply to withdraw missiles behind some artificial line in Soviet territory where they are supposedly, if temporarily, out of range of Europe.

Second, the agreement should be *bilateral,* affecting only U.S. and Soviet forces. The British and French (and Chinese) nuclear forces, as last-ditch ultimate deterrents, serve functions fundamentally different from either U.S. or Soviet intermediate-range forces. Moreover, considered in light of the overall nuclear arsenals of the superpowers, their numbers are not substantial (a few hundred warheads each, compared to perhaps 20,000 for both the U.S. and the USSR). Soviet efforts to make these third country forces a stumbling block for an agreement—while plausible-sounding—represent a tactical unwillingness to agree at this time, not a legitimate security concern.

Third, any limitations must provide for *equal rights* for each side. The U.S. cannot politically, and should not strategically, agree to limits that enshrine a Soviet advantage, whether or not we intend immediately to match Soviet levels in all categories.

The administration has, by some of its rhetoric about nuclear victory and limited war in Europe, tended to stimulate public opposition to deployment and to obscure the substantial virtues of its INF proposals and the importance of carrying through on deployment if no agreement is reached. There are elements of the U.S. position, notably the mix and level of deployments, that should be noticeable in the context of Soviet agreement to the basic principles outlined above. But the fundamental current problem in reaching the stage of detailed negotiations is Soviet rigidity and political maneuvering, behaviors that arise from factors outside the talks. The Soviet leaders realize their large SS-20 force gives them strategic and political advantages that would be offset by the deployments agreed on by NATO in December 1979, and they are — in a sense, quite understandably — unwilling to give up these advantages by limits on their own forces while they can still hope to foster a unilateral NATO halt to its deployments by exploiting public concern in the West about the dangers of nuclear war. Only when it is clear that the deployments will go forward unless there are serious limitations on Soviet forces is it plausible to expect that the Soviets will talk seriously about limitations.

Given this reason for the impasse in the talks, the critical issue during the coming year for arms control — as well as for the strength of the Alliance — will be successful implementation of the INF deployment. For the most part, the outcome depends on European domestic politics, and the United States can make the greatest contribution by enhancing its reputation for responsible and steady leadership — and by having made and pressed a concrete and reasonable proposal. However, it is also obviously important that the United States itself not pose political obstacles. For that reason, congressional action in delaying full funding of the Pershing II missile was particularly inappropriate and should not be repeated.

In sum, the prospect is for arms control to be a slow and incremental process. But for all its limitations arms control has the potential for affecting, in important ways, the scale of programs, the shape of force structure, and even deployment and operational patterns; but not for producing drastic or abrupt changes. Because the strategic competition is not a conflict of abstract or idealized superpowers, but a concrete contest of the United States with the Soviet Union over vital differences about the organization of society and the relations of nations, the prospects for progress on arms control are linked to the prospects for dealing effectively with the Soviet Union. Broadly speaking, we have for the future two devices to keep deterrence working. The first is prudent programs focused on stability and the second is arms control. These are closely linked, for programs are necessary to make agreements possible, and agreements are necessary to channel the competition into less dangerous areas.

9

COLIN S. GRAY

Arms Control: Problems

The SALT decade of 1969–79, and the revival of a formal Soviet-American arms control process from late 1981 until the present, provide persuasive evidence that, sadly, arms control negotiations should be understood to be as politically necessary as they are strategically unpromising. For reasons detailed and explained below, the arms control process is unpromising because the structure of American, and more generally Western, defense politics does not permit steady behavior conducive to the promotion of arms control agreements that would serve the interests of national and international security. No matter how ill-equipped the United States may be to participate in an arms control process with a totalitarian state, such participation must be judged necessary because the electorates in Western democracies have come to view evidence of activity on behalf of arms control as evidence of commitment to peace.

The Reagan administration attempted in 1981 to pursue the strategically rational course of charting and funding its defense program before it committed itself to the arms control negotiating fray. This approach was a domestic and inter-Allied political failure of no small dimension or importance. In practice, notwithstanding the inherent merit of its approach, the administration forfeited the moral high ground of being seen to care about arms control—and *ipso facto* to many people, about peace. When the administration made dramatic and ambitious bids for public confidence by means of attention-seizing proposals for disarmament in intermediate-range nuclear forces (INF) and then in the Strategic Arms Reduction Talks (START), those bids looked as though they had been prompted by a concern to respond to public disquiet. Inevitably, some of the credit the administration might have expected to receive for such visible (and genuine) evidence of commitment to arms reduction was forfeited because of the widespread belief that the timing and the character of the proposals advanced were dictated more by a felt need to appease domestic and allied critics than by a genuine commitment to arms control.

The East-West arms control process has always been about politics, and particularly (in the Soviet perspective) about influencing defense politics in Western countries, rather than restructuring the military balance according to technical criteria of stability. Understandably and inevitably, the Soviet Union engages in the arms control process in order to press for political advantage. Such political advantage may flow from the character of the superpower relationship implicit in the fact and detail of an agreement; from the impediment an arms control process can be to domestic American support for nuclear weapons modernization; from the influence that an agreement is expected to have upon the relative competitive performance of the two sides; or from the disharmony that can be promoted within the Western Alliance as a consequence of tempting the United States, or European members of NATO, with agreements that have very different appeals in different NATO capitals.

This article is not hostile toward, or even suspicious of, arms control in the abstract. The Western (largely American) theoretical literature on arms control is rich with designs and suggestions that, if effected through international agreement, would indeed greatly strengthen the stability of deterrence. Unfortunately, as a general rule, the problems with arms control are not of a theoretical kind and they do not lend themselves to solutions by the exercise of strategic imagination. In short, there are structural reasons, having to do with the character of the American and Soviet polities and the nature of their political rivalry, that effectively preclude their accomplishing anything of far-reaching importance for strategic stability through an adversary-partnership in joint arms control ventures.

There is always room for improved theory, but arms control theory must be far less deductive, more political, and less technical than characteristically has been the case in the past. The late Bernard Brodie was very much on the mark when he advised that

strategic thinking, or "theory" if one prefers, is nothing if not pragmatic. Strategy is a "how to do it" study, a guide to accomplishing something and doing it efficiently. As in many other branches of politics, the question that matters in strategy is: Will the idea work? More important, will it be likely to work under the special circumstances under which it will next be tested?[1]

Just as the American strategic theoretical literature in the late 1950s and early 1960s on the subject of limited war had very little indeed to say about the stability of the (U.S.) home front,[2] so that literature, in its excitement with the possibilities of arms control, neglected to investigate circumstances wherein arms control negotiations would be more political theater (or political warfare) than substantive.[3] It is a sad reflection on the state of public education that today, notwithstanding ten years of intensive SALT experience, the immediate arms control policy challenge for Western governments is the need for negotiating designs of sufficient domestic political appeal to legitimize the arms acquisition programs essential for national security (they are also essential if progress is to be made in arms control).

This, truly, is a policy area with no villains. Soviet leaders are behaving responsibly, according to their own lights, and have been true to their theory of security. American leaders have felt compelled, *faute de mieux,* to endorse expectations concerning arms control negotiations that they should know will not, and cannot, be met: this is pragmatic recognition of the political reality that democracies today will not tolerate arming without parleying. Also, arms control per se, as a body of theory and as a partial approach to security issues, can be neither villain nor hero. One cannot be for or against arms control in the abstract.

Because of the great appeal of arms control—of the idea of cooperation among potential enemies—very few commentators, let alone officials, have proved willing to address the structural problems that attend American endeavors to secure progress in this field. The on-off arms control debate of the past fifteen years, and particularly of 1979 in connection with the ratification controversy over SALT II, has been noticeably barren in the realm of fundamental inquiry and argument; many commentators have chosen not to address the more basic questions pertaining to the viability of the multifaceted East-West arms control process.[4] One suspects the reason for this failure to be that they feared that the answers produced by the evidence and logic of such inquiry would be politically and even ethically (if arms control is considered a moral value) illegitimate and unacceptable or, at the very least, profoundly unfashionable.

The hiatus in formal East-West negotiations that resulted from the Soviet invasion of Afghanistan on Christmas Eve of 1979 might have enabled the United States and its allies to reconsider, at appropriate and necessary leisure, the wisdom in the arms control policies pursued over the previous ten years. Indications to the effect that an important shift had occurred in official American policy thinking vis-à-vis the merits of, and proper approach toward, arms control were provided in 1981.[5] Nonetheless, by 1983 it has begun to be apparent that, only in part for reasons of their own making, Western governments might be in the process of committing old arms control negotiating sins in (some) new ways.

This article is not a critique of current policy in START and INF. Indeed, given the constraint of public opinion, there is much to praise in the approaches adopted by the Reagan administration and by NATO as a whole. Instead, in a later section, this article addresses seven basic problems that operate to inhibit the ability of any U.S. government to advance national and international security through attempts to effect some sort of cooperative management of the arms competition through formal arms control.

Negotiation, Arms Competition, and War

The history of arms control negotiations in this century, be they the Washington Conference on the Limitation of Armaments in 1921–22 or SALT I (1969–72), demonstrates very plainly that substantive arms control agreements are possible only when the negotiating parties have very strong political incentives for mutual accommodation, and when the extant military balance is judged tolerable. As a general rule, a superpower will not negotiate from a position of weakness (though this rule can be broken for overriding domestic political reasons, as with the United States vis-à-vis START and INF today), while it may be unable to negotiate successfully from a position of great strength. By way of illustration, the Soviets would not negotiate on strategic nuclear arms in 1964, when President Johnson made the first approach to what became the SALT process—yet as Soviet commentators are fond of saying, "it was no accident" that they did agree in 1968, having corrected much of the imbalance that characterized the early 1960s, to participate in negotiations.

The major problem today is that the United States lacks bargaining power in the coin of the realm for negotiations— dynamic deployment programs under way. The United States is seeking to cut dramatically into the weapons category that the Soviet Union views as the very basis of its defense—intercontinental ballistic missiles (ICBMs)—on the strength of the *promise* of a far more capable, modernized American strategic nuclear arsenal in the future. If the U.S. government and NATO mean what they say concerning Soviet strategic advantages today, then it should follow that the policy goal of equitable agreement cannot be pursued in the near term with any plausible prospect of success. The Soviet Union is not at all interested in reaching fair and balanced agreements that would have a mutually stabilizing effect on the competition. It is interested in securing recognition of the extraordinary effort it has expended upon its strategic nuclear buildup of the past two decades.[6] The Soviet government will not permit the United States to secure a strategic balance through negotiation that it is unable, or unwilling, to achieve through unilateral effort.

Inevitably, when a U.S. government advances radical arms control proposals that require substantially disproportionate disarmament on the Soviet side—unequal reductions for equal results—it invites domestic criticism to the effect that it is not "serious" about arms control. "Serious" proposals, presumably, are those that pass the test of equality and negotiability. However, because of the huge Soviet arms buildup over the past decade, the situation today does not permit the U.S. government responsibly to seek a reduction in, or even the "freezing" of, the current (im)balance. It follows that, barring the emergence of quite extraordinary political or economic pressures for agreement, the state of the strategic balance does not lend itself to arms control discipline at the present time. Equitable agreements, by U.S. definition on INF or in START, most probably are not negotiable in the early 1980s.

Because Western governments dare not admit this—or, more accurately stated, believe that they dare not admit this—and because the Soviet government has no incentive to admit it, the arms control process descends into political theater for influencing fearful minds in democracies. It is unfortunate that a *formal* arms control process has come to be associated closely with reducing the risk of war. Because of the great technical difficulty in comparing armed forces between countries, negotiations are compelled to focus upon those units of military account that are the easiest, or the least difficult, to assay. Those units of account, be they "launchers,"[7] delivery vehicles, warheads, or even throw-weight, are indeed not without significance, but they are relatively unimportant to the risk of war at the force levels currently deployed by both sides.[8]

What has happened over the past decade and a half is that, for the best of reasons (at least in the United States), the arms control process has been accorded an unmerited measure of importance for its potential contribution to reducing the risk of war. Reductions in forces, even deep reductions, are unlikely to be relevant to the risk of war. What is relevant to the risk is the survivability of forces (a problem area that, to date, has been exacerbated rather than alleviated by the arms control process) and—above all else—the stability of the command function[9] and the enduring reliability of intelligence information that the command function needs for rational policymaking.

SALT and START have not merely neglected to focus upon true stability issues; they have also served to focus public attention, unhelpfully, upon relatively unimportant questions. That focus has produced political irritation in Soviet-American (and U.S.– NATO-European) relations quite out of balance with any inherent merit in the arms control enterprise. It is tempting to put forward the proposition that when Soviet-American political relations are good and improving, an arms control dimension to those relations is likely to provide positive reinforcement; while when Soviet-American political relations are poor and deteriorating, an arms control dimension is likely (indeed certain) similarly to provide negative reinforcement. That proposition is probably correct. However, it needs to be supplemented by the following judgments: although the arms control process has come to be seen as an essential element in East-West relations, so limited is the underpinning of East-West common interests that the potential for the process to have a net negative effect on political relations must always be high.[10]

The voluminous public commentary on arms control of recent years is near-silent with regard to two rather obvious negative features of the SALT, START, and INF ventures. First, as noted above, the negotiations of necessity have focused upon the least important aspects of the forces under discussion. Second, arms control negotiations serve, unhealthily, to keep the narrowly military aspect of East-West relations constantly at the forefront of political notice. Moreover, to combine these two points, the negotiations require both sides to be sensitive to military comparisons that often are strategically irrelevant. Imbalances in particular categories of forces that are quite tolerable *de facto* rapidly become intolerable if the "disadvantaged" party is pressed to accept them *de jure* in a formal agreement.

On balance, SALT, START, and INF to date probably have had a net negative effect upon East-West political relations. While much is uncertain in the realm of political-military analysis, there can be no doubt that arms control negotiations cannot produce effects beneficial to international security if they are conducted in a context of implacable political hostility. The hope of the late 1950s that arms control negotiations, conducted on a narrow front by the technicians of strategic stability of East and West,[11] could diminish the danger of war regardless of political tension has long since been shown to be fanciful.

Arms control policy in the United States, like the body of analysis that it imperfectly reflects, tends to contain a fallacy at its center. The error lies in the understanding of why wars occur. This is no small matter, because the principal explicit American purpose in the pursuit of arms control has been, and remains, to reduce the risk of war. Contrary to widespread belief, the danger of war does not lie, and has never lain, in the arms race itself. This is not to deny that first-strike anxieties, fed by observation and anticipation of new weapons and tactics of the arms race rival, logically should reinforce estimates of hostile political intentions.[12] However, granting the possibility that there is a partially self-fueling aspect to the multidimensional East-West arms competition, that competition was initiated, has been sustained, and can be terminated only by political motives. Estimates of relative military prowess will help determine the risks the states elect to run and, *in extremis,* the outcome of deliberations on whether or not to fight; but the occasions for crisis and war are political only.

Demands that the superpowers should "halt the nuclear arms race" focus attention upon the symptoms rather than the cause of the problem. So long as political rivalry and hostility are not abated, there can be no sufficient basis for an arms control process to accomplish anything more substantial than a registration of the facts of military competition. Nuclear armed forces could, of course, pose a threat to peace for reason of their technical characteristics and as a consequence of major imbalance in their respective operational prowess. As a general rule, however, these dangers cannot be alleviated through arms control. States cannot legislate strategic doctrine through arms control (since strategic doctrines are inspired by strategic cultures that, by definition, have deep roots);[13] they cannot compel design and deployment of a robust architecture for command and control; and they cannot, and would not wish to, require that all parties compete with such vigor as to preclude the design of a plausible theory of victory by others.

Should the United States and the Soviet Union ever "go to war," to employ the old-fashioned term, it will not be because the hands on the clock on the cover of *The Bulletin of the Atomic Scientists* finally reached midnight, signifying a terminal superpower failure to control the nuclear arms competition. Instead, war will come because of a chronic crisis of control within the Soviet imperium; because of some "Balkan trigger" that ignites a wider conflict; because of some overlap between the superpowers in areas of critical geopolitical interest, and so forth. Whether or not the nuclear arsenals of both sides are reduced 25 percent, 33 percent, or 50 percent below their current levels may well be a matter of profound irrelevance to the political judgments and misjudgments that, in malign combination, produce a war.

Problems

The seven problems with arms control negotiations as a policy instrument for the United States that have been selected for discussion here are all of an enduring kind—they do not refer to the difficulties of any particular administration but are rather inherent in the structure of arms control as a policy area. These problems are thus realities to which each administration must pay attention if its efforts at arms control are to avoid doing more harm than good to national and international security.

The arms control paradox. The more the military relationship between two states is in need of arms control discipline, the more difficult such (reciprocal) discipline is to effect. States compete in armaments because they believe they may have to fight each other. Political rivalry fuels anxiety and suspicion, virtually precluding agreements that carry the promise of meaningful military reductions. States compete in armaments in order to support their contending foreign policy activities. So long as they cannot agree to settle their foreign policy differences, they will not deem it prudent to restrict greatly their freedom of action with regard to unilateral defense preparation. If the superpowers could reach a genuine geopolitical accommodation, which would have to entail a rather basic change in the character of the Soviet and/or American systems, then there would be no reason for the nuclear arms competition to continue. Radical solutions to the nuclear arms competition—Jonathan Schell's *The Fate of the Earth* provides a recent example[14]—either ignore critical political difficulties or simply assume a magical transformation in the terms of international political conduct.

Objectives. Because American policymakers have been unwilling, or unable, to consider the structural problems of arms control, they have not settled upon solid and publicly well-understood policy objectives in this area. Indeed, they have themselves provided ample evidence of ambivalence as to which American objectives are realistic and which are not. A senator confronted with the SALT II treaty, for example, had a major problem of evaluation. Should such a treaty be judged on the basis of its accuracy as "a photograph of the existing balance" (as Henry Kissinger characterized the interim offensive forces agreement of SALT I)?[15] Should it be judged on the basis of its contribution to future strategic stability—although there are different definitions of the requirements of stability?[16] Should it be assayed as to its equitability? But how should equitability be judged—with reference to *extant* forces, that is to say in recognition of past and current effort expended, or with regard to consideration (by whom?) of developing a tolerable, even balance between the forces?

From the very outset of modern arms control theorizing and policymaking in the United States in the late 1950s, the U.S. government has advocated what Robert Ranger has called "technical" arms control, but it has been compelled, in practice, to accept "political" arms control.[17] This divergence of public aspiration from the reality of what could be accomplished has fed public disillusion; it has also driven senior officials to tout their SALT accomplishments in ways that support the extravagant promises previously made. The unfolding story of START and INF in the 1980s bids fair to remind people of the lesson that should have been learned from the SALT decade: because of the political rivalry between the negotiating parties, arms control agreements can provide little more than a politically symbolic expression of joint interest in preventing nuclear war.

Writing in 1980, Richard Burt, now a senior member of the Reagan administration, advised that arms control would—and could—be of little importance for national security:

Whatever approach the United States follows, there seem to be strong arguments for deemphasizing the role of arms control. . . . SALT, as the

American-Soviet nuclear competition begins to revolve around nuclear force management issues, has become irrelevant in a new strategic era. The risk is that by continuing to base American strategic policy on SALT, the United States will be impeded from seeking unilateral solutions to such problems as force survivability and endurance.[18]

He was correct then, and his words are still correct today — at least with reference to "technical" arms control attempts to restructure the strategic balance in the interest of stable deterrence according to the American definition. Where he erred, understandably given the period in which he was writing, was in understating the need that American and NATO-European governments have for a visibly "live" East-West arms control process as political cover for the weapon deployments necessary for national and international security. Much of the dislike of SALT II expressed by its more conservative critics rested upon the belief that that treaty was not "real" arms control. As often as not those critics were right, but for the wrong reasons. They were correct in noticing that SALT II made no dent of importance in the strategic weapons programs of the two sides; but they were wrong in failing to notice, as a general rule, that SALT II would not serve the basic traditional goals of arms control — in particular the goal of reducing the risk of war (through contributing to the stability of deterrence).

There is much to recommend the old adage that if you attempt the impossible you are certain to fail. As long as the United States lags in a major way in the relative development of weapons programs, negotiating with a state that takes a severely political-instrumental view of negotiations and that has a deep-seated (indeed cultural) preference for unilateral rather than cooperatively negotiated measures for national security, America should probably not embark boldly upon a quest for "real" arms control. The goal is not attainable. So long as Western publics are told that the arms control process is very important, they can hardly be expected to acquiesce passively when far-reaching Western proposals are shown to be nonnegotiable. They will insist upon compromise (on the American side) — even though the actual strategic merits of heavily diluted proposals will be marginal at best. In such a situation, any administration will be tempted to avoid the charge of intransigence by negotiating what it can negotiate and overselling what it has negotiated so as to conceal the gap between initial goals and final accomplishment.[19]

Arming to parley. At the level of theory, few people have difficulty understanding that a demonstrated will and ability to compete effectively in armaments is the source of bargaining strength in negotiations. Yet in practice, U.S. governments have difficulty managing competently the parallel activities of arms control and strategic policy. Administrations argue, with good reason, that successful negotiations must be based upon real military capability, not on ideas of strategic stability. Arms control negotiations do not comprise a debate over strategic theory.

Critics argue variously that negotiations are used as an excuse for the purchase of weapons; that "bargaining chip" programs tend to find a supporting constituency (witness the cruise missile); that new American weapons programs with major counterforce first-strike qualities increase Soviet anxieties and strengthen the "hard-liners" in Moscow; and that arms control agreements, to date, have achieved only the registration of the status quo and the legitimization of "competition as usual." Some of these criticisms are not without merit. Also, there is considerable reluctance in Congress to fund any weapon that an administration chooses to defend mainly in terms of its postulated value in arms control negotiations. In response to the argument that it cannot be convinced of the strategic value of a weapon that it is willing to trade away, an administration is driven to the awkward position of arguing both that the weapon in question is essential if negotiations are to succeed, and that it intends to proceed with deployment virtually regardless of the outcome of the arms control process.[20]

In practice in a democracy, the idea of arming to parley, notwithstanding its intellectual respectability, is nearly untenable at an emotional level. As a consequence, governments frequently fall for the temptation of escalating their rhetorical commitment to arms control in order to minimize the reality of weapon programs justified in part, sometimes even in good part, with reference to the problematical joys of arms control agreements yet to be secured.

Strategic-technological prediction. Laurence Martin has suggested that

entering into over-simplified agreements about particular aspects of a complex strategic environment . . . entails the danger of losing the flexibility with which to adapt to change. . . . The rigidity you legislate today may deny you the evasive manoeuvre you want to take tomorrow.[21]

The formal arms control record comprises a legacy for the future, even with its interruptions and despite the occasions on which it has been partially discredited (as in 1979–81). United States performance in arms control since 1969 suggests that American policymakers may be unable to protect those possibilities of "evasive manoeuvre" needed for stability in deterrence. The terms of any arms control agreement constitute a guess about strategic requirements in years to come.[22] While improvement in prediction is always possible, it is less than obvious that policymakers in the early 1980s are any more able to predict which weapons options they should protect for the 1990s than were their predecessors who made predictions in the early 1970s for the 1980s. Over the years, there has been little observance of the principle that even if arms control cannot alleviate (let alone solve) serious strategic problems, it should not be permitted to exacerbate those problems.

Treaties that effectively preclude the active defense of strategic forces, prohibit construction of new fixed launchers, and place ceilings on the number of delivery vehicles far lower than the number of warheads that could be directed against them do not serve the goal of deterrence stability. The existence of such treaties does not reduce the risk of war; to the contrary, the exacerbation by treaty constraints of the problem of survivability of land-based missile forces tends instead to increase that risk.

Negotiating on the home front. It is commonplace, and true, to note that the major negotiations on arms control policy occur within the United States (and presumably the Soviet) government, rather than between the United States and the Soviet Union. It is very difficult indeed for a U.S. government to hold the line even on important details, not to mention on matters of principle, in its arms control negotiating posture. Set in the context of a society that tends to value negotiations and agreements per se as beneficial to peace and security, the structure of the U.S. policymaking process on arms control makes it virtually impossible for arms control policy to support strategic planning objectives in a purposive fashion. Careful, integrated analysis of possible arms control positions in the light of U.S. strategic needs should be conducted by the Joint Chiefs of Staff. These options should then be weighed against, or in support of, the political criteria that dominate the views of other players. More often than not such careful analysis is not performed or, when performed, is treated as just another input to policymaking.

The United States government has a truly impressive ability to negotiate itself, internally, out of (or away from) arms control positions that have substantial merit for deterrence stability. In short, the character of U.S. government organization, and the attractiveness to the electorate of arms control per se, must raise the question of whether the United States can perform steadily and competently in the field of arms control negotiations. The evidence to date is not encouraging.

Soviet-American asymmetries. States can reach agreement even if they do not have the same styles of behavior. However, the asymmetries between Soviet and American strategic cultures and styles are so deep and extensive that the arms control process may well serve to increase rather than decrease political suspicion. The Soviet Union views arms control as an instrument of political struggle and as a framework not so much for regulating strategic relations to strengthen deterrence stability (a Western concept),[23] but rather as a vehicle for the more effective pursuit of strategic advantage. Soviet doctrine requires steady enhancement of war-waging prowess—in support of the Soviet idea of deterrence—which works to undermine the political viability of the arms control process in the West. Being true to itself, the Soviet state, on occasion, has lied over the performance characteristics of some of its weapons, has cheated on some treaty terms,[24] and has deployed new weapon systems (the SS-19, for example) that were blatantly incompatible with what the U.S. government believed—and the Soviet Union knew the U.S. government believed—were legally permitted.

The issue here is how the enduring (mis)behavior traits of the Soviet Union should be allowed to affect East-West relations. It is one thing for the United States to live with a Soviet government behaving in usual Soviet ways; it is quite another for the United States to choose to place itself in a legal and political position where it feels compelled to acquiesce in, or even explicitly excuse, Soviet misbehavior.[25] The domestic Western imperative (if such it is) of arms control has rendered East-West relations hostage to American tolerance of highly questionable Soviet strategic activity. For fear of "rocking the boat" of arms control and, *ab extensio* in the public mind, of peace, U.S. freedom of action to call violations what they are (with respect to the Geneva Protocol of 1925, the ABM Treaty and Interim Agreement of 1972, the Biological Weapons Convention of 1975, and the Helsinki Agreement of 1975) has been greatly restricted.[26]

Verification, compliance, and sanctions. American public debate on arms control of recent years has focused heavily upon the question of verification. Because of the basic differences between an open and a closed society, and the derivative fact that the Soviet Union has made secrecy a strategic asset in negotiations, it is entirely appropriate that the United States should endeavor to negotiate only those agreements that are verifiable with high confidence. While the general problem of verifying treaty compliance is inherent in the structure of the Soviet-American arms control process, a rather more serious matter is the issue of what the United States should do when it discovers either clear or ambiguous evidence of noncompliance. What has been the policy on sanctions for evident or apparent noncompliance? The record to date suggests that the United States does not really have a policy in this area—unless tacit acquiescence merits description as a policy. In fact for many years there has been a very pronounced difference between American official public rhetoric on the importance of verification, and actual U.S. behavior when examples of apparent noncompliance have been discovered.

No U.S. government has been willing to make a real diplomatic fuss over actual or likely Soviet SALT violations. The reasons for this are very familiar: much (though not all) of the evidence is ambiguous; many of the key treaty terms are ambiguous; the whole

architecture of the arms control process is deemed too important
to imperil for minor infractions; and, along the same line of
thought, it is often held that "Soviets will be Soviets," and the
health of East-West political relations as a whole cannot be jeopar-
dized because of a few small technical violations; and so on and so
forth. There are any number of politically attractive excuses for
American failures to call the Soviet Union to account, or in the absence of a persuasive accounting to exercise the sanction of walk-
ing out of the arms control process. Quite aside from whatever
strategic disadvantage may flow to the United States as a consequence of excessive and illegal Soviet zeal in arms competition, by
failing to develop a genuine sanctions policy the United States invites a measure of Soviet disrespect that is not conducive to future
strategic stability.

What Can Be Done?

Notwithstanding this assessment of the enduring realities of East-
West arms control, the United States need not, indeed politically
cannot afford to, abandon arms control as a policy instrument.
However, for the United States to design and conduct an arms
control policy that will be of net benefit to national security, full
account should be taken of the problems discussed above. The
point is not to complain about Soviet political and strategic
culture, nor to bewail the great difficulty that a democracy has in
pursuing a steady negotiating course. These are enduring facts of
life and must be accommodated in Western statecraft. The
analysis presented here suggests the following conclusions:

- Western publics should be educated about the problems, as well
  as the promise, of arms control. Agreements that are very
  modest in content should be acknowledged as such.

- U.S. arms control proposals should always make strategic sense
  for American defense planning—whether they be trivial or
  very substantive. Negotiating positions that have merit only as
  public political rhetoric should be eschewed—no matter how
  tempting for near-term effect. They are bound to result, eventually, in the charge that "the U.S. is not serious about arms

control," and they will encourage demands for compromise that will be difficult to meet if they make only political sense.

- An American government should never enter the arms control arena if it is afraid to leave it. The United States should be prepared to walk away from negotiations if the Soviet Union plainly will not meet the reasonable negotiating requirements of U.S. security, and if the Soviet Union is unable satisfactorily to explain apparent evidence of treaty noncompliance.

- Because of the nature of their rivalry, the superpowers must always view their military capabilities as inherently of far greater importance than the fact of arms control agreement. Fortunately, it is a general truth that the higher the quality of the U.S. strategic nuclear deterrent, the better should be the negotiating hand of the U.S. government. (It is, of course, possible that the U.S. bargaining hand could be so strong that neither side would discern incentives to negotiate.)

In short, the arms control process per se is unpromising for the stabilization of deterrence because in practice the U.S. government in particular, and Western democracies in general, seem unable to deal with the important problem areas that have been discussed here. Every new administration promises to do better than its predecessors, as should be expected; but the enduring ill effect of these problems upon policy performance suggests that they may well be inherent in the arms control process as it must be conducted by a democracy.

V

The Nonnuclear Dimensions of Strategy

10

AMORY B. LOVINS

L. HUNTER LOVINS

Reducing Vulnerability: The Energy Jugular

Massive attacks by nuclear-armed missiles are not this country's only strategic problem. National security is threatened not only by hostile ideology but also by misapplied technology; not only by threats imposed by enemies abroad but also by threats that America heedlessly—and needlessly—has imposed on itself. Despite its awesome military might, the United States has become extremely vulnerable, and is becoming more vulnerable, to the simple, low-technology disruption of such vital infrastructure as energy supply, water, food, data processing, and telecommunications.

Terrorism, technical mishap, or natural disaster that damaged the domestic energy system could be nearly as devastating as a sizeable war. Covert paramilitary or nonmilitary attacks on key infrastructure are so cheap, safe, and deniable that they may prove a fatally attractive instrument of surrogate warfare. The

horizontal proliferation of nuclear weapons technology means
that the delivery vehicle of choice for a miniature nuclear bomb
may now be a Liberian freighter or a fishing boat, a delivery van
or a U-Haul truck — modes that can be anonymous and therefore
undeterrable. And *non*nuclear strategic attacks may likewise
come in unfamiliar and unstoppable forms, appearing as sudden,
complete, but perhaps seemingly accidental breakdowns of infrastructure vital to national life. American prosperity could end
"not with a bang but a whimper," as the lights go out and the
machines stop for a long time because our less visible dangers
have been ignored.

The community of strategic planners needs to take fuller account of our self-imposed fragilities. Significant attacks upon
energy systems are now occurring at a rate of about one a week
around the world (not counting El Salvador, where they occur
more or less daily). They are becoming more frequent, serious, and
sophisticated. Yet federal energy policy is increasing U.S. vulnerability to such attacks, while ignoring alternatives that would
make the American energy system both more resilient and
cheaper.

Appropriate responses to threats against our overcentralized infrastructure are quite different from those required to defend
against missile attack, though they would also improve nuclear
and general military preparedness. Those responses, and the
threat itself, were therefore ignored for decades. No analysis had
comprehensively examined this strategic blindness until late
1981, when the Federal Emergency Management Agency released
a study of U.S. energy vulnerability.[1] The findings of that study
have important implications for any meaningful understanding of
our national security.

What Is Energy Security?

Military planners have long appreciated that secure energy supplies are vital to maintaining military capabilities, civilian
prosperity, and political stability. Threats to energy security,
however, have recently been defined — especially since the
1973–74 Arab oil embargo — as the risk that oil imports may be
cut off. Innumerable conferences, books, and articles have treated

this risk. And it is certainly real and important. One aircraft, or even two people in dinghies, could probably shut down 85 percent of Saudi oil exports for up to three years (the period required to manufacture key components of the loading terminals).[2] Such an attack could be repeated once the damage was repaired. But insecure oil imports are only one of many forms of energy vulnerability. Foreign oil provides only a tenth of America's energy; yet most of the other nine-tenths is as easy to shut off, faster and in larger pieces.

This pervasive energy insecurity has evolved by haphazard ricochets from one vulnerability to another. America shifted from wood to coal in the 1800s in search of more secure and abundant supplies; thence to oil and gas—now three-fourths of our energy—after the 1919 coal strike; thence to oil and gas pipelines after World War II U-boat attacks on coastal oil shipments and labor problems with railway coal shipments. In 1973–74, policymakers rushed to embrace any domestic energy sources, however vulnerable, that could replace embargoed Arab oil: massive electrification, an expanded nuclear power program, "coal by wire," and Arctic and offshore oil and gas. The 1979 Iranian revolution in turn sparked the abortive synthetic fuel program.

The oil crises of the 1970s, far from raising consciousness about the fragility of *all* centralized energy systems, focused attention exclusively on the vulnerability of oil imports. Most proposed substitutes have further *reduced* energy security. The domestic energy system is now so vulnerable that even eliminating oil imports—which could be done in the 1980s by making buildings and cars more efficient—would barely begin to reduce America's inventory of critical energy choke-points.

Generic Causes of Vulnerability

Complexity. Many modern energy systems are so complex that their modes of failure often cannot be foreseen. Rare, even bizarre, surprises do happen. Critical systems should therefore be designed not only to be reliable against calculable kinds of technical failure, but also resilient in the face of the incalculable: lunatics, guerrillas, social turmoil, freak weather, and those unexpected high-technology failures that are held to be impossible until, like the 1965 Northeast blackout, they happen. Yet this design philosophy of resilience for a surprise-full future is unfortunately very rare in modern energy engineering. If a relay failure blacks out New York, the engineers' usual response is to redesign the relay to fail less often — while doing nothing about the centralizing, monolithic architecture that caused the cascading grid failure in the first place.

Control and synchronism. Many structural features of modern energy systems make major failures more likely. For example, energy is generally hauled for hundreds or thousands of miles, and exploitation of more remote fuel deposits is increasing the distances. Along those energy lifelines are strung vital pumps, valves, switches, etc., which demand split-second computer timing and instantaneous communications. Electrical delivery demands a continuous, direct connection, and large, precise generating machines spread across a subcontinental area must rotate exactly in step with each other, threaded together by a frail network of aerial arteries. Gas grids, too, must maintain a certain minimum pressure; otherwise they can collapse, extinguishing pilot lights and causing an epidemic of fires and explosions. (Thus a city's urban redevelopment problem could be solved by interrupting its natural gas supply, then turning it back on again.)

Hazardous fuels. Energy is often delivered in concentrated, powerful forms that are themselves hazardous. In 1976, an exploding oil tanker in Los Angeles Harbor shattered windows 21 miles away. A standard tank truck of fuel oil contains energy equivalent to 0.3 kiloton; a standard marine tanker of liquefied natural gas, 0.7 megaton. Tanks, tankers, and pipelines rich in flammable or explosive fuels pervade our urban and industrial heartland.

Inflexibility and interdependence. Different fuels, or even different compositions of the same fuel, are seldom interchangeable, so shortages of one type cannot be made up by simply substituting others. Most energy transportation systems, too, have only limited flexibility, reversibility, capacity, speed, and convertibility.

Moreover, many supposedly independent energy systems actually depend on each other. Home oil and gas furnaces need electricity for pumping and ignition. So do gas station pumps, most water systems, most coal mines and oil refineries, and half of all domestic oil extraction. All heavy machinery needs lubricants from the oil industry. Nearly all coal transportation uses diesel fuel. Most power stations use standby diesel generators to run vital safety devices.

Specialized requirements. The extreme capital-intensity of most modern energy systems makes them high-value targets; reduces the financial slack that allows routine maintenance, built-in redundancy, and spare-parts inventories; and reduces adaptability to unforeseen changes in demand patterns. Such systems also often take a decade or so to build, increasing financial and technical risks, and depend on highly specialized skills for operation and maintenance. Without a few key people, many computerized pipeline systems or power plants become inoperable. Such dependence has helped to bring down governments in Britain (the 1974 coal strike), Iran (oil strikes and blackouts in 1978), and Chile (blackouts in 1973). Political disruptions of energy supplies have also threatened the stability of El Salvador (1972, 1980–), Portugal (1972), Puerto Rico (1973, 1977–78, 1981), Colombia (1977–), Israel (1981), and Peru (1981–). A strike of Salvadoran power workers in 1980, which cut off all power and half the water in the capital for only twenty-three hours, shut down 95 percent of the nation's industry and created a national emergency. In 1983, when striking power workers blacked out sweltering Delhi, the government capitulated in five hours.

Energy systems can be not only severed but also misused: for example, by introducing noxious substances into the gas grid or oil storage depots; adding substances to oil that cause it to rot or make it unrefinable; or altering the frequency or voltage in electrical grids so as to destroy generators and end-use devices over a wide area. Many electrical grids are controlled by open communications links that, in the private estimation of some utility engineers, could probably be taken over and manipulated by amateurs.

Difficulty of repair. Reestablishing collapsed energy systems can be very difficult, as the July 1977 New York City blackout revealed. Many devices cannot be restored to service without some unaffected energy source from outside (e.g., to restart power stations and resynchronize electric grids).

Major spare parts are often special-order items with lead times of months to years. Spare parts that are stockpiled alongside original components may be destroyed with them; spares stored elsewhere may be impossible to get to the site in an emergency. The national inventory of critical components — special motors and valves, extra-high-voltage transformers and switchgear, and a host of other key items — is very small, typically only enough to cope with failures in one or two plants. Essential repair skills, once available within energy companies, are now generally contracted out to small, specialized crews of very limited capacity. Making spare parts from scratch may require an intact industrial, transportation, and communication infrastructure that presupposes universally available energy.

All these constraints on repair, restoration, and recovery can enable a seemingly minor interruption to enmesh an industrial economy in waves of rapidly spreading chaos. Coordinated attacks designed to hamper recovery could cause abrupt backward lurches in our standard of living. The most powerful and sophisticated nations on earth might suddenly find themselves grappling with the problems of daily survival that have long been confined chiefly to the poorest nations.

War and terrorism add new dimensions to this threat. Although analyses are inconclusive, some experts believe that the electromagnetic pulse from a single high-altitude thermonuclear burst over the central U.S. could instantaneously burn out virtually all unhardened electronic circuitry in the country, including power grids and their controls, computers (which control oil refineries and oil and gas pipelines), electronic car ignitions, telephones, radios, and televisions. Some analysts suspect that all operating nuclear plants could even melt down uncontrollably.[3]

Terrorist and criminal groups, too, are showing ever more sophisticated tactical and technical skills, and are acquiring such modern munitions as miniaturized silent firearms, precision-guided rockets, poison gases, specialized vehicles, electronic countermeasures, night-vision devices, and industrial lasers. Even the tiny fraction of key energy facilities now hardened against small groups with light arms could not withstand a modern terrorist assault. At many sites, standoff attack with a rifle could cause damage of national significance.

Specific Vulnerabilities

Liquefied energy gases. Liquefied natural and petroleum gases (LNG and LPG) are increasingly common items of commerce. A modern marine LNG tanker contains, at −260°F, enough gas to form a flammable gas-air mixture several hundred times the volume of the Great Pyramid of Cheops. Spilled LNG boils into gas so cold that it remains heavier than air. The plume can drift along the ground for miles before it ignites in a conflagration like a hundred *Hindenbergs*. Radiant heat from such a fire would cause third-degree burns and start fires a mile or two away. Despite safety precautions, there have been several significant LNG accidents and many near misses.[4] Most LNG facilities have minimal guards, no alarms, and key structures vulnerable to light arms.

LNG is shipped by marine tanker into terminals, one of which is in Boston Harbor. Each terminal contains several LNG tanks, each equivalent in energy content to over half a megaton. The U.S. has about 50 additional LNG storage depots aboveground, each equivalent to more than 130 kilotons. LNG is also delivered by trucks, each with a quarter kiloton of energy content, routinely traveling over key bridges and through urban centers. Under suitable circumstances, one LNG truck falling off of Boston's Southeast Expressway could fill with flammable air-gas mixture the entire Boston subway system, or the city's major tunnels, or enough of the sewer system to blow up virtually every street in the city. LPG is shipped by marine tanker, high-pressure pipeline, rail, and ubiquitous trucks. Each LPG railcar contains energy equivalent to about three-fourths of a kiloton, releasable in a violent fuel-air explosion that can hurl large shrapnel and cause second-degree burns by radiation up to a mile away.[5] LPG and LNG trucks could readily be hijacked and detonated next to a high-value target. LPG and LNG facilities are often next to or surrounded by such targets already: cities, ports, refineries, oil depots, the Calvert Cliffs

[Maryland] nuclear power plant. In 1981, an FB-111 aircraft crashed a quarter mile from New England's second-largest LNG/LPG facility—two miles from the center of a town of 27,000, two and a half miles from a nuclear submarine base, and three-quarters of a mile (well within the range of radiant third-degree burns) from Pease Air Force Base with its huge fuel depot. Because the plane did not score a direct hit, the General Accounting Office's devastating 1978 report on the risk of disastrous LNG explosions and firestorms continued to be ignored.

Oil and gas systems. Nearly three-fourths of America's energy comes from oil, gas, and natural gas liquids. (So do most rubber, plastics, fertilizers, paints, solvents, and medicines—all the products of petrochemical plants, 60 percent of which are tightly clustered along the Texas Gulf Coast.) In 1982, a fourth of the oil used was imported, and less than a fifth of that came from Arab OPEC nations.

Extraction and transport. Middle Eastern oil fields are valued at more than one gross world product–year. Oil extraction in the Persian Gulf is astonishingly concentrated. Saudi Arabia has until recently lifted oil at nearly the rate of the United States, but from about a thousandth as many wells—with a single supergiant Saudi field lifting oil faster than any other *country* except the U.S. and the USSR. Just the five hundred–odd miles of eastern Saudi pipelines carry a sixth of the non-Communist world's oil. All such facilities are militarily indefensible, and many have been under attack throughout the Middle East for more than a decade.

The lumbering supertankers that bring Middle Eastern oil through strategic straits to Europe, Japan, and North America managed to destroy themselves without assistance at a rate averaging three per month in early 1980.[6] During eight months in 1981, twenty-one of them were boarded and robbed near Singapore by pirates in small native boats; one was even hijacked in the Strait of Malacca.

Oil platforms off the U.S. coast, often proposed as a substitute for imported oil, are sitting ducks laden with highly flammable fuel under pressure. A single platform may cost upwards of $50 million, carry over forty wells, and feed mainland pipelines through a single frail link. The Coast Guard in New Orleans has contingency plans that, in good weather, can bring a protective vessel to any of 3,000 platforms in eight hours. A competent terrorist could destroy such a platform in eight minutes. Gulf of Mexico fireboats might handle up to three modest platform fires at once—if not bottled up by sinking a barge in a single canal. In the North and Beaufort seas, fire fighting, protection, and repairs are often rendered impossible by hundred-foot waves.

Storage. The average barrel of oil takes about three months to get from the wellhead to the final American user. Usable storage capacity in between represents at most a few months' normal demand. The oil system is so tightly coupled that if normal flows are interrupted, refineries typically run out of crude oil in three to five days, and pipeline customers run out of products in five to ten days.[7] Oil stockpiles therefore represent high-value targets. On December 19 and 22, 1982, respectively, major oil depots in Venezuela and Kenya went up in smoke in apparent accidents. Rhodesia's main stocks were blown up in 1978, increasing the national budget deficit by 18 percent overnight. Attacks on oil depots have succeeded in Mozambique, Britain, and Italy; partly succeeded in Namibia, The Netherlands, West Germany, France, and the U.S.; and been narrowly foiled in Chile and Israel. The U.S. Strategic Petroleum Reserve—the only major oil or gas facility in the country where some serious thought has been given to security—is mostly underground; but one person could render it useless in three nights by knocking out the three pipelines meant to deliver SPR oil to refineries.

Processing plants. Oil refineries are typically the most vulnerable, capital-intensive, and indispensable element of the oil system downstream of the wellhead. Just as three-fourths of domestic oil is lifted in four states, over half the refinery capacity is concentrated in three (Texas, Louisiana, and California), and more than 69 percent is in six states. This concentration is increasing. The Office of Technology Assessment noted that in 1978, destruction of the seventy-seven largest U.S. refineries would have eliminated two-thirds of U.S. capacity and "shattered" the economy.[8] This would not, however, require dozens of nuclear warheads—only a wrench, rifle bullet, grenade, or turned valve at each of seventy-seven plants. Many design trends are making refineries ever more vulnerable to the simple, unstoppable sorts of sabotage that have already occurred in several U.S. plants. Thus simple damage to a coking unit of a TOSCO refinery on the first day of a California strike did many millions of dollars' worth of damage and shut down the whole refinery for more than three months. "Physical disaster," reported the company's president, "was narrowly averted" by luck and by the prompt action of supervisory staff.[9] In 1980, when an extortionist threatened to set off a remote-control bomb at a $250 million refinery in Edmonton, Alberta, the Imperial Oil Company paid up—reportedly $1 million.

Natural gas processing plants are similarly vulnerable and even more concentrated. A single plant in Louisiana handles 3.5 percent of America's natural gas, equivalent to the output of more than twenty giant power plants. About 84 percent of all interstate gas in the country flows from or through Louisiana. So concentrated are the pipelines and their controls that a few people could shut off, for upwards of a year, three-fourths of the gas and oil supplies to the eastern U.S. in one evening's work without even leaving Louisiana. The head of a major oil production company recently told us, "With a hundred pounds of dynamite, distributed among about eight places, I could cripple the country."

Pipelines. Oil and gas pipelines depend on prime movers (usually electric motors or gas turbines), pumps or compressors, and complex computer controls and telecommunications equipment. Few if any pipeline companies have, or know where to get, enough skilled people to run the pipeline grids manually by turning valves and controls. Pipelines are easily located and cut using low technology; gas pipelines can be made to explode and rip themselves up automatically for miles. Many key pipelines are co-located, and have vital but easily cut junction points. River and swamp crossings are very hard to repair. Many times longer than the Equator, crossing remote and rugged terrain, major pipeline systems are indefensible. They have already been successfully attacked in most parts of the United States.[10]

Pipelines move about three-fourths of the crude oil used by U.S. refineries, a third of the refined products sent from refineries to consumers, and nearly all natural gas. The pipeline grid, especially interstate, is not flexible enough for rerouting to bypass major damage. Cutting just three domestic oil pipelines (Trans-Alaska, Colonial, and Capline) would stop a flow totaling nearly five million barrels per day—substantially more than all 1982 net oil imports.

East Coast refineries get crude oil only from tankers, not from pipelines. Their output is supplemented by a few product pipelines too big to replace with tankers. Six hits could sever pipeline service between the main oil fields and the East and Midwest; ten could cut off 63 percent of U.S. capacity for piping refined products. A single pipeline system (Colonial) carries about half the barrel-miles of refined products pipelines in the country, yet it has only recently acquired a duplicate (but soft-target) control center. Security arrangements for major pipelines and their control systems are so lax that a 1979 General Accounting Office audit found easy public access to major terminals, computers, and power sources: some pumping stations were the sites of juvenile beer parties.[11]

Arctic pipelines are especially vulnerable. The Trans-Alaska Pipeline System (TAPS) is four feet in diameter, cost eight billion dollars, moves one-seventh of all crude used by U.S. refineries, displaces oil imports worth nearly $600 a second, and has no substitute. Over half of its nearly 800-mile length is held aloft on stanchions. It crosses readily accessible rivers. State highways lead to five of its eight pumping stations. The line crosses three mountain ranges and five seismic areas. Interrupted pumping for three winter weeks would congeal nine million barrels of hot oil, turning TAPS into the world's largest Chapstick. (Laboratory tests give hope that the pumps may be powerful enough to get the oil moving again, but nobody is eager to try a full-scale experiment.) Trouble in the plumbing or tanks at either end of the line, or in the gale-prone Valdez Narrows at the southern end, could do the same. The uninsurably vulnerable labyrinth of pipes feeding oil into TAPS would take at least eight months to rebuild plus two to ship from Japan.

TAPS has been lightly bombed twice, shot at, and sabotaged by other means; the U.S. Army found it indefensible. But its operators still perceive no security threat.[12] In 1977, the southernmost pumping station—the least vital and the easiest to fix—was blown up by operator error. The line was shut down for ten days, then ran at half-capacity during nine months of intensive repairs.

Three-fourths of America's energy reaches its destination only because nobody tries very hard to stop it. The highly complex, centralized oil and gas system is designed for a "technological paradise" in which everything works according to the blueprints. The future may not be like that at all.

Power stations and electric grids. Central-electric systems deliver 13 percent of U.S. energy and consume a third of all primary fuels, including four-fifths of the coal burned. Electricity is essential to most people's lives—even, in many cities, to seeing and breathing. The lack of electrical storage makes any disruption instantaneous and widespread (as when a 1982 Oregon relay failure caused blackouts in Arizona). Yet electrical supplies are even more vulnerable than oil and gas supplies. A 1981 General Accounting Office audit found that sabotage of eight easily accessible substations could black out a typical U.S. region, while sabotage of only four could leave a city without power for days and with rotating blackouts for a year. A worker in a major Eastern utility recently remarked, "I could shut down my grid with a coat hanger."

The three U.S. regional power grids are probably just as brittle, for three reasons. Having no significant storage capacity, the grid requires immediate bypassing of failed transmission links (the main cause of failures); failed generating plants (a minor cause) must also be very rapidly replaced by spare capacity; and these corrective actions absolutely require that key transmission segments be available and that switchgear and computerized controls and communication links work properly.

About 82 percent of U.S. electricity comes from 900-odd large thermal power plants; most of hydroelectricity's 12 percent comes from a few large dams. These complex, billion-dollar facilities are tempting targets and very slow to mend. Their key components are so huge, yet so delicate, that in 1978 someone with a bludgeon was able to damage dozens of coils, many beyond repair, on three of the world's largest electric generators in the bowels of Grand Coulee Dam. Lost production was estimated to cost $35 per minute.

Centralized generation places heavy burdens on the transmission system, switchgear, and controls — the most frequent target of attacks in numerous countries (including the U.S.). Such assaults are now a characteristic target of Soviet-trained guerrillas.[13] Transmission and substation attacks have been frequent and coordinated: during 1978, on average, an American utility was bombed (in most cases more symbolically than seriously) every twelve days.[14]

The officially encouraged trend toward more and bigger power stations, more remote siting (e.g., in Western coalfields), and longer, higher-voltage transmission lines is increasing the instability and potential uncontrollability of large grids for which no adequate control theory yet exists.

Nuclear facilities. Nuclear power plants, reprocessing plants, and spent-fuel storage depots contain prodigious amounts of long-lived radioactivity. They are valuable and highly visible economic and political targets. They also facilitate the manufacture of nuclear bombs by providing fissionable materials, information, skills, equipment, and organizational structures suited to that purpose.[15] Such bombs can in turn be used to attack nuclear facilities.

More than a hundred significant attacks on, incidents of sabotage at, and security breaches in nuclear facilities have already occurred worldwide. More than seventy nuclear power plants are operable in the United States, fewer than sixty under construction. Each large plant, when operating, contains over fifteen billion curies of radioactivity (equivalent to the fallout from some 2,000 Hiroshima bombs) plus heat, mechanical energy, and chemical energy that could facilitate its release. Despite extensive precautions, the plants remain vulnerable. For example, none of the safety devices can work if electricity from outside the plant and from its own emergency generators is cut off.[16] Straightforward attacks could cause unstoppable releases comparable in radiological effect to a sizeable nuclear bomb, with lethal ranges of tens or even hundreds of miles.[17] The saboteur could deliberately choose the worst weather conditions, the ripest fuel, and the reactor upwind of the biggest city.

A bomb yielding one kiloton or less, detonated thousands of feet from a nuclear power plant, is probably enough to cause an un-controllable meltdown. Shortening the range to a few hundred feet (within public access to many sites) would release virtually all of the reactor core. The long-term radiological consequences of bombing a reactor with a crude nuclear explosive in the tenth-kiloton range would probably be similar to those of a one-megaton ground burst at ranges up to a few hundred miles. Longer-range effects would exceed those of the ground burst. Tens of thousands of square miles could be seriously contaminated for centuries.[18]

Is the Threat Real?

Readers unfamiliar with the hundreds of actual attacks, in over forty countries, cited in *Brittle Power* may feel that such energy-related threats to national security are implausible. One might also have been excused for thinking that regionwide power black-outs were unlikely until 1965, or the hijacking of three jumbo jets in a single day until 1970, or the take-over of more than fifty embassies until the 1970s. But given the potential conse-quences, nobody would want to be in the position of the British in-telligence officer who, on retiring in 1950 after forty-seven years' service, reminisced: "Year after year the worriers and fretters would come to me with awful predictions of the outbreak of war. I denied it each time. I was only wrong twice."[19]

Some military planners already know better. Goering and Speer stated after World War II that the Allies could have saved two years by bombing the highly centralized German electric-power system. In contrast, 78 percent of Japanese electricity in World War II—like most Vietnamese electricity later—came from small, dispersed hydroelectric plants that, in contrast to the centralized thermal plants, sustained only 0.3 percent of the bombing damage.

The accidental blackout of virtually all of France in 1978, of Israel in 1979, and of most of southern Britain in 1981 has re-newed interest in less vulnerable designs for the energy system. Even the Red Army is said to seek energy decentralization as a preparedness measure—though the Politburo forbids this be-cause it would reduce the Party's political control. Several coun-tries are analyzing, and at least Sweden, China, and Israel are systematically seeking, the strategic benefits of energy decentralization.

Yet the Reagan administration, despite its concern for national security, is emphasizing—and subsidizing with more than $10 billion per year—precisely the most vulnerable energy technologies. Federal plans call for a trillion dollars' worth of new power stations and grids in the next twenty years (including trebled or quadrupled nuclear power capacity), vastly more Arctic and offshore oil and gas, an Arctic gas pipeline, a new inland version of the Strait of Hormuz to be created in the Powder River Basin of Wyoming, and a synthetic fuels industry—an option so vulnerable that both times it has been tried before (Nazi Germany and contemporary South Africa) it was promptly and successfully attacked.

These brittle devices are supposed to form the backbone of America's energy supplies well into the twenty-first century—a period likely to bring increasing uncertainty, surprise, unrest, and violence. The United States cannot afford vulnerabilities that so alter the power balance between large and small groups in society as to erode not only military security but also the freedom and trust that underpin constitutional government.

Such escalating energy insecurity, however, is not necessary. It is not even economic. Alternatives exist—and are cheaper anyhow. Design lessons from biology and from many kinds of engineering suggest twenty or so principles of a design science of resilience. Embodying those principles in practical, available, and cost-effective technologies can make energy supply so resilient that debilitating failures become impossible. Best of all, this enhancement of national and individual security, far from costing an "insurance premium," would actually put money back in our pockets. A resilient energy strategy would enhance American preparedness, make it less necessary, and at the same time save several *trillion* dollars and about a million jobs over just the next twenty years.

Designing for Resilience

An inherently resilient system should include many relatively small, fine-grained elements, dispersed in space, each having a low cost of failure. These substitutible components should be richly interconnected by short, redundant links—rather as a tree has many leaves, and each leaf has many veins, so that random nibbling by insects cannot disrupt vital nutrient flows. Failed components or links should be promptly detected, isolated, and repaired. Components need to be so organized that each element can interconnect with the rest at will but stand alone at need, and that each successive level of function is little affected by failures or substitutions at a subordinate level. Systems should be so designed that any failures are slow and graceful. Components, finally, should be understandable, maintainable, reproducible at a variety of scales, capable of rapid evolution, and societally compatible.

Redundancy and diversity. These principles are already being applied in data processing, where tens or hundreds of microcomputers can be organized into a network that can do the same job as a large mainframe computer but with far greater reliability, resilience, and data security. The failure of some components or interconnections does not interfere with normal operation: each task being done by a failed part is safely completed by others. Multiple failures may make the system a bit sluggish, but it will perk up again as soon as the parts are repaired (which is done without shutting the system down). Commercial "distributed processing" systems organized in this way can make the mean time between failures arbitrarily long—thousands of years, for example—at a trivial extra cost, more than paid for by avoided downtime.

Energy systems offer equally striking examples. When the engineer running the power system in Holyoke, Massachusetts, saw the 1965 Northeast blackout rolling toward him, he quickly isolated the city from the grid and powered it with a local gas turbine. The money saved by not having to black out Holyoke paid off the cost of building that power plant in four *hours*.[20]

The advantages of diverse energy supplies became clear in West Chicago in 1980 when Department of Energy officials had just finished cutting the ribbon on a photovoltaic-powered gas station. Just then a thunderstorm blacked out the area—leaving only that one station pumping gas.[21] Likewise, in the bitter winter of early 1977, while the Midwest reeled under an acute shortage of natural gas, consumers in equally chilly rural New England were virtually unaffected—because the gas used there (LPG) came in bottles. Therefore not everyone ran out at once, and systemwide collapses of distribution pressure were not possible. As in Israel, the independent, highly dispersed gas storage was all but invulnerable.

Efficient energy use. The most striking contribution to energy resilience, however—the most "bounce per buck"—comes from more efficient energy use, for many reasons. Efficiency is the fastest and cheapest way to eliminate the most vulnerable marginal supplies (such as Persian Gulf oil), making their failure inconsequential. Those failures that efficiency cannot altogether prevent it makes slower, more graceful, less severe, and more fixable. It also buys time to improvise substitutes, and stretches the job they can do.

For example, if you live in a superinsulated house in Minnesota, and your heating system (assuming you even need one) fails in January, you won't know it for weeks. You'll find out only because the indoor temperature will slowly drift down from 72°F to the high 50s—but no lower, because of the "free heat" from bodies, windows, lights, and appliances. Thus neither you nor your pipes will freeze. If a few neighbors come in to take refuge from their sieve, their body heat alone will restore your house to 72°. If they bring a few kids, the house will overheat and you'll have to open the windows. Alternatively, any improvised point source of heat could keep the whole house warm—such as burning junk mail in a #10 can.

On a national scale, a light-vehicle fleet getting, say, 65 miles per gallon (15 worse than the city performance of an advanced Volkswagen Rabbit prototype tested in 1981) would make oil stocks last four times as long as they could today. The tanks of the vehicles would constitute a highly dispersed Strategic Petroleum Reserve, already delivered in usable form. An average car with a half-full tank could run for about three weeks without filling up at all. The "pipeline inventory" between the wellhead and the gas pump would last, not for days or weeks as at present, but for nearly a year—buying precious time to mend major damage to the national oil system or to improvise alternative supplies.

Likewise, cost-effectively efficient use of electricity would enable small and improvised supplies—industrial cogeneration,
wind, small hydro, even the car and truck alternators and generators that now total a sixth as much capacity as all U.S. power stations—to maintain fairly normal production and amenities and
provide abundant nuclei for restoring damaged grids.

Any more efficient use of U.S. vulnerable energy sources would
increase the ability of inherently resilient energy sources—the
diverse, dispersed, uninterruptible, renewable sources—to meet a
larger fraction of total energy needs. Those sources, chosen
carefully and built sensibly, are already more reliable and less
costly than the centralized, nonrenewable sources they would
gradually replace.[22] Within a few decades, appropriate renewable
sources could replace, largely or wholly, the vulnerable supplies on
which the U.S. now depends. Using energy in an economically efficient way[23] can thus buy the American energy system time to
complete comfortably the transition from living on energy capital
to living on energy income.

From vulnerability to resilience. That transformation is
well under way. Since 1979, the United States has gotten more
than a hundred times as much new energy from savings as from
all expansions of energy supply combined. Of those expansions,
more new energy has come from renewable sources (now nearly 8
percent of total U.S. supplies) than from any or all of the non-
renewables.[24] That is, sun, wind, water, and wood (which now
delivers about twice as much energy as nuclear power)[25] are collectively outcompeting and outpacing oil, gas, coal, and uranium,
or any one of them—and higher energy productivity is far outpacing them all. Even in the electric utility sector, more new generating capacity has been ordered since 1979 from small hydro plants
and windpower than from coal and nuclear plants.

Americans spent some $15 billion on efficiency and renewables
just in 1980. The problem of secure and affordable energy supplies
is starting to be solved—but from the bottom up, not from the top
down; Washington will be the last to know. Community programs[26] are vital to this transition from high-cost to lower-cost
and from high-risk to low-risk investments. But even the
strongest community sentiment would not be enough without eco-

nomic rationality. The marketplace is confirming that efficiency and appropriate renewable sources, the keys to energy security, are also the best buys in the narrowest economic terms—the options that would win in a truly free market, even if all their security benefits were valued at zero. Removal of the severe price distortions caused by federal subsidies, and a few limited federal policy initiatives to ensure that potential resiliency benefits are not lost through poor or incompatible designs, could make the American energy system resilient even faster. But this will require greater willingness than the Reagan administration's to expose *all* technologies to free competition.

A New Security Paradigm?

These principles of energy security suggest broader conclusions for strategic planners: Exclusive attention to overt military threats risks building some very expensive Maginot Lines while the back door swings wide open. Better security does not always cost more money; at least in the case of energy—and probably of food and water, too—it costs less. And most importantly, better security may not require, and may not even be able to tolerate, central management.

The past decade's experience proves that effective programs to make energy secure and affordable tend to work on the same political scale as the Founding Fathers' concept of a local militia. Might not other kinds of security also be best obtained on a scale more local than national? Real security, after all, must include not only reliable supplies of energy, but also of food and water; a sustainable, flexible system of production and exchange; a healthful environment; free expression and debate; a legitimate system of self-government. But all these things can be more responsively provided at the scale of a county commission, a town meeting, a city council, or a block association than of a federal Congress or president.

Does the central government indeed hold any monopoly on providing security? Our government spends about $10 thousand a second on a stronger military establishment; but success seems elusive. In 1947 the U.S. was militarily invulnerable, while today, thirty thousand nuclear warheads later, it lies entirely exposed to devastation. Clearly, military might is an insufficient basis for security. But with the freedom to act as individuals and communities, we can largely provide real security for ourselves by building it into the infrastructure, the economy, and the polity of every locality in the land—by building a society so resilient that it defends itself. Perhaps security, in its broadest sense, can come only from the bottom up—from individuals and communities— and not from bureaucracies.

But security, whatever its source, and whether on the scale of the village or the globe, cannot be taken from or denied to others; it must be shared. Achieving security is never a zero-sum game. If we ourselves enjoyed the elements of a secure life while others did not, we would live in fear that they might seek to take from us what they lack. Real security, then, comes not from a siege mentality, but from making both ourselves and our neighbors more secure.

11

ROBERT KUPPERMAN

Vulnerable America

It may seem inconceivable that we will one day look back upon the Cold War era as a time of relative peace and stability—a time when the only major global threat was that the two largest powers would annihilate each other. But in fact that bipolar order has even now deteriorated into a much less certain, much more fluid international environment. As power and influence have become increasingly diffuse, the traditional mechanisms of international political restraint have become decreasingly effective. It is far less clear who can do what to whom, why, and with what effect.

The mysteries of atomic weaponry are neither as secret nor as difficult to master as we had once hoped. The number of near-nuclear and nuclear powers is expected to grow significantly by the end of the century. As a result, we face the very real danger of a nuclear holocaust triggered by the aggression of rogue states or by catalytic conflict in the Third World. Chemical and biological weapons—less expensive and easier to fabricate—may yet become the poor man's bomb, a means by which radical sub-national and national groups can attain the extortion potential of a nuclear device.

The tools and techniques for mass destruction have so proliferated as to force our planners to think about the unthinkable. The proposals before the nation span the spectrum between unilateral disarmament and unabated nuclear arms competition. More and better of everything is clearly not the answer but neither is it axiomatic that less is always more secure. In fact, reduced nuclear arsenals in conjunction with the proliferation of small nuclear forces present a very real danger that minor errors in verification or marginal cheating by the other side can propagate overwhelming strategic advantages. Clearly, we need to rethink the options for stable and substantial arms reductions and possibly contemplate some kind of buffering mechanism—such as a limited ballistic missile defense—that could eliminate the first incoming warheads in the event our faith in bilateral agreements or our own verification capabilities proves misplaced.

The specter of nuclear holocaust, however, tends to be almost a hypnotic preoccupation. Lost in the national security debate is the fact that the United States faces very real—and much more imminent—threats at the other end of the conflict spectrum in low-intensity warfare.

Our crisis managers devote themselves to planning for big disasters—fantasizing about the nation's capacity to cope with nuclear carnage. The sad truth is that the U.S. is not prepared to respond to most kinds of emergencies—from natural disasters to industrial accidents—much less an induced and strategic disruption or organized response to a carefully selected, technologically sophisticated attack on our industrial base. No up-to-date inventory exists of medical, logistical, civil engineering, food, temporary shelter, or trained manpower resources—all of which are essential to deal, for example, with the terrorist-induced blackout of a major city lasting for weeks. Our capabilities to mobilize industry and redirect the flow of materials from a civilian economy to a national defense footing are virtually nonexistent. The fact is that despite a massive nuclear and conventional arsenal—among the largest in the world—we are dangerously vulnerable to attack.

In today's changing global environment, the vulnerability of our industrial and service infrastructure to disruption represents a slowly developing (hence ignored) crisis. Although the facts are in plain view, the will and precautions necessary to counter the threat lag behind.

The Low-Intensity Threat: Terrorism

The most likely danger confronting us may not, after all, be the threat of nuclear holocaust. In fact, it is difficult to conceive why any nation would risk certain retribution (and probable escalation) for an overt act of war when unconventional forms of attack offer such unique advantages. Employing limited firepower, they can be profound in leverage and just as disruptive. The initial uncertainty about the origin of attack — or even whether an attack has occurred — often limits the range of diplomatic and military responses. With the collapse of the traditional networks of intra- and international relations, the temptation to rely on unconventional action mechanisms may become irresistible. For the relatively weaker countries, the high-leverage/low-cost element of low-intensity warfare is essential because they cannot afford to compete economically or militarily. For the more powerful, the high-leverage/low-risk factor is decisive because the costs of large-scale conventional or nuclear confrontations are unacceptable. Hence, the "action" we may expect to see over the next two decades will be at the margins, below the level of war but with the power to cripple governments or topple nations.

The techniques of unconventional warfare are hardly a new dimension of international rivalry. Disinformation, overt or covert thefts of high technology, export of undesirables as refugees, or support of movements of national liberation have long formed part of the spectrum of low-intensity conflict. What is new, however, is an international climate that offers a strategic rationale for such tactics.

An increasingly important tool of conflict at the low end of the spectrum is terrorism.[1] Hardly a day passes without a terrorist incident occurring somewhere in the world; it permeates the fabric of contemporary civilization. And the significance of the terror act has been raised exponentially by several different but interrelated factors. First, the tools available for destruction are much more lethal and much more frightening than ever before. Second, the media attention focused on terrorism is immediate, global, and usually undisciplined. Third, motives for terrorist attack today span a spectrum that includes, at the extremes, personal grudges and superpower ambitions of global hegemony — and there is little certainty as to which underlying motive may really be at play in any particular case. Finally the United States (unlike others in the Western Alliance) has no internal consensus on how to respond either to acts of supercriminal violence or to coercive political threats. It has no common philosophical basis for accepting the high costs (in lives, materials, pride, and power) of occasional failure in dealing with terrorism, and it has no internationally recognized commitment to firm, retributive deterrence of such violence.

Although the United States has not so far been a primary target of attack, recent events prove that we are far from immune. The 1979 seizure of the American embassy in Teheran demonstrated that the U.S. is not only a visible target but a vulnerable one as well. America failed diplomatically and militarily to deal with the terrorist tactics of a rogue nation and a national disaster was the result. Threats from a Libyan death squad against the president represented a direct attack on the foundations of our democratic society. In the end, it was irrelevant whether or not a Libyan "hit" team actually existed; the threat itself forced the president to retreat into a "steel cocoon" and appeared to paralyze the American government. The attempted assassination of General Kroesen in Germany and the kidnapping of General Dozier in Italy represented an attack on a cornerstone of U.S. foreign policy: the NATO alliance and the decision on theater force modernization. Using the media as a springboard, the terrorists attempted a "cushion shot" to capitalize on the political stresses in the Alliance and the growing worldwide antinuclear movement.

The full extent of our vulnerability was made most dramatically evident when an anonymous killer in Chicago contaminated a few bottles of Tylenol with a small amount of commercially available cyanide. That single act not only cost a number of individuals their lives and the pharmaceutical industry 100 million dollars; it also generated widespread anxiety in the general population and outright terror in a small portion. That individual gave the United States a profound lesson in the disruptive potential of the strategically vectored terrorist attack.

Terrorist assaults, like a martial art, can turn our chief strengths — our democratic tradition of fairness and restraint, the openness of our news media — against us. They can also directly attack, with potentially devastating results, our technological and economic infrastructure.

The Modern Vulnerability

The greatest strength of modern Western society, its strong technological base, is also its Achilles' heel. In a remarkably short span, Western man has translated his observations of the natural world into forms of control over energy and materials, and has exercised that control for his own benefit and comfort. The rate of change of knowledge—and the technologies that flow from it—has been dramatic, making possible conurbation on an unprecedented scale. In effect, we have reached a point of no return; we no longer can go back to a preindustrial, agrarian society without severe cultural disruption.

Urban man has become wholly reliant on the technological infrastructure for the continuity of goods and services necessary to his survival. But at least in the United States, that infrastructure is the product of accretion, patched together with little continuous planning and with no provisions for survivability against attack. The design and placement of individual systems, such as electric generation and distribution, water reservoirs, oil and gas refineries, pumping stations, and pipelines reflect the priorities of a past era. The efficiency of these systems lies in their size (large and few) and centralization. Today, their lack of redundancy, duplication, and dispersion creates appealing and leverageable nodes of attack.

Taken together, the systems form an intricate, interdependent, and extremely fragile infrastructural web. The ad hoc process of growth has resulted in critical "choke-points" where major utilities come together; hence, the failure of any one system can mean the disruption of many others. For the embracing systems, like electrical power, there are no available damage control options, no way to halt the feedback (the asynergies) into the other networks. A major power failure—perhaps the most extreme case—could paralyze the sanitary and water systems, the food supply chains, computerized networks (e.g., banking and insurance), the manufacturing sector, transportation; in short, nearly every vital service of the affected area.

The broad problem, cutting across all industries, arises from the fact that the costs of protecting against every natural or accidental disaster are prohibitively high: in any technologically based, democratic society, some degree of risk must always be accepted. As Louisianans discovered, their levees are designed to contain the yearly flood waters, not the once-in-a-century flood. Californians protect their schools and hospitals against the intermediate earthquake, not the massive one. In general, we rely on the statistical conclusion that the effects of most kinds of disasters can be isolated, and are temporary and reversible.

The special danger today, however, stems from induced as well as natural disasters of a vastly different magnitude. The vulnerability of the society's life-supporting physical networks invites focused sabotage and low-intensity warfare attacks, which, if successful, could conceivably exceed the self-healing limits of the society at large.

These kinds of attacks have already begun. Since 1970, there have been over 200 attacks worldwide directed against electric utilities from California to Puerto Rico, from France to the Philippines. At home, the New World Liberation Front has targeted Pacific Gas & Electric some seventy times, albeit with minimal damage. Nuclear power stations in France, Spain, Germany, and the U.S. have been unsuccessfully attacked. A raid on an FALN safehouse prior to the 1980 Democratic National Convention turned up detailed plans of the power system of Madison Square Garden, possibly signaling a plot to black out the facility and disrupt the electoral process. To date these terrorist attacks have been largely ineffective, but they raise the prospect of very large disruptive impacts caused by few human and material resources.

Without providing a blueprint for destruction, one can describe a number of areas of extreme vulnerability. The nation's energy system, especially the electric power system, is the most vulnerable target (see ch. 11). Beyond that, even critical components in the U.S. defense production system itself are vulnerable to attacks of quite elementary sabotage. For example, this country maintains only two very large extrusion presses on which the titanium-based aircraft industry depends and only one facility where all of the gun tubes for both the army and navy are produced. The United States maintains a large reserve of critical strategic materials—

invaluable in the event we need to refight the Second World War. However, it stockpiles none of the critically important intermediate goods, such as heavy transformers or natural gas pumping stations, that are essential in countering current threats against our infrastructure.

The only utility system that possesses the necessary redundancy and decentralization to be truly survivable is the national telecommunications network—which is currently being dismantled by judicial edict. An indispensable element of secure telecommunications is the ability to maintain local contact in time of disaster by rerouting connections through the nationwide network. It is questionable whether this flexibility can be maintained in a patchwork regional system. This case presents a classic example of potential conflict between socially desirable goals and national security. In pursuit of antimonopoly policy, the courts have required an integrated telecommunications system to decentralize both in facilities and in management. Unless the new regional telecommunications systems are carefully modernized for interoperability and for survival, the U.S. thus may lose in the national security arena more than it gains from the social benefits of deregulation. For example, if each regional telephone system ignored state-of-the-art advances or rejected commonality of connections, U.S. civil telecommunications capabilities could be Balkanized, encouraging the military services to develop their own integrated systems for nonemergency use.

These problems of vulnerability, combined with those in our energy systems, endanger more than our standard of living or industrial productivity; they also have long-range national security implications for military preparedness and mobilization capability. The military, like the civilian sector, operates on the assumption that a reliable technological infrastructure is guaranteed. Given the strategic vulnerability of that infrastructure, one may appreciate how fragile our actual military capability might be.

The problem is aggravated by growing evidence that terrorist organizations are developing and refining training for attacks on our energy and industrial infrastructure. Some governments may have the necessary contingency response plans, trained personnel, and dedicated equipment to guarantee the continuity of goods and services in their societies; the United States does not.

Preparedness Limitations

The emergency preparedness/civil defense apparatus in the United States is designed to cope with either the unimaginable or the unimportant. No preparation is made for superdisasters because they are perceived to be beyond human managerial skills or credible planning. It is true of devastating earthquakes, the hundred-year rain over Lake Pontchartrain, or even the terrorist detonation of a nuclear weapon in a major American city. Since no government would be blamed for failing to organize, say, the aftermath of a nuclear holocaust, our government officials can freely exhibit bravado when faced with theoretical carnage. At the opposite end of the spectrum, little disasters present no substantial problems. Whether they are managed efficiently or poorly, little disasters usually go away on their own and, in any case, fade quickly from the public eye.

The real danger is posed by the intermediate disaster. This country is completely unprepared—physically or politically—to deal with the reconstructive phases of disasters with widespread geographic or technological effects.

The problem of inadequate emergency preparations is not limited to malevolent acts against the United States. Our technological infrastructure is not only vulnerable; it is also aging and rapidly deteriorating. We face the prospect of condemned bridges, impassable roads, grid-locked electrical systems, and unreliable networks to distribute food, water, and energy. The market economy offers few incentives to make the investment required for a complete systematic overhaul; and in the current climate of public budget constraints, the political temptation to defer maintenance of capital infrastructure is overwhelming. With so much money tied up in debt service on existing capital investments, only minor and minimal adjustments are made to upgrade these systems.

Where are the national strategies and meaningful contingency plans to cope with the decay of our industrial infrastructure and ultimately of our mobilization base? It is unfortunate that while the image of civil emergency preparedness has been maintained as a political necessity, the capability for planning and execution is largely illusory. Civil defense, in its classic sense, is clearly a worthwhile notion, but in the absence of any real capacity to deal with the lesser disasters, the concept has little meaning. We are victims of denial—and not only for disasters on a massive scale.

In fact, there is no embracing plan for crisis management, no national means of command and control linking the myriad of state and local agencies charged with meeting disaster and civil defense responsibilities. The first line of response in any disaster is the local police and fire officials who are largely cut off from the federal bureaucracies. Indeed, much of the nation's emergency management apparatus is an assortment of aging programs built on twenty-year-old technology.

The Federal Emergency Management Agency (FEMA) is assigned overall responsibility for disaster management and relief. The legislative intent behind FEMA and its predecessor agencies is to build a "bridge" between national security concerns and domestic emergency management.

FEMA is therefore charged with responsibilities ranging from disaster relief to crisis management, from continuity of government to industrial mobilization for conventional war and civil defense against nuclear attack. It is asked not only to fulfill critical national security and civil emergency functions, but to cope with the administration of social programs such as flood insurance. All are important, but administrative duties distract the agency from its first order of business: civil emergency preparedness. And it is a sad truism that FEMA, like its predecessors, has an overabundance of responsibility and a corresponding dearth of authority and resources.

Another classic example of a federal bureaucratic structure poorly positioned to handle emergent crises is in the field of counterterrorism. The Justice Department is the lead agency for incidents of domestic terrorism, while the State Department has jurisdiction over terrorist acts against U.S. interests abroad. Although this may appear to be a rational division of responsibility, it proceeds from the assumption that our primary goal is to apprehend the culprits. If the electricity goes out along the Eastern seaboard, we may be able to count on the FBI to handcuff the perpetrators—a satisfying prospect that does not, however, redress the main problem. In effect, the tendency towards political denial that a problem exists is rooted in—and perpetuated by— the mismatch between the responsibilities of federal agencies and their problem-solving capabilities. The agencies thus typically take the path of least resistance in coping with a crisis; bureaucratic niceties become substitutes for careful planning and thoughtful crisis management.

As we begin to recognize the enormously complex and threatening nature of modern crises, it becomes clear that we can no longer rely on ad hoc processes of automatic reaction. *Crisis management* should become inseparable from *crisis preparedness*. Politicians may become emotionally devastated by disaster; the crisis manager must not.

A Role for Professionalism

One of our most serious problems is that at present we have no clearly defined authority structure to set priorities, determine the command, control, and jurisdictional parameters of effective management, and allocate available resources among competing needs. The typical crisis manager is usually another kind of victim: he is often pulled away from his normal duties after emergencies already exist, given few guidelines, limited resources, and poor information. Without having participated in any of the prior planning stages—if indeed there were any—he is the relief pitcher called in to bring order out of chaos. Not surprisingly, the result is that frenetic activity and an obsession with minutiae substitute for strategy. Under present conditions crisis managers appear busy and react to the flow of events, but they have no embracing concept of how to deal with disaster.

We need a professional cadre of disaster managers who do not change hats on nonemergency days and who are intimately familiar with both the planning and execution phases of disaster response. Ideally, when a real crisis hits, no difference should exist, either operationally or emotionally, between the current reality and the previous training simulations. The same people who planned for and managed the last crisis should be prepared to handle the next.

The Executive Office of the President is the only logical organizational placement for these professional crisis managers. Under the present structure, the emergency management apparatus is at the independent agency level, with power only parallel or subordinate to that available to many other federal institutions involved in various aspects of crisis management. Only from the White House can action authority and management responsibility be readily and visibly delegated. Such a group should maintain perhaps 1,100 professionals at a national command center and some 200 liaison, logistics, and organizational experts in the field, and would have responsibility for coordinating between the White House and the relevant state and local agencies.

One major function of such a group would be to provide continuous and realistic contingency planning to prepare for the variety of accidents and incidents that can occur, a basic requisite of any effective crisis management. Such planning is designed not to prepare in detail for every potential crisis, but to develop modes of operation and analytical models to cope with crisis, to gain an awareness of available resources, and to arrange the logistics involved in using them. Gaming exercises, computer simulations, and adversary "Red Team" attacks would all provide training and testing at many levels of threat.

Technology and Interactive Decision Making

The use of intelligent, interactive computer systems* has not been adequately explored as a means of developing planning, training, and operational bases for crisis modeling and management.[2] The distinctive feature of computer conferencing systems is ease of use, breadth of applicability, and great flexibility. Rather than requiring knowledge of a computer language, they actively present the user with a "menu" of things that he can do, allowing him to select the appropriate items. Working with liaison agents in the field, he can redefine choices and correct mistakes. In this way the nature of the choices presented to users and the form and content of resulting information can be changed relatively rapidly to suit a

---

*An analogue to robotics, interactive computer systems offer a man-machine relationship that, properly constructed, may actually create an interactive learning process. Interactive computer systems combine human inputs with highly sophisticated processing centers to sort data, perform statistical analyses, and set forth decision-trees. By employing sophisticated models of warfare, environmental matters, or flows of people and resources, for example, it becomes possible to process data in ways that maximize the information content of both the human and computational actors.

specific crisis and the preferences of the decision-makers managing it.

The significant feature of these systems is their underlying concept of dynamic modeling. To keep the process vital, both the designers of the interactive models and the decision-makers must stay in close contact to understand each other's requirements and limitations. This places a new demand on the available talent pool — one that is just coming to be recognized as our schools move towards computer awareness and utilization curricula. Computer-based interactive techniques will be able to clarify problems of collective judgment as well as the communications and resource allocation problems that occur when making policy operational. Moreover, the hardware systems in use here will allow the more routine but equally important functions of efficient teleconferencing, model building and testing, and training.

But all such sophisticated management and communications systems will be for naught unless senior government officials at least become familiar with the kinds of decisions they may have to make. Without leadership interest, new institutions and machines can make few contributions to the problems confronting top-level policymakers at times of crisis.

Proposals for Reform

The civil and military infrastructure on which this country depends for its survival is a highly visible and systematically vulnerable target for low-intensity warfare. As the increasingly fluid global environment multiplies opportunities for such warfare, that vulnerability is increasing. At the present time, the United States has few defenses against this kind of focused attack. Our strategic planners have tended to be shortsighted, measuring the strength of our defense simply in terms of weapons systems or troops. Our logistical base in fact, if not in prevailing policy, is only as strong as our domestic technological infrastructure. If that network is disrupted by sabotage or neglect, the United States will hardly be able to mobilize, let alone effectively conduct, the canonical extended NATO conflict.

The following is a reform agenda to correct this serious vulnerability:

- *Reorganize the Federal Emergency Planning Agency.* As an independent agency, FEMA at present lacks the authority to perform essential tasks of planning for and coping with the effects of natural disasters, industrial accidents, or highly disruptive acts of terrorism.

  The first, most important reform, therefore, must be to relocate FEMA in the White House, reporting to either the vice-president or the national security advisor. The agency should be reorganized as an elite group, reducing its current staff to 200 professionals drawn on a rotating basis (for, say, 4-year interleafed tours) from various agencies involved in responding to crises. Half of this reduced staff would remain in the White House to do elite planning and crisis management; the other half would operate in the field, working with industry, local, state, and federal officials in the reconstructive phases of disaster.

  The balance of FEMA's current staff of 2,400 should be reassigned to the constituent agencies responsible for various disaster functions: people involved in federal insurance and in natural disaster relief should be reassigned to the Department of Housing and Urban Development; those involved in liaison with fire departments should be moved to the Department of Commerce; Civil Defense planning professionals should be relocated to the Department of the Army; and so on.

  This would leave an elite staff that would perform only essential functions, operating under the imprimatur of the White House with bureaucratic authority to perform essential tasks. Among other responsibilities, this reconstituted FEMA should be intimately familiar with the set of contingency plans to cope with disaster, knowing what the nodes of vulnerability are and understanding the resources needed to manage the crisis and the logistical difficulties involved in using them.

  There is no question that information technology plays a particularly important role in improving both our emergency preparedness and our ability to cope effectively with crisis. The professional crisis manager must have a modernized "situation room" from which to handle the various problems of resource allocations and command, control, and communications during times of crisis. Modern digital equipment for more reliable communications, computer conferencing capabilities to allow multiple inputs without physical proximity, and interactive use of computers for problem analysis are largely unutilized tools in disaster management.

- *Develop a program of command post and field training exercises.* An effective crisis management structure requires joint planning to iron out jurisdictional issues between the agencies involved. For crisis planning and management these include most agencies in the government in various ways, from the Internal Revenue Service (for tax relief) to the Defense Department (for relief functions and maintenance of civic order). Joint "gaming" exercises and computer simulations, both at the FEMA command center and in the field, are essential to developing smooth working routines in crisis conditions. These simulations should provide training and testing opportunities at many levels of threat.

- *Develop analytical models to explore the vulnerable and critical nodes of the technological infrastructure.* Current efforts at system modeling are conducted in a number of agencies, including FEMA, the Department of Energy, and the Department of Transportation, among others. Current efforts, however, do not take into account the asynergies resulting from mutual interaction between systems. An electric power failure implies automatically the failure of many other systems. Indeed, any major failure would have ripple effects across the infrastructure spectrum. It is thus critical that we clearly understand the nature of these interactions. Without such understanding, we have no effective way to isolate the incident or contain the damage.

- *Rethink implications of infrastructure vulnerability for national defense capability.* While the U.S. has made some provisions for redundancy, it tends to prepare for the wrong crises. The estimated $15 billion worth of materials stored in the Critical Strategic Materials Stockpile might be useful if we had to refight World War II, but it is not tailored to deal with the range of crises we currently face.

FEMA should take immediate planning steps under the Defense Production Act to reconfigure the stockpile with a view toward protecting ourselves from technological disruption. This might include, for example, stockpiling semifinished and finished goods instead of raw materials or critical components, such as very large custom-made electrical transformers—the procurement of which takes several years and without which widespread economic and social disruptions would occur.

VI

Space and Defense

12

HANS MARK

Arms Control and
Space Technology

For well over two decades, arms control and the development of space technology have been intimately related. It would hardly be an exaggeration to call the major arms control agreements of the past decade stepchildren of the space program. Without space technology, no satellites would have been launched into earth orbit; and in the absence of satellite reconnaissance, such large-scale arms control agreements as SALT I and SALT II would never have been verifiable because the Russians have never agreed to adequate on-site inspection. There is every reason to believe that this relationship between arms control efforts and space technology will continue. Furthermore, recent technological advances will soon make it possible to conduct operations in space that have heretofore been impossible. In view of these developments, it is very important to examine various arms control proposals that have recently been made and to define clear criteria that will allow discrimination between those that are to the advantage of the United States and those that are not.

The technological changes that must be dealt with fall into two categories. The first, and more immediate, is the development of new methods to destroy satellites in orbit. The Russians have already deployed one such system, and the United States is in the process of developing another. Given our own heavy dependence on satellites not merely for surveillance but also for command-and-control and communications, such antisatellite systems pose a significant problem. The second change is the emergence of technologies that may make an effective defense against ballistic missiles possible. This development could alter the strategic equation in a manner that fundamentally affects the concept of the strategic balance that has been the cornerstone of U.S. defense policy for almost forty years.

Antisatellite Weapons Systems

At present the primary functions carried out by national security–related satellites are surveillance and communications. Both the United States and Russia have developed comprehensive technical means for gaining information about what the other is doing. Satellite surveillance is of fundamental importance because it reduces the uncertainties that our political leaders must face in making important decisions related to the national security. It is really for this reason that both the Russians and ourselves agreed not to attack each other's "national technical means of verification"—which was the euphemism then employed for photoreconnaissance satellites—in the 1972 arms control agreement (SALT I). It was only in 1978 that President Carter publicly announced the fact that the United States possessed photoreconnaissance satellites for the purpose of verifying arms control agreements.[1]

It is significant that in spite of this agreement, the Russians were already well along during the late 1960s in the development of an antisatellite system designed to shoot down the surveillance satellites of the United States. The Russians made such a heavy investment because they recognized that these satellites are much more important to the United States than the equivalent systems are to the Russians. It was a graphic illustration of the problems that an open and free society such as ours has in dealing with a closed, iron-fisted tyranny. The Russians have many ways other than earth satellites of gaining information about the United States, but the same is not true for the United States. This is why the Russians have already developed and fielded an antisatellite system that is now operational. With this step, they opened the era of warfare in space, and they did it for much the same reason that the Confederate army during the Civil War developed the means for shooting down Union reconnaissance balloons. The U.S. satellites perform a very valuable function; the Russians know this and they therefore wish to have the capability to deny us this function.

The Russian antisatellite system — which was tested successfully for the first time in 1972 — is a relatively primitive device technically, but it has nevertheless proved to be effective in a number of tests. It depends on the weapon-carrying satellite to maneuver into the same orbit as the target satellite, execute a close approach, and then detonate a conventional shrapnel-type explosive warhead to destroy the target.

Probably the best way to defeat such a "co-orbiting" satellite system is to detect the antisatellite vehicle as it approaches and then maneuver the target out of harm's way. This can be done because co-orbiting systems of this type must have very slow approach velocities. All that is necessary is that the target satellite have a detector capable of picking up the homing radar on the antisatellite device and possess enough propulsive capability to maneuver out of range of the exploding shrapnel. Such measures are technically feasible, but they do require that the satellite carry some extra weight that is not directly connected to its primary mission. Since weight is always at a premium on spacecraft, this price may often be very high indeed. Thus making satellites survivable is a very difficult business: the usual engineering trade-off between offensive and defensive capabilities — such as between guns, armor, and speed on a warship — becomes very much more complicated.

There is every reason to believe that new methods of destroying orbiting satellites will be developed in the coming years that do not have the drawbacks of the Russian co-orbiting satellite system. The United States is now working on an antisatellite system based on the technology of "miniature homing vehicles," which use on-board sensors to follow the moving target satellite and "home" in on it, destroying it without the use of a large nuclear explosion. These vehicles would be launched using small but very powerful solid fuel rockets carried on fighter aircraft such as the F-15. The miniature homing vehicle is not a co-orbiting system but rather approaches the target on a direct trajectory, and it relies on the homing sensors and a very accurate guidance system to get close enough to the target so that the destruction mechanism can be effective. The relative closing speed of the miniature homing vehicle and the target satellite is very great compared to a co-orbiting system. Therefore, much greater demands are placed on the capability of the guidance systems (that is, the on-board trajectory computer and the thrust vector control system) to make the weapon work properly.

It is, of course, the closing speed problem that presents the largest technical difficulty in the development and design of space-based weapons. Unlike conventional aircraft, which need to move with speeds of only a few hundred miles an hour to sustain forward flight, a spacecraft must have a velocity of 17,000 miles per hour in order to sustain itself in earth orbit. It can easily be seen, therefore, that unless an attacking spacecraft is in nearly the same orbit as the target (that is, it co-orbits with the target), very high relative velocities will be encountered. These high relative velocities mean, in turn, that a formidable fire control problem must be solved.

This consideration has led many people to speculate on the possibility that lasers might eventually be the best weapons for the conduct of warfare in space in which the primary objective is to destroy the enemy's satellites. Lasers have the great advantage that the energy used to destroy the target travels with the speed of light—which is always very great compared to the speed of the target in any practical situation. Therefore, the fire control problem is greatly simplified as compared to the case where the destructive energy is carried by a projectile that travels with a speed comparable to that of the target.

Although the principle on which lasers are based, the stimulated emission of electromagnetic radiation, was discovered in 1917 by Albert Einstein,[2] the first successful laser was not produced until 1961 by T. H. Maiman and his collaborators.[3] In addition to understanding the principle, means had to be developed for applying in practice what Einstein had discovered in theory. The essential problem of the laser was then, and is still, that it is not very efficient. This means that not much of the energy used to produce the laser beam actually winds up in the beam in such a way that it is capable of doing damage of military interest. Operational gas dynamic lasers today have efficiencies of the order of 5 percent—that is, 5 percent of the energy required to produce the laser beam actually goes into the beam. Although beams having fairly high energies—of the order of several hundred kilowatts to perhaps one megawatt—have been produced, the lasers capable of doing this require large and complex installations. There are, however, some very promising concepts—especially in the area of chemical lasers and free electron devices, which would have much higher efficiencies than currently available gas dynamic or chemical lasers. Thus there is good reason to believe that much more progress can be made by doing the necessary research and development in this field.

In spite of these difficulties, very significant progress has been made since 1961 in the creation of lasers with the capacity to do damage that might be of military interest. We have developed lasers that have destroyed missiles and aircraft in flight in an experimental setting. We have also put a large laser on a large transport-type airplane—the Airborne Laser Laboratory—which has demonstrated the ability of lasers to destroy missiles from airplanes. In conducting experiments with the Airborne Laser Laboratory, we have learned much about the fire control problem and the technology of packaging lasers to minimize weight and size. Both of these areas will be important when the time comes to place high-energy lasers in space.

Even though it is difficult to produce lasers capable of doing damage to "normal" targets, antisatellite lasers may become practical because their intended targets —the satellites—are usually very flimsy and vulnerable structures. It can be shown, for example, that a ground-based laser that can deliver a beam power of the order of ten megawatts and that has reasonably good optics can do enough damage to certain satellites in near-earth orbit to put them out of commission. It turns out that most solar cells in use today for satellite power systems would be very vulnerable to damage from a ground-based laser of this type. Lasers in the ten-megawatt power level have yet to be built, but there do not seem to be any compelling technical reasons why this cannot eventually be done. If such a laser is actually fielded by a hostile power, then measures will have to be taken to protect satellites against attacks from this device. In the near term, say for the next decade, the threat from a ground-based laser of this type is the most serious that is posed by laser technology. In the long run, however, the threats that might be caused by the existence of space-based lasers should also be considered.

Survivability of Satellites

What can be done to protect orbiting satellites and launch vehicles such as the Space Shuttle against the near-term threats that have been described? In view of the value of surveillance satellites, succeeding administrations in this country have expressed continuing concern over the problem of satellite vulnerability. Actually doing something concrete, however, turns out to be distasteful and expensive because of the very stringent weight constraints under which satellite systems are designed. Meaningful defensive measures almost always compromise the capability of the satellite to perform its primary mission beyond the point that has been considered profitable. It is probable, nevertheless, that satellites can be built that can deal somehow with the near-term threats. The possibility of maneuvering out of the way of co-orbiting anti-satellite systems has already been mentioned, and this technique sometimes has the advantage that additional maneuvering capability enhances the primary mission of the satellite, though this is not always true. Furthermore, maneuverability is less likely to work against a direct trajectory weapon or a laser. It is probable that most satellite systems could be hardened against the kind of ground-based laser that has been described, but it would be more difficult to defend against space-based lasers that could get much closer to the target satellites.

Nothing has been said so far about the employment of nuclear explosives to bring down satellites. Nuclear explosives detonated in the earth's magnetosphere produce large numbers of high-energy charged particles (electrons and protons as well as heavier ions) that are trapped into relatively stable orbits around the earth by the earth's magnetic field.[4] These particles can seriously damage many kinds of satellites when the satellites are exposed to the particles above the atmosphere. Since these energetic particles quickly spread around the entire globe, it does not matter very much where the original nuclear explosion occurred.

In 1962, a nuclear explosion above the atmosphere (Starfish) with a yield in the range of one megaton was able to put a number of satellites out of commission temporarily. This happened essentially by accident, and if several weapons of this size were properly placed by design at the right locations and detonated, much more damage could be done. If a satellite is close enough to a nuclear explosion, then the X rays emanating from the blast will kill the satellite, and nothing can be done about this for ranges up to hundreds of kilometers.

Thus, if a belligerent power is willing to invest a few nuclear weapons at the beginning of a conflict, it is very unlikely that any of the surveillance or communications satellites that the other side has in orbit will survive. It is true that there is probably some kind of a political "threshold" against using nuclear weapons that might deter their use for this purpose. Also, nuclear weapons and their delivery systems are expensive, and it is possible therefore that an aggressor would want to use them against targets of higher value than satellites. Finally, large nuclear detonations may also kill the aggressor's own satellite surveillance system, thus deterring him from using nuclear explosives. However, there is no guarantee that these factors will serve as deterrents, so the military planner must live with the fact that it is impossible to protect orbiting satellites against a determined and intelligently planned attack using nuclear weapons.

Having said all this, we are still left with the problem of developing the technical means for protecting satellite systems and, probably more important, evolving the military doctrines that govern what should be done. In the case of satellite vulnerability, it is very probable that the correct answer will be actually to develop two sets of military satellite systems, one designed for "peacetime" applications and the other to be fielded only after a high level of hostilities is reached. The "peacetime" system would be designed so as to maximize the capability to provide warning, intelligence, and communications until such time as the decision to employ nuclear weapons were reached. Clearly, the value of information up to that point is extremely critical, and therefore the capability to secure this information should not be compromised. Once a nuclear conflict starts, then the requirement for information changes drastically and there is good reason to believe that new requirements for information following a nuclear exchange could be fulfilled by a "wartime" satellite system that would be less capable but also less vulnerable to destruction than the "peacetime" system. Very probably the right way to fulfill the objectives just outlined is to keep the satellites out of the hardened "wartime" system on the ground and then launch them using a launch system designed to survive an initial nuclear exchange.

The existence of the MX missile offers us the opportunity to develop a "wartime" satellite system that could fulfill many of the information requirements political and military leaders would have during a nuclear conflict. The MX missile is a capable space launch vehicle that can place about 5,500 pounds of payload in a near-earth 30° inclination orbit and somewhat less—perhaps 4,000 pounds—in a polar orbit. The technology exists today to build reasonable and hardened payloads in this weight class for photography and various purposes associated with the gathering of electronic intelligence. It is also possible to develop a manned "space plane" in this weight category, which would be used for surveillance if all ground receiving stations and the relay communications systems used by them became inoperable. (Remember that the "Mercury" spacecraft weighed only 3,600 pounds and that with current technology it should be relatively easy to build a space plane capable of going into orbit and then returning in much the same manner as the Space Shuttle does today.) Once a set of payloads of this kind is available, they would be placed on top of MX missiles and deployed in standard intercontinental ballistic missile (ICBM) silos. (Since the Titan II system is now being dismantled, it has been suggested that the fifty-four Titan II silos might be employed for this purpose.) The MX missiles are designed to remain in standby conditions for long periods of time, and it should pose no real problems to design the payloads so that they can be kept in a ready-to-launch posture for long periods as well. The employment doctrine of this system could vary with the precise situation, but one contingency is clearly a surprise first-strike nuclear attack on the continental United States. In this case, the MX missiles carrying the reconnaissance payloads would be launched on warning of the attack—that is, when the peacetime sensors said the attack was on the way. The wartime satellite surveillance system launched using the MX missiles would then be in place to assess the damage done by the exchange on both sides. Another scenario would be to declare an attack on the peacetime systems an act of war and to launch the wartime satellites with a strike that would retaliate against the destruction of the peacetime systems. These are only two examples of how the wartime system might be employed, and it is obvious that there are many more.

Space Stations

Everything that has been said so far deals with the relatively near-term future—that is, the next decade or so. In the longer term, it is almost certain that both the Russians and the United States will develop manned orbiting space stations for various purposes. Ultimately, these stations will also have to be defended, and in the decades that it will take to develop them it is likely that space-based laser weapons will become technically feasible. It is not possible to predict with any degree of certainty just what the stations will be used for, but it is likely that some of their functions will be of sufficient value that they will have to defend themselves just the way military aircraft must defend themselves today.

It is likely that some of these stations will become space-based command posts to operate the defense systems against ICBM and submarine-launched ballistic missile (SLBM) attacks that might be launched during the same period. There is every reason to believe that the technology to field such defensive systems will become available and that this must be considered in the new strategic equation. The very accurate guidance and control technology that characterizes the miniature homing vehicle anti-satellite concept can also be employed to bring down reentry vehicles carried by ICBMs and SLBMs; the technical problem turns out to be more difficult but still manageable. In addition, there is the possibility that large space-based lasers could be employed to shoot down ICBMs and SLBMs during their launch phases when

they are easy to detect and when the relatively "soft" booster vehicles can be the primary targets rather than the very "hard" reentry vehicles. This is clearly an even more difficult proposition;
but since the lasers are likely to become available, it is not too
early to think about how they can be effectively deployed.

There are some who believe that the application of the technologies just outlined will have a really profound effect on world
stability because it will change the doctrine of "mutually assured
destruction," which is the intellectual framework for the employment of our current nuclear strategic forces. Once it becomes
possible actually to defend the launch sites of ICBMs and SLBMs
with a high degree of certainty, then clearly new doctrines must
be evolved and new concepts of "stability" must be thought
through. Although it is not possible to foresee the future, there is
at least some hope that these new concepts will lead to a world less
beset by fear of nuclear war than it is today.

Arms Control Prospects

Could arms control be used to secure the safety of satellite
systems? In 1978, President Carter asked General Secretary
Leonid Brezhnev to start discussions on an agreement to limit
testing and development of antisatellite systems. The president
recognized that concluding such a treaty would be in the best interest of the United States because we depend much more heavily
on our satellite systems than the Russians depend on theirs. Two
rounds of talks were held, one in 1978 and the second in 1979. No
agreement was reached, and the negotiations were halted when
the Russians invaded Afghanistan late in 1979. In both negotiating sessions, the objectives of each side were clear and very
different. We feared the existing Russian antisatellite system and
we wanted the Russians to stop their tests. The Soviets feared our
lead in technology once the Space Shuttle would become operational; therefore, they sought to negotiate limits on it. In view of
these very different objectives, there never was any serious
prospect that an agreement could be reached.

Is there any prospect that an antisatellite agreement *can* be
reached and, if so, what form should it take? One problem is
verification. The difficulties of verifying the existence of an anti-

satellite system decrease as we move from development to testing and then to deployment. Development, as in most instances, is impossible to verify and tests could be conducted in such a way that all but the final operational tests could be kept hidden. We have been able to watch the operational tests the Russians have been conducting for over a decade, but it should be remembered that this has been easy because of the technical nature of the Russian system; verifying the operational test of a system such as the one currently being developed by the United States would be much more difficult. Suspected deployments of both kinds of systems can, of course, be observed. It is, however, not possible to determine with complete confidence that these deployments are actually antisatellite systems rather than some other weapons system for which similar equipment is used.

In view of the situation just outlined, it is unlikely that an antisatellite agreement can be reached that would prohibit further operational testing. There are, however, some objectives that both the United States and the Russians will share in some future bilateral negotiations. One approach might be for the world's two major "spacefaring" nations to take the lead in the development of a set of "rules of the road" that could eventually be expanded to the kind of comprehensive international agreements that now regulate the telecommunications business. These rules would govern the maneuvers satellites could execute, the closest distances of approach, and the kinds of orbits various satellites could occupy. It is possible that such an agreement could be useful, and there is actually some chance that it could be successfully concluded. This kind of treaty would control space operations rather than testing or technology development and would therefore be relatively easy to verify.

The Russians currently have before the United Nations an initiative that calls for the banning of all weapons from space. This is precisely the kind of sweeping initiative that the Russians have also made in the field of nuclear weapons, and it is equally meaningless except for propaganda purposes. Unfortunately, there is little that we can do about such Russian moves except to explain as patiently and as often as we can to all concerned why the Russians are free to take such initiatives and why a free and open society such as ours is not. Whatever else we do, we should not accept the Russian proposal for space at face value or base any agreements on it. There is good reason to believe and to hope that many people understand the cynical and manipulative policy that Russia follows in this area so that the advantage gained by the Russians in taking such evident propaganda steps is small.

Strategic Implications

The technologies that would make possible military operations in space also have much broader implications for arms control and nuclear strategy. For the past forty years, offensive weapons in the form of ICBMs, SLBMs, and to some extent the manned bombers carrying nuclear weapons have been at the center of attention. It is a fact that there is no defense right now against land-based intercontinental ballistic missiles and submarine-launched ballistic missiles, and that even a militarily significant number of manned bombers will still be able to penetrate the best defenses that the Russians have. It is this technological circumstance that has created "stability" through the doctrine of mutually assured destruction. But there is at least some reason to believe that the situation is slowly changing and that the balance may once again be moving toward the defensive. The existence of "smart" weapons and high-energy lasers makes it possible to imagine a time in the future when an aggressive power launching a nuclear first strike could not be sure that enough of the missiles launched would reach their targets to deliver the intended knockout blow. It is at least possible to imagine that a fleet of large Boeing 747–type aircraft armed with high-energy lasers or high-powered air-to-air missiles could patrol the oceans and shoot down submarine-launched ballistic missiles as soon as they broke the surface. (The missiles would then still be in powered flight and would be most vulnerable to laser damage.) It is at least possible to imagine that a decade further in the future, space-based lasers could do the same with land-based intercontinental missiles. Finally, it is at least possible to imagine that a nonnuclear antiballistic missile system could be deployed in the continental United States and could shoot down most of the reentry vehicles that the lasers in space and on airplanes had not already destroyed.[5]

All of the things outlined in the last paragraph depend on pursuing technologies that are already in various stages of advanced development. One can argue about the time scale on which these developments are likely to occur, but it is almost certain that eventually all of them can be done.[6] There are no insuperable technical problems that cannot be dealt with given enough time and money. It is, of course, this point that was made so eloquently by President Reagan in his remarkable speech on this crucial subject on March 23, 1983. There is every reason to believe that the president's statement marks the start of a new era in strategic thinking.

It is ironic that the existence of effective defensive weapons against the presently available nuclear-armed ballistic missiles would, in a certain sense, achieve the objective of the people who want to abolish nuclear weapons. Defensive weapons of this kind would greatly reduce the danger of the catastrophic destruction and the huge casualties inherent in any war fought with nuclear weapons. Furthermore, if really effective defensive weapons existed, then the fear of nuclear war would disappear and, we are told, the world would breathe easy and get on with the business of life.

Thoughtful people who are interested in peace and stability know that the proposition is not all that simple. Many people in this category actually fear the advent of such defensive weapons because no one can be sure what would replace the relatively stable situation created by the doctrine of mutually assured destruction. There is simply no way that an accurate forecast can be made about the new situation that will be created by the application of defensive weapons technology. There are some who argue that we should attempt to slow the development of these technologies by seeking agreements to limit the development and testing of defensive weapons with the Russians. To some extent, the 1972 antiballistic missile (ABM) agreement was motivated by these considerations. Now, however, there is not much doubt that a treaty to limit the technology of defensive weapons would be self-defeating. If we are prevented from developing the technology by a treaty with the Russians, this is not likely to hinder the French, the Japanese, the Israelis, the Germans, and possibly a few others as well from going ahead with it. It is very important to remember that, in contrast with nuclear technology, the things that must be done to develop these defensive technologies are not expensive, nor do they require unique facilities. Therefore, the prospect that the French and the Japanese—not to speak of the Russians—will acquire them before we do is very real indeed.

Another interesting consequence of the advent of defensive technologies is that it will increase the influence of certain "non-nuclear" powers with respect to those that possess nuclear weapons. An interesting case in point is Japan. The Japanese have shown great skill at the sort of technical steps that must be taken to create defensive systems capable of providing Japan with substantial protection from nuclear attacks. Electronics, computers, and to some extent the fluid mechanics necessary to create high-intensity laser systems are the fields that must be mastered. Should Japan be able to develop such weapons systems in the next decade or so, then it is very likely that the Japanese will become much more independent of the United States than they are at present. Despite all our current economic disputes with the Japanese, we retain a measure of leverage based on the Japanese recognition that their independence and their freedom of action depend, to a large extent, on the "nuclear umbrella" we provide for them. The same statements can be made about Germany and some of the other advanced industrial nations in Western Europe. If Germany and Japan could actually defend themselves against nuclear attacks with some certainty, a completely new situation would be created.

What will be the political consequences of the increasing independence of these nations from the protection that they currently enjoy because of the existence of American nuclear forces? Will the world be more stable or less stable as a result of the technical developments that are likely to occur in these nations? These questions cannot be answered with any certainty right now. What is certain is that we must begin to take these considerations into account when we make our strategic plans.

The time has come to return to the original question posed at the beginning of this paper. In view of what has been said about the prospects for antisatellite weapons and related defensive weapons against reentry vehicles equipped with nuclear warheads, can any general statements be made regarding criteria for the establishment of arms control agreements with the Russians that might be to the advantage of the United States? There seem to be four conclusions that might be relevant to making this important judgment:

- We must continue to seek genuine arms control agreements with the Russians that limit and reduce the *deployment* of nuclear weapons of all kinds with adequate verification measures. While this subject has not been discussed in detail in this paper, the search for such agreements is very properly still the centerpiece of the Strategic Arms Reduction Talks (START) negotiation process initiated by President Reagan. It is important to recognize that treaties limiting *deployments* are much more likely to be to the advantage of the United States than those that limit *testing* or *development*. The Soviets can easily outspend us in deploying weapons, but they are not as good as we are at the development of new technology. Thus we must maintain the freedom to stay at the forefront of new developments and make the necessary investments to retain this technological lead.

- We must avoid entering into any arms control agreements with Russia or any other country that limit the *development* and in some cases the *testing* of any weapons based on new technology. This is especially true of nonnuclear antiballistic missile systems and high-intensity lasers. It is not possible to monitor and verify the development process adequately, and in many cases testing for these new weapons systems can probably also be successfully hidden.

- We must vigorously pursue the technologies that will lead to the creation of defensive systems against nuclear ballistic missiles. Since it is very likely that not only Russia but other technologically advanced nations will develop these things, we must try to maintain our present lead so that we will be able to judge the possibilities of these weapons as accurately as possible.

- We must begin to examine carefully what kind of international arrangements would be most advantageous to the United States in the event that the doctrine of mutually assured destruction can no longer be sustained because of new technical developments.

These are somber conclusions that many people may find difficult to accept. Nevertheless, they are based on straightforward extrapolations of technical developments that will occur in the coming years. It is especially difficult to comprehend that the decreasing importance of nuclear weapons in the scheme of things will not necessarily increase world stability or lead to world peace.

We are still, as President Kennedy once said, being "tempered by a hard and bitter peace." In such a situation, it is important to recognize our strengths, to use them to preserve technical leadership, to seek friends and allies where we can, to know our adversaries, and, above all, to have faith in our own ability to deal with the problems we face. This is the way great nations have always behaved, and we can do no less without risking the loss of our heritage of freedom and ultimately our identity as a great nation.

13

NEWT GINGRICH

JOHN MADISON

Space and
National Defense

The importance of outer space for both commercial and military
uses should be evident to anyone familiar with the precision of
photographs taken by U.S. satellites over the Soviet Union, the
quality of satellite radar photography that records naval ship
movements on the oceans, or the valuable technical information
now available from weather satellites. Space is thus rapidly
becoming a major arena of competition, both commercially and
militarily.

Although space has become increasingly important in human
affairs, no conflict has yet occurred there. However, consider the
analogy of the first club and the first spear: both were probably in-
vented to kill animals for food or protection, but both became converted into assets for war. Because of that tradition of tools
becoming weapons, the United States' attitude toward human conflict puts us in a peculiar dilemma regarding space.

Americans have an idealistic vision of the world that leads them to favor the demilitarization of space. On the other hand, space-based systems are critical to the effective employment of U.S. military forces throughout the spectrum of conflict. These space systems are crucial to national security, and they must be survivable—at a minimum—to make a contribution.

At present, our space satellites are more powerful than similar Soviet satellites, but they are also more vulnerable. As a peace-oriented nation, we have built efficient peacetime systems, producing large and complex multimission satellites that are far more efficient than similar Soviet satellites. We have better satellite photography, better communications, and more sophisticated equipment than the Soviets. But our satellites are more vulnerable because our systems lack the redundancy necessary for survival in conflict. The fact is that we have committed a large fraction of our war-waging capability—including command-and-control operations and systems for navigation, communication, and intelligence—to satellites we cannot defend.[1]

The problem is serious for a number of reasons, the first of which is that in all probability one of the first arenas of conflict in a major war will be space. Certainly, the Soviet commander who knows that his American opponent in the Persian Gulf area is using satellite reconnaissance to find out where the Backfire bombers are based, is going to be very tempted to destroy those satellites. Similarly, if the American naval battle group commander knows that the Soviets are using satellite reconnaissance to discover the targets at which they can launch their Backfire bombers, he is going to be tempted to destroy the Soviet system of satellites.

This problem is particularly serious in that if the Soviets eliminated our space-based assets they would in fact strike a far greater blow to us than we would if we eliminated theirs—for two reasons. First, the Soviet Union is a land-based power with fixed communications systems across the country. It doesn't need the real-time communications across water that we do because of our commitments in areas such as the Indian Ocean, the Pacific Ocean, the North Atlantic Ocean, and Europe. And second, as a potential aggressor able to plan its first moves, the Soviet Union has less need for intelligence satellites than we do as a probable respondent.

War Fighting or War Preparing?

There are three central questions involved in planning for survival in space. First, how can we minimize violence in space, given the reality that the great powers disagree about fundamental values and interests? Second, how can we structure our behavior, in relation to future agreements we may reach with the Soviets, to minimize in a conflict the risks to American national survival? Third, assuming we do everything we can to avoid conflict and still minimize the risks to ourselves, what developments are likely to occur in the next generation that relate to conflict in space?

It is clear that, following from the basic theory of deterrence, the best way to avoid a war is to be prepared to fight one. But in thinking about what war fighting in space would be like, we must recall Clausewitz's teaching about the differences between peacetime military preparedness, organized in peacetime and influenced by it, and preparedness for fighting in actual wartime conditions. Peacetime preparedness is concerned only with administrative requirements such as training and maintenance of the fighting forces. Actual conflict, on the other hand, involves operational requirements such as the *use* of the forces for successfully conducting war.

The Defense Department, however, is still dominated by peacetime concerns instead of actual military preparedness. The United States tends to focus on a concept of efficiency that makes sense only as long as there is no violence and no conflict. The development of the Space Shuttle, the design of complex and irreplaceable systems, the absence of backups, and the lack of a rapid launch capability are all brilliantly designed to work efficiently in peacetime.

Unfortunately, the very characteristics that make them efficient in peacetime make them unlikely to work in wartime. In peacetime, efficiency means accomplishing tasks with minimum inputs, avoiding "waste." In wartime, efficiency means the exact opposite: it means redundancy ("waste"), having backups, preparing for the unexpected.

In combat conditions, one's opponent will make unanticipated moves that may provoke unplanned losses.[2] In war everything is uncertain, calculations have to be made with variable quantities, and all military action is intertwined with intangible forces and effects. War is a continuous interaction of opposites. In response to unanticipated situations it may be necessary to move very quickly or risk heavy losses. In these circumstances, planning for such contingencies can be done only by violating many cardinal rules of efficiency in peacetime.

Soviet War-Fighting Capabilities

If the American approach to space has ignored the need for a genuine war-fighting capability, what would the development of a space war-fighting system entail? The answer, frighteningly, can be found merely by looking at the Soviet system. The best example of the Soviet space war-fighting capability is their satellite launch capability. During the last four years the Soviet Union has launched satellites at an annual rate six times greater than that of the United States. They have launched three times as many satellites on military missions as we have. During the Falkland Islands crisis, which lasted about ten weeks, the Soviets launched nine such satellites; they have, in fact, a launch-on-demand capability.[3] Even United States high technology cannot compensate for this differential in launch potential.[4]

Soviet Military Power, a report prepared by the Defense Department, indicates that 70 percent of all Soviet space systems serve purely military purposes and that another 15 percent have dual civil and military roles.[5] Many routine military activities depend heavily upon communications and weather forecasting provided by other satellites. Other Soviet space systems are used to calibrate radar systems and to monitor the earth's gravitational field (in order to provide increased missile guidance accuracy).[6]

The Soviets have a continuously evolving space program of enormous depth and integrity. Even in manned spaceflight, where the Space Shuttle may give the United States an advantage in the future, the Soviets have more experience today. They now have accumulated about 52,518 hours of manned spaceflight compared to 23,900 hours by the United States.[7] And they have launched relatively complex space systems for communications, navigation, photographic and electronic intelligence-gathering, early warning, ocean surveillance, nuclear explosion detection, meteorology, and geodesy.[8]

The United States has focused heavily on the application of advances in microelectronics and microcircuitry research to space systems; we get about four times as much product per pound as the Soviets because our systems are more efficient, reliable, and sophisticated. The Soviets, on the other hand, decided at a very early stage that they would focus on relatively simple, single-purpose satellites. They use simpler rockets. They produce them faster than we do. They have more of them. They launch more satellites. Their satellites are less survivable, but that doesn't matter because there are more available. Recently their annual payload weight placed in orbit has been ten times that of the United States.[9]

The U.S./Soviet space systems are almost perfect models of Clausewitz's war-preparing and war-fighting paradigms. Our very technical sophistication and rationality makes our systems more efficient in peace and less survivable in conflict. The Soviets' crudeness and duplication makes their space efforts inefficient in peace and very effective in war. They would survive; we would not.

Policy Dilemmas of Antisatellite Warfare

After looking realistically at American capabilities and activities in space, the Soviets decided to deny us those advantages by developing a ground-based co-orbital antisatellite system (ASAT). Since October 1968, the Soviets have conducted twenty tests of the ASAT system, and the U.S. secretary of defense has publicly warned that it is operational. It can maneuver to within one kilometer of a target, explode, and destroy the target's operating systems with its fragments. Even more alarming, it can destroy a target shortly after launch. We would have a warning of no more than two ASAT orbits' time before losing one of our satellites.[10]

The Soviet ASAT system poses major problems for the United States. Suppose we lost a satellite and thought the Soviets did it but were not certain. If, for example, we lost real-time communications over the Indian Ocean, or lost all reconnaissance capability to check on the Soviet Backfire bombers coming out of Afghanistan, what would the president do about it? What would he do in response to a violent act committed covertly against an inanimate object? With ASAT technology there would be no bodies in a

Lebanese camp and no tragedy of young men dying aboard a ship near the Falkland Islands. Would he really risk 225 million American lives in response to a purely technological offense? How would he explain that to the American people? What sense of outrage would there be? All that would be known would be that a piece of electronic hardware had stopped functioning, for reasons not immediately ascertainable. Would this be an act of war, or a random event? The Soviets would offer no provocation; they would declare across the planet that they didn't know what happened, and that they didn't understand why the Americans were blaming them for the weaknesses and failures of American electronics. The president would face a diplomatic quandary and a massive military problem, but he would get little help from either the administrator of NASA or the secretary of defense to clarify the situation.

American Advantages and Opportunities

In addition to the problem of our lack of survivability in space, our failure to think through the classic problems of war in space denies us great opportunities. The pressure of opponents (both domestic and foreign) to a military presence in space has blocked the United States from its natural advantages. We are never going to match the Soviet infantry, armor, tactical aircraft, major combat surface ships, or submarines. But in space we have the capacity to outstrip the Soviet Union beyond the hope of competition. Furthermore, the effort to pull away from the Soviet Union in space will lead to precisely the investments that would give us an unbeatable commercial lead over the rest of the world in a variety of profitable and job-creating technologies.

The use of military research and development to gain commercial advantage is not new. Our development of various computer systems and programs in the late 1940s and the 1950s in the Defense Department led to incredible superiority over our competitors. Similarly, the decision to build systems in space that are protected and are capable of doing the things we want them to do will give us a modern industrial infrastructure in a whole range of industries, including computers, space-launched systems, and space-manufactured systems. These developments will allow us to be the dominant nation in making space an avenue of human opportunity.

To the degree that we have been unable to pursue our natural advantage as a high-technology nation, we cripple ourselves in our long-term military competition with the Soviets. We leave ourselves militarily more vulnerable, and by weakening our deterrent capabilities we increase the danger of war—not in space, but on earth.

Some Prescriptions

To address the problems set forth above, the United States should undertake a number of corrective measures. First, the U.S. military should practice operating without satellite communications and intelligence. It should use backup systems that function when satellites do not. The Soviets still operate ground systems along with new space systems in order not to be entirely dependent upon the latter.[11] At the very minimum, developing alternative and redundant systems would counter the current Soviet efforts to develop an antisatellite capability.

Second, the United States should develop and deploy an antisatellite system. To preserve peace through deterrence, we must match the Soviets' very real ASAT capability. The U.S. ASAT system under development uses rockets launched from fighter aircraft to destroy satellites on a direct trajectory. That system must be completed.

Third, the United States should respond to the development of Soviet antisatellite capabilities, and to the possible danger from other systems such as laser and particle beam weapons, by preparing for war fighting in the manner advocated by Clausewitz. We cannot guarantee 100 percent survivability by hardening our satellites, but we can make it very expensive for the Soviets to defeat our systems. We should consider active defense in space—that is, satellites that protect themselves, either by changing their orbits to avoid oncoming systems or by sending out alternative signaling devices so that Soviet homing systems will go to decoys rather than to the original satellites. We should also develop active protection systems that might fire short-range anti-ASAT rockets. Resembling proven Sidewinder heat-seeking air-to-air missiles, they would have a range of about thirty kilometers.

Fourth, in keeping with Clausewitz's notion of war-fighting redundancy as essential to national survival, the United States should aggressively and immediately begin developing a redundant system in launch and satellite capability. The basis of this system might be the MX missile.

Fifth, the United States should aggressively develop those emerging technologies in which we have the maximum advantages. Unhappily, the United States is ill-prepared to seize the initiative and exploit the promise of technology. The U.S. space policy is essentially reactive in nature, often contradictory in its stated objectives, and excessively concerned with maintaining self-imposed restraints in the hope of avoiding an "arms race" in space.[13]

The Strategic Challenge of Space

The Soviet intent to dominate space is clear. The United States should communicate to the Soviets that if they are willing to talk about an across-the-board disarmament program, we will be perfectly happy to trade some of our high-technology space-based capacity against their land-based ICBMs, mobile missiles, air defense systems, land army, or large blue-water navy.

We must impress upon the Soviets that we have the capability and the will to compete outside the realm in which they excel: the ability of a totalitarian police state, through a command bureaucracy, to order its citizens to work long hours for low pay to produce massive weapons systems. As long as the Soviets want to compete, we must continue to exploit our strengths. One of these is the ability to mobilize a free people, through private corporations, to integrate technology and people synergistically and thus produce high-technology systems the Soviets can't match.

Space is an area of natural advantage for the United States. Failing to use that advantage would amount to a unilateral concession at a time when the Soviets are feverishly arming in all conventional arenas of warfare. Calls for limitations on American efforts in space in reality amount to an agreement that we will contest the Soviets only in arenas where they are strong, while we avoid competition where the advantage is ours.

The Soviets have issued a challenge. Their activities in space and programs under development clearly reveal their intentions to exploit space for their own strategic military advantage.[14] As a free society, however, our efforts in military preparedness must rest on a high-technology program designed to serve both military *and* commercial/scientific uses, creating a base from which we could expand rapidly in wartime. Without the scientific and commercial purposes, we cannot sustain a military effort on the scale we need—nor would we want to, because it would be too bureaucratic, too centralized, too lethargic, and too unlikely to innovate.

The marriage of military and commercial effort has a long history in the United States. In the 1920s and 1930s, the development of the commercial airline industry, aided by subsidized airmail, gave us an extraordinary potential for building an air force. The army air corps was able to grow rapidly from 1939 to 1943 because many small companies competed in many ways to give us the richest range of choices of any nation for the development of air power. Today, a serious military space program should begin with the development of a space station with a large capacity for scientific and commercial as well as military uses.

By nature, an aggressive, totalitarian state will always exceed a free society in peacetime military spending. In considering how to spend money, developing a war-fighting capability in space involves trade-offs between survivability and primary, peaceful use. Reflecting their essentially nonaggressive nature, free societies will tend to emphasize primary use and de-emphasize design features that promote survivability. The reason is that survivability adds nothing at all to capability in peacetime and is usually the first to suffer when budgets get tight. Paying for the war-fighting capability is like buying auto insurance—if you don't expect to have an accident, it doesn't seem worth the price.[15] The United States, however, must be willing to pay the expense of insuring its own survival.

Finally, the U.S. should clearly be concerned about the end of the ICBM era, an era hypnotically sustained by the marriage of two very different things. One was the capacity to produce weapons of mass destruction. The other was the capacity to produce elegant systems that left the atmosphere and returned by way of an arc.

If ICBMs are rendered obsolete, we will all be safer. The reason is not that the world will be made safe by the disappearance of nuclear missiles — nuclear warheads can be delivered by airplane, cruise missile, merchant ship, or Greyhound bus. What makes ballistic missiles especially dangerous is their unique ability to wreak massive destruction in thirty minutes. As each cycle has passed, the length of time for reasonable men to avoid annihilation has been diminished greatly. The emergence of the MIRVed solid fuel missile sitting on its pad, capable of instant launch, has made our era probably the least stable period in human history. Therefore it is to everyone's advantage to find systems of defense that obviate the effectiveness of the ballistic missile system. We would be a more secure planet if it took three hours instead of thirty minutes to deliver annihilation.

To help us step back from the brink, the United States should have a major program to develop for use in space all the possible defensive measures to make those missiles vulnerable once they leave the atmosphere. The defensive power of lasers and particle beam weapons in space will therefore not be degraded by the atmosphere. With them, we could destroy missiles in their arc, and, in the long run, could threaten to destroy enough missiles to end the possibility of a successful first strike. The world for the first time since 1945 could take a significant step back from rather than toward the brink of catastrophe.

President Reagan's proposal to develop a space-based defensive system is a key move toward a more stable world. The Reagan program represents a decisive change in American strategy. Throughout the nuclear age American strategic thinking has been dominated by the concept of a mass destruction offense overpowering any defense. Now for the first time an American president has suggested that a successful defense is possible against a mass destruction offense. While the decision to develop defensive measures against ballistic missiles is more important for nuclear strategy than for the use of space, it will have a significant impact on our thinking about military activity in space.

The Reagan administration has taken prudent steps toward a realistic policy for America's activities in space. It needs to expand and continue its current vision and programs. Freedom can survive on earth only if America can defend itself in the high frontier of space. That is what is at stake.

VII

Conclusion

14

SAM NUNN

The Need to Reshape
Military Strategy

Although the threats facing the United States have changed, our fundamental national security objectives have remained constant since the late 1940s. These objectives are:

- protecting the American homeland;

- preventing the Soviet domination of the Eurasian land mass;

- ensuring our access to overseas resources and foreign markets.

In the aftermath of World War II, the United States clearly possessed the most potent military and economic capability on the globe. In the 1950s and 1960s, the United States enjoyed a nuclear advantage, and the threat of escalation to nuclear weapons remained credible. During this period, our nation attempted to field

This paper was delivered as the first annual David M. Abshire Endowed Lecture at the Georgetown University Center for Strategic and International Studies and was published in the CSIS Significant Issues Series, vol. 4, no. 5. Copyright © 1983 Center for Strategic and International Studies, Georgetown University.

A huge increase in force levels would be needed to provide any reasonable assurance that the United States could carry out the military strategy now in the posture statement. But these additional forces would cost many billions more than we expect to allocate to defense spending. We will be fortunate in the current economic circumstances to maintain real growth in defense spending of between 5 and 7 percent per year. This obviously poses a serious dilemma.

A sound military strategy must be predicated on a calculated relationship between ends and means. Based on this definition, there would appear to be three alternatives: (1) alter our global national security objectives, (2) increase the resources for defense, or (3) change our military strategy.

Are we prepared as a nation to redefine our vital interests and, therefore, our military objectives? Do we write off Europe, or the Persian Gulf, or Northeast Asia?

If we are not so inclined—and I submit that we are not—are the Congress and the American people prepared to increase greatly the military budget over the current Reagan plan? The answer to this is obvious.

If we cannot afford to give up our national security objectives and we are not willing to spend huge additional funds for defense, then we are left with the third alternative: change our military strategy.

In determining a realistic and sound military strategy and in allocating our finite resources, we must begin with certain realities.

First, any new strategy must be comprehensible and convincing to the American people and their elected representatives. It must be understandable and clearly related to what this nation wants to protect and to the means available to do so.

Second, the threat of nuclear responses to nonnuclear aggression is becoming less credible. There is a growing aversion to nuclear weapons in the Western world that is beginning to be reflected in the various peace and freeze movements.

Certainly, there are some unilateral disarmers in the freeze movement, but there are also many sincere people who are searching for a defense and arms control policy entailing less nuclear risk. To them, I say frankly—we must place the conventional

conventional forces capable of coping simultaneously with major conflicts in Europe and Asia while holding sufficient military forces in reserve to handle a smaller contingency elsewhere. This was often labeled the two-and-a-half-war strategy.

In the wake of the Vietnam War, the Sino-Soviet split, and the emerging relationship between the United States and the People's Republic of China, our military strategy was adjusted to one of being prepared to fight one war in Europe or Asia, while also being able to fight a small war elsewhere. This was sometimes over-simplified by calling it a one-and-a-half-war strategy.

During the 1970s, America was confronted with significant changes: the advent of nuclear parity, greater American dependence on foreign resources and foreign trade, and vastly improved Soviet conventional military forces.

Since 1979, the announced purposes of U.S. military strategy have been substantially inflated, reversing the trend in the post-Vietnam era. Starting with President Carter's commitment to protect U.S. interests in the Persian Gulf, we have asked our military forces to take on new and demanding tasks in addition to traditional U.S. military obligations in Europe and the Far East.

Secretary of Defense Caspar Weinberger has testified that this administration's "long-term goal is to be able to meet the demands of worldwide war, including concurrent reinforcement of Europe, deployment to Southwest Asia and the Pacific, and support for other areas." Some would say that this amounts to a three-and-a-half-war strategy.

Despite these expanding obligations, U.S. force levels have remained essentially static. The inevitable result has been a widening gap between forces on hand and forces needed to achieve our military strategy. The Joint Chiefs of Staff in 1982 recommended force levels that could cost up to $750 billion more than the $1.6 trillion requested in the administration's Five-Year Defense Plan.

In short, our military strategy far exceeds our present capability and projected resources. General David Jones, former chairman of the Joint Chiefs, recently stated, "The mismatch between strategy and the forces to carry it out . . . is greater now than it was before because we are trying to do everything." As Army Chief of Staff General Edward C. Meyer has commented, "We are accepting tremendous risks with the size of the forces that we have, to do what we have pledged to do."

- provide a much broader firebreak between conventional and nuclear war;

- confront the Soviets, rather than ourselves, with the grim choice of being denied the fruits of military success or assuming the terrible risk of crossing the nuclear threshold;

- counter attempted Soviet conventional aggression in a manner that would leave the Soviet empire and the Soviet military establishment in a far weaker position at the end of hostilities;

- refuse a NATO occupation of the Soviet Union. As the late Field Marshal Bernard Montgomery remarked, "There are only two ageless principles of war—don't invade Russia and don't invade China."

In developing a viable conventional strategy, we must focus on Soviet weaknesses and Western strengths.

Exploiting Soviet Weaknesses

In wartime, Soviet force planners would confront a number of inherent weaknesses, including the tenuous land lines of communication connecting European Russia with Soviet forces in the Far East, the unreliability of their Warsaw Pact allies, and the lack of easy Soviet naval access to the high seas. We should establish a set of new military goals that would exploit these weaknesses.

First and foremost, I suggest a broad military goal that I would label "Keeping Russian Forces in Russia." We have looked at the huge Soviet land mass as an asset to the Russians. It can also be converted into a serious liability for them. Across this huge land area, the Soviets have tenuous lines of communication and limited access to the sea. They have potential adversaries on most of their borders.

We should let the Soviets know that if they invaded Europe or the Persian Gulf, we would seek to tie down their forces in the Far East and in other areas of the Soviet Union. We would seek to accomplish this not through direct assault on these forces but rather through the destruction of their lines of communication. I am under no illusions that this will be an easy task, but every step we horse before the nuclear cart. Nuclear parity means that we can neither tolerate serious deficiencies in our nuclear deterrent nor continue to tolerate long-standing deficiencies in our conventional forces.

The bottom line is that even with the modernization of our nuclear forces, the nuclear "crutch" on which we have leaned for so long is no longer sufficient to compensate for conventional weaknesses. The conventional leg of NATO's defenses must come out of its cast. We must prepare our conventional forces to deter and defeat conventional aggression.

Third, any new U.S. strategy must be based on a partnership with our allies. Indeed, no discussion of U.S. military strategy can ignore America's historic and continuing dependence on powerful allies as a means of fulfilling our own national security objectives. Today, the United States enjoys in Europe and Asia a network of allies whose combined economic power and potential military power exceed our own, although none devotes as much of its national wealth to defense as the United States. As NATO specialist Tom Callaghan has stated, "The Alliance must pool its enormous industrial and technological resources, eliminate all unnecessary duplication of defense efforts, and share the financial burdens and economic benefits."

Fourth, hard choices are unavoidable. We lack the budgetary and manpower resources to do everything we now wish to do simultaneously. Two years ago, the Reagan administration announced a program to modernize most of our strategic nuclear forces; increase and modernize our conventional force structure; build a 600-ship navy; and improve readiness, sustainability, and military pay across the board. It is now obvious that the Reagan program cannot be fully implemented.

Needed—A Viable Conventional Strategy

With these dilemmas, questions, and realities in mind, I believe that our principal military challenge is the development of a military strategy and military forces that deny the Soviet Union any prospect of achieving its objectives through conventional aggression. While maintaining a nuclear deterrent, such a strategy would:

take to add to our own capability for this mission greatly increases deterrence, both militarily and psychologically.

While I do not believe the West should count on the Chinese to open a second front if the Soviets invade Western Europe, I do believe the Soviets would think long and hard if they believed that their Far East forces could be isolated.

Our military capabilities also should send an unmistakable message that Eastern Europe will not be a sanctuary if the Soviets invade Western Europe. Eastern Europe is a potential Achilles' heel for them.

It should be made clear to the Soviets that, in the event of European war, violence will not be confined to Western Europe—that their forces in or passing through Eastern Europe will be subjected to attacks ranging from deep aerial strikes to commando and partisan raids.

To wage war against NATO, the Soviets must move massive forces and supplies from Western Russia across Eastern Europe including Poland and Czechoslovakia, countries whose peoples have long resented—and occasionally resisted—membership in the Soviet empire. In a war we should not permit Moscow to count upon their continued, even if enforced, loyalty. In the 1950s, we trained and fielded special stay-behind forces dedicated to disrupting Soviet military activity in occupied territory and to promoting indigenous popular resistance. This concept should be revived; the very recreation of such forces would strengthen deterrence by putting the Soviet Union on notice that it could not expect a free ride in Eastern Europe in the event of an invasion of Western Europe.

Another element of keeping the Russians in Russia would depend on our navy. In peacetime, the navy plays a vital role in the nuclear deterrent and operations in support of American interests overseas. In wartime, the primary goal of our naval forces should be to deny Russian use of the sea.

This has been described as "gaining sea control" or "defending the sea lines of communication." I would put it more directly and simply as "sinking the Soviet fleet, and bottling up the remnants." I would include the Russian merchant marine and fishing fleet, which operate in concert with the Soviet navy.

By sinking and blocking their fleet we would gain sea control, protect the lines of communication, and also, at war's end, leave no viable opposing navy to threaten us, whatever the outcome on land. This task is no longer a matter of battle force against battle force in a World War II manner, but primarily our submarines and aircraft operating against enemy submarines, land-based air, and surface ships.

As part of this task, our naval forces, assisted by land-based air, should have the mission of controlling the choke-points that limit Russian access to the sea. The best way to keep the Soviet navy in its proper place is to keep it bottled up in the Norwegian, Baltic, and Black seas, and the Sea of Japan.

Even if we have to repaint some air force planes navy blue and gold, we must insist that our naval strategy be based on full utilization of land-based air. I do not believe that we should take on Soviet naval power through massive employment of our carrier-based air power directly against heavily defended ports and naval installations in the Soviet homeland.

Enhancing Western Strengths

We must also design our strategy to take advantage of our military strengths. The United States and its allies possess marked advantages over the Soviet Union in ocean access, tactical air power, antisubmarine warfare capabilities, the training of our military manpower, and advanced technologies such as precision-guided munitions, microelectronics, and cruise missiles.

If properly exploited, our technological advantages can in no small measure offset the Soviet Union's long-standing superiority in numbers. By properly exploited, I mean utilizing our technological know-how not just to improve weapon performance but also to enhance cost-effectiveness, operability, maintainability, and reliability.

One area in which our technological prowess can be brought to bear is in tactical air power. U.S. tactical air power has long enjoyed advantages both in quality and in pilot skills. We should dedicate ourselves to the goal of achieving tactical air superiority in any theater of operations deemed vital to the United States within a few days after the outbreak of hostilities.

By providing improved conventional munitions for delivery from standoff ranges as a top procurement priority, we can apply our technological genius to multiplying dramatically the military effectiveness of our existing aircraft. We must also maintain our advantages in tactical intelligence and command and control.

This stepped-up tactical air capability should be accomplished primarily through the Guard and reserve forces. The Guard and reserves in all four services have demonstrated repeatedly that it is possible to maintain a degree of readiness and combat skills equivalent to or even superior to that of their active duty counterparts.

If we truly want to increase U.S. defense capabilities within reasonable budget resources, we should also plan to increase the role of our reserve forces in many other areas. Countries as disparate as Israel, Sweden, and the Netherlands have shown what is possible with properly trained and properly equipped reserve forces.

Integrated active and reserve forces could yield the United States a less costly, yet more combat-effective, force structure characterized by larger, readier reserves. The time has come to stop parroting the virtues of the total force concept and make it a reality. Truly ready reserve forces are perhaps the best defense bargain available.

Tasking Our Allies

I have outlined a number of changed military tasks for U.S. forces. When implemented, these new capabilities would greatly enhance NATO's ability to carry out its long-standing doctrine of forward defense.

The imperative question must now be posed: If U.S. forces are to undertake these new tasks and continue to provide an effective nuclear deterrent, what should be the role of our allies?

Before discussing Europe, I must add that the Japanese clearly must be consulted with respect to their announced goal of defending the air lanes and sea lanes within 1,000 miles of their homeland. That is something we should expect from our Japanese allies, and that is something their own prime ministers have announced as their goal.

We clearly must rethink NATO's present doctrine of forward defense. The political desirability of conceding as little European territory as possible to an invader is not at issue. What is at issue is whether that objective is properly served by the current organization, disposition, and operational doctrine of NATO forces dedicated to Europe's forward defense. I do not believe that it is.

A large gap exists in NATO's ability to implement the sacred principle of forward defense. NATO is thus confronted with a choice: either to drop the concept of forward defense as part of its doctrine, or to convert forward defense from a theory into a reality by reallocating the NATO defense burden.

U.S. ground forces are and must remain a vital part of the defense of Europe. To implement properly the new Army—Air Force doctrine of Airland Battle, our forces must emphasize maneuverability and flexibility, lighter reinforcements, special operations forces, communications, and second echelon attack.

The Allies, however, must increasingly provide the basic ingredients for Europe's initial forward defense, including heavy ground forces, more effective utilization of their vast pool of trained reserves, and the possible employment of barrier defenses. In short, if U.S. forces in Europe are to assume the primary responsibility for disrupting and destroying Soviet second echelon forces, European units must assume the primary responsibility for holding the first echelon in check. In my judgment, the United States should take steps over time, in close consultation with its allies, to make these shifts. If the Europeans do not adjust, military gaps that presently exist will quickly become even more pronounced. If it is politically essential that forward defense remain a key part of NATO's strategy, it is no less politically essential that our European allies explain to their citizens why they are not providing the forces to implement the forward defense of their territory.

The Persian Gulf

Each of the changes I have proposed would provide U.S. forces with more flexibility to meet contingencies outside Europe, including the Persian Gulf, while still contributing to the defense of Europe.

We should, however, take a closer look at the Rapid Deployment Force: its purpose, its size, its composition, and its command arrangements. When this is done, I believe we will find that the RDF should be built mainly around the navy, marine, and light army forces that already have long experience and training for just such purposes.

We should not plan to slug it out tank for tank with Soviet forces in areas along the Soviet periphery. We must structure our forces for tasks that are achievable. This means emphasizing light, strategically mobile reaction forces designed to beat the Russians to the vital ground and thereby confront them with the choice of backing off or firing the first shot in a war between two nuclear-armed states. We should also strongly emphasize tactical air and other military capabilities designed to isolate Soviet field forces by severing their lines of communication.

Arms Control

Arms control must be an inseparable component of any military strategy in the last quarter of the twentieth century. Our arms control efforts must, like our military strategy, reflect certain realities.

We must recognize that a coalition military strategy demands a coalition arms control strategy. Our arms control efforts must enjoy the confidence of our allies as well as our own citizens. We must develop a bipartisan approach to arms control that has some hope of continuity beyond one's administration.

I have suggested a number of proposals in the last several years toward these goals. They include creation of a bipartisan commission to oversee our arms control efforts, improving hotline communications between the United States and the USSR; regular visits and exchanges between U.S. and Soviet defense and military leaders; establishment of a U.S. and Soviet manned crisis control center to help prevent an accidental nuclear war; the Cohen-Nunn guaranteed build-down proposal in which both sides would eliminate two warheads for each new one added; and a proposal to reduce significantly battlefield nuclear systems in NATO. In regard to battlefield nuclear weapons, the increasing obsolescence of many of them and the continuing absence of any persuasive doctrine for their use make certain battlefield systems prime candidates for a unilateral reduction. Such a reduction would signal our good-faith bargaining position and present to the Soviets a challenge to reciprocate—or to explain to the European public why they refuse.

An Urgent Need

The U.S. political, economic, and military margin for error has diminished significantly since World War II. Our principal adversary is stronger but so are our allies. We now face the need to reshape our military strategy. In so doing, we need to engage our minds as well as our pocketbooks. More money for defense is a necessity, but spending more money without a clear sense of ultimate purpose or priority will not result in sound strategy or adequate security.

I recommend a military strategy that places a premium on out-thinking the potential aggressor, a strategy that

- seeks to apply our strengths against his weaknesses, not our weaknesses against his strengths;

- requires a greater contribution by the Allies, and substantially greater cooperation among us all;

- includes fully exploiting our technological advantages, including tactical air and improved munitions;

- makes better use of our reserves and National Guard;

- in particular seeks to avoid depending on nuclear weapons to deter conventional attack.

In an era of nuclear parity, defense and deterrence are inseparable. The ability, actual or perceived, to wage war successfully is the best means of avoiding the necessity to wage it at all. This should be the driving force behind our objectives, our goals, and our strategy. As General George C. Marshall observed: "If man does find the solution for world peace it will be the most revolutionary reversal of his record we have ever known."

In a nuclear age our task is clear but awesome—we must reverse the record of history.

15

R. JAMES WOOLSEY

The Politics of
Vulnerability: 1980–83

As the Soviet Union has steadily improved its strategic nuclear and other military forces in recent years, it has become increasingly clear to Americans that the United States is vulnerable in a sense that was never true before the advent of nuclear weapons.

This type of vulnerability had its first major impact on the U.S. political debate following the Soviet development of nuclear weapons in the late 1940s and then, again, during our last great national paroxysm of concern about strategic and nuclear issues at the end of the 1950s and the beginning of the 1960s. But this third time around our reaction has been different and less sure-footed.

Our primary response, as a nation, to the first evidence of our new vulnerability was overwhelmingly positive. Acheson, Vandenberg, and other farsighted statesmen built a bipartisan consensus for the NATO Alliance even at the same time as our fears helped produce bitter political recriminations about other issues—e.g., "who lost China," and the responsibility for the Korean War.

The second major wave of public concern—over the Soviet space and missile programs, fallout, atmospheric nuclear testing, nuclear crises, the missile gap, and so on—was fueled initially by the Soviet launch of Sputnik in 1957 and then by Khrushchev's missile rattling, the Berlin crisis of 1961, and the Cuban missile crisis of 1962. Our response as a nation to those events, and to the sense of national vulnerability and fear they produced, was extraordinary. We made a major and effective national effort in education with the National Defense Education Act; undertook the space program that led to the moon landings; and initiated two extraordinarily successful and well-managed strategic programs: the Minuteman ICBM and the Polaris submarine and missile. Neither was arms control neglected; the Limited Test Ban Treaty was negotiated and the first steps that led later to the Non-Proliferation Treaty were taken. Indeed most Americans believed that it was not inconsistent for us both to build our national strength—whether with new high school science and math courses or with increased activity at the submarine construction yards—and also to work out agreements with the Soviets where such were possible and reasonable.

During the intervening years, however, the United States government was largely occupied by Vietnam and by undertaking significant increases in its domestic programs for health, social security, and other social needs. In foreign policy, the years and the language of détente led a number of Americans to believe that peace had broken out in some fundamentally new way between the U.S. and the Soviet Union.

Events at the end of the 1970s starkly interrupted our reveries. Although there had been some concern as a result of earlier events, the Soviet invasion of Afghanistan, together with the fall of the Shah and the Iranian hostage crisis of 1979–80, bludgeoned American consciousness at virtually the same time that our concern finally became focused on the results of the Soviet military buildup of the 1970s. These events, and the impression of national weakness and drift they produced, played a major role in the 1980 presidential election.

The Reagan administration took office riding upon what many of its members and supporters thought was a political wave as large as that which had begun to surge in the election of 1932—

i.e., the first evidence of a political sea change. In its first year the administration concentrated heavily on domestic economic issues such as its program of tax reduction; it proposed major funding increases in ongoing defense programs, but left the clear impression that it would deal with arms control, Democrats, and other matters of secondary importance in its own good time. Events, its own mistakes, and its opponents conspired against such a schedule.

At the heart of the administration's delays in coming to a position for both intermediate-range nuclear force (INF) talks and strategic arms talks (formerly SALT, now START) was a sound principle—namely, that arms control and strategy should work hand in hand. Many in the Reagan administration reasoned that they could not reasonably develop an arms control position until they had in mind what strategy they intended to accomplish and what major steps they planned with respect to strategic systems.

But the delays in reaching arms control positions proved to be very costly politically. The administration announced its approach toward the INF talks—the "Zero Option" to prohibit intermediate-range nuclear missiles in Europe—in November 1981, over a year after the 1980 election. This delay, although shorter than the delay required to develop a position for the strategic talks (described below), apparently resulted almost entirely from the difficulties of getting started in this new area of arms control and from internal administration disagreements. Even though there were no external causes for the delay, it took considerable time for the stasis to be broken by the then-weak National Security Council (NSC) machinery. Those who remembered previous Republican administrations' behavior—either the domination of arms control policy, from the NSC, by Henry Kissinger or the expeditious decision making in the same forum (flavored with a considerably greater amount of due process) under his successor, Brent Scowcroft—were amazed to hear of senior-level meetings on arms control where people just sort of came and talked and went away.

In 1981 it seemed that, in many ways, the administration's laissez-faire views on the economy had carried over into important aspects of national security policy. Indeed cabinet and subcabinet-level officials during this period seemed determined to air their individual views on nuclear issues without giving careful thought to how their various musings would strike the public or affect the political debate. The low point was probably the public disagreement between the secretary of state and secretary of defense over whether U.S. plans did or did not call for a "demonstration" launch of one or a few nuclear weapons in the event of a conventional Soviet attack in Europe. But other officials also made their share of disturbing contributions to the public discourse — e.g., from the White House staff came an estimate of a "40 percent" chance of nuclear war, and from a Defense Department official came the suggestion that hand shovels could readily deal with the problem of nuclear fallout. To the public, including many friends and supporters of the administration, it seemed that the government was taking the subject of nuclear war rather too casually. To those who wished to exploit such slips for their own purposes, the administration's willingness to let a hundred flowers bloom on this most sensitive subject was highly welcome and gleefully exploited.

In the field of strategic arms control the delay in reaching a government position was even longer than it was for the INF talks and, at least in this country, even more politically devastating. From the beginning, the issue that bedeviled the strategic arms control decision was the problem of finding a basing mode for the MX missile and making arms control policy fit with it.

During the 1980 political campaign the Reagan administration-to-be had become committed to the MX missile but opposed to the basing mode (the multiple protective shelter, or MPS, system) that the Carter administration had developed for it. This was probably in no small part because of political problems that were being created in the western states by the MX's imminent deployment there. In any event, the new secretary of defense convened a committee early in 1981, chaired by Nobel laureate Professor Charles Townes of the University of California, and asked it to develop a basing mode for the MX. The new administration had spurned the Carter administration's solutions; but, given the decision to modernize the U.S. ICBM force using a missile weighing nearly 100 tons, and given the need to mesh that deployment with an approach toward arms control, the Carter administration had done its work reasonably well. The MX, based in MPS, and SALT II were not an ideal package, but the Reagan administration was soon to learn how difficult it was to produce an alternative.

The Townes Committee from the beginning saw that the problem it had been handed was an extremely difficult one and not at all susceptible to quick solution. As it labored through the late winter, spring, and summer it came up with several possible ways to base the MX that, over the long run, might give the missile a mode of basing to ensure that it would be adequately survivable in case of attack. The committee suggested that the most promising technical solution was to base the missile in an aircraft having great fuel efficiency and designed to be able to patrol (primarily over ocean areas) for long periods of time. Its technical studies convinced the committee that an aircraft could be designed to be roughly the same weight as a 747 or C5A but to have approximately ten times the fuel efficiency—by using composite materials, turboprop engines, and a specially designed wing. It further felt that such fuel efficiency would make it feasible to keep a portion of these aircraft on airborne alert continuously (as was done, at considerable cost, with B-52 bombers for several years), giving a potential attacker a significantly different problem than would be faced by trying to attack land-based or sea-based missiles or bombers on airfields. Such an approach was highly innovative, however, and the committee recognized that the survivability of such an aircraft would depend upon a careful assessment of future Soviet electronics, intelligence systems, and weapons that might be able to threaten it—and the possible countermeasures to these threats. Thus the Townes Committee recommended that other long-range solutions be investigated, including deep underground basing. It also suggested an investigation of basing the missiles in closely spaced and hardened silos so that any Soviet attack planner would face the complication of "fratricide," the phenomenon wherein one of his attacking warheads would destroy or disrupt the trajectory of others. In addition to these long-range possibilities, a significant majority of the committee was sufficiently concerned with the need to provide a hedge (in case none of the long-term solutions worked out), and sufficiently impressed by the need not to delay the MX program unilaterally in the face of Soviet strategic deployments and pressures on the NATO Alliance, that it made an additional recommendation: it called for MX deployment to begin in a small number of shelters, designed in such a way that these could be expanded into an MPS system if no other long-run alternative worked out.

As a technical and strategic group with a limited charter (essentially, "find a survivable basing mode for a 100-ton missile"), the Townes Committee did a creditable job. It seriously considered the notion—outside its formal charter but certainly not outside the realm of reason—of recommending the cancellation of the MX and the development, in its stead, of a small, single-warhead ICBM. Such an ICBM had been attracting able and articulate supporters for some years from across a wide range of the political and strategic spectrum, among them Herbert York, Paul Nitze, Senator John Glenn, Congressman Albert Gore, Albert Wohlstetter, William Van Cleave, Jan Lodal, and Henry Kissinger. But no particular basing mode for a small missile commended itself then to the committee as superior to basing in continuous-patrol aircraft, and that mode was not significantly more difficult for a 100-ton missile than for a small one.

These deliberations took several months and, when they were over, two things became quickly apparent. The recommendation of the majority of the committee to begin a limited, expandable deployment of the MX in shelters was popular in the air force but not in the administration. The continuous-patrol aircraft was popular in the administration (at least at the top) but not in the air force.

The air force and the administration each then proceeded to kill the other's solution to the MX basing problem. The administration rejected the idea of beginning a limited, expandable MPS deployment and instead vacillated among other short-term basing modes—putting the MX in Titan silos, in Minuteman silos, or in C5A aircraft. None of these seemed reasonable to the Congress in light of the uncertainty about a long-term solution. One after the other, all such interim solutions died aborning. The air force, and some civilians, were concerned about the need to develop countermeasures to protect the continuous-patrol aircraft. In any case, the air force was opposed to developing a fourth new big aircraft just when it was working to develop two new strategic bombers and a new long-range transport. It feared that one of them would be killed in Congress. It also wanted an MX basing mode with lower annual operating costs than would be required by *any* kind of basing in an aircraft. Thus the air force and members of Congress who were impressed by its skepticism ended the brief life of continuous airborne patrol.

These political difficulties were augmented by the fact that the Townes Committee had made no effort to broker a solution politically with the military services, the Congress, or other interested parties. Such had not been its charge. But it was now the end of 1981, and the administration had no way to base its new ICBM and no position on strategic arms control.

By the beginning of 1982, the administration and the air force finally began to work together and reached a tentative decision to proceed with a single basing mode for the MX—namely, closely spaced basing of MX silos, subsequently termed "dense pack." This basic concept had been one of the long-term ideas that had been suggested, but merely for preliminary technical investigation, by the Townes Committee. About the same time, the administration decided to postpone further the presentation of a strategic arms control proposal to the Soviets in light of the recent Soviet-sponsored crackdown on Solidarity in Poland. Thus it was May of 1982, one and one-half years into the administration, before the original START proposal was made by the president. During 1982 a new committee, of somewhat different composition but still under the chairmanship of the redoubtable Charles Townes, was asked by the Department of Defense to assess the technical feasibility of the dense-pack basing mode for the MX. Thus the second Townes Committee's charter was even more limited than that of the first. By the end of the year it had given the concept a carefully hedged and cautious technical approval.

The original START proposal advanced by the Reagan administration in May was not the initial public success that the "Zero Option" had been for the INF talks. The START proposal was rather complex—in this regard somewhat like the SALT II agreement it was designed to replace. The original proposal also was silent on a number of points, proposed delaying bomber limitations to a later phase of the talks, and lacked a single clear underlying principle. The administration thus left itself both without a proposal that could be readily explained to the public and open to the accusation that it was seeking to use arms control to restructure Soviet military forces significantly and quickly by demanding large reductions in Soviet forces while proposing no effective limitations on U.S. forces (such as bombers) in return.

By this time in mid-1982 both the nuclear freeze movement and

the work on the American Catholic bishops' pastoral letter were in
full swing. Both were closely followed in the media and both were
widely taken to represent significant shifts in opinion on nuclear
issues — one on the part of the public, the other on the part of a
major (and heretofore relatively conservative) religious institution. The midterm elections in November 1982 could not be
characterized as a catastrophe for the administration, but they
were doubtless not a pleasant experience. The administration held
its majority in the Senate, although a number of Republican senators were narrow victors in the face of challengers who supported
the nuclear freeze and who heavily criticized the administration
and its supporters on nuclear questions. Freeze resolutions, in
different forms, were passed in a number of states and localities.
And, most importantly, the administration lost twenty-six seats in
the House of Representatives. The shift in support in the House
was greater, moreover, than the margin of fifty-two votes suggested by this shift in twenty-six seats, because many congressmen who retired and were replaced by new members from their
own party had been generally more conservative on defense issues
than the newcomers.

In the lame-duck session following the 1982 election the administration — forced by the timing of congressional deadlines — sub-
mitted its dense-pack basing mode for the MX to Congress for approval. This timing and the complexity of the proposal (including
especially the features dealing with fratricide) doomed it. It was
roundly defeated in the House 245 to 176 on December 7, 1982.
Development and production funds for the MX in the fiscal year
1983 budget were held up by the legislation until the administration reported to Congress on strategic and arms control questions
and until affirmative votes for the MX funds were obtained in both
houses.

Thus by the beginning of its third year, the feeling of confidence
that had been present in early 1981 — the conviction that the administration had both the time and the public and congressional
support to work its will on strategic programs and arms control
matters — had wholly evaporated.

In these straits, the administration took the requirement for a
report to Congress as the occasion to form a presidential commission with a very broad charter to report to the president on the

same issues. The commission, chaired by Lt. Gen. Brent Scowcroft (USAF, ret.), who had been President Ford's national security advisor, was also charged to consult with Congress in developing its overall recommendations. Thus the commission that began to meet in January of 1983 under Scowcroft's chairmanship was formed in response to the political chaos of the previous two years on strategic and arms control questions. It was faced with a potpourri of technical, strategic, and policy questions and a political situation in which the executive branch was committed to the MX but the House of Representatives was thought to be 50—100 votes more opposed to the continuation of the MX program than the members of the previous lame-duck session, who had decided by 69 votes in December to freeze the MX funds.

As the Scowcroft Commission began to deliberate, several matters became clear. First, the modernization of the U.S. ICBM force was at the heart of the strategic, arms control, and political deadlocks. Other strategic programs were important—particularly improvement of our strategic command, control, and communications—but solutions to the other problems appeared to be reasonably on track and not exceptionally controversial. Second, a modernization program for the ICBM force was important; over the long run this was primarily necessary in order to ensure that the ICBMs would be survivable and could serve as a hedge against problems that might develop at a future time in the survivability of the submarine or bomber force. It struck a number of commission members, however, that the short-term nature of this survivability problem—the "window of vulnerability" that had been much discussed in 1979 and 1980—had been rather exaggerated. Careful study of some recognized phenomena indicated that the various parts of the strategic forces would probably contribute to one another's survivability for a period of time. In the case of the ICBMs it was particularly important that it would be very difficult currently to launch simultaneously an attack on the U.S. ICBM force and the U.S. bomber force.* Third, whatever solution was adopted for ICBM modernization, it would have to be integrated closely with a reasonable approach toward arms control. Only if this were done could any modernization program have a decent

---

*See the discussion by William Perry in ch. 6.

chance of public and congressional support. Fourth, the major political problem was the conflict between the administration and the Democrats in the House of Representatives, although the Senate could certainly not be ignored; early consultations with key members of both houses and a careful consideration of their views were essential pieces in the puzzle.

But what, indeed, was the puzzle? The commission implicitly decided rather early that its objective had to be to develop a framework for U.S. strategic force modernization and arms control that could stand the test of time. Only an approach toward both modernization and arms control that had some chance of surviving from one administration to another would be able to reverse the nation's now-chronic pattern of perpetual strife and resulting stalemate on these questions. Each administration, when it came into office, had fallen into the practice of making major changes in its predecessor's strategic modernization programs and in its approach to arms control. Conservatives and liberals were also now in the habit of organizing mass movements, and building up their direct mail lists, by attacking one another's approaches toward strategic modernization and arms control. One could foresee an endless series of conservative campaigns similar to that in 1979–80 against SALT II and a similar series of liberal campaigns analogous to the nuclear freeze, with neither side ever being able to muster the congressional consensus needed for either modernization or arms control (including particularly the two-thirds of the Senate needed to approve arms control treaties). Not only did all this bewilder the public and undermine any reasonable chance of obtaining the necessary degree of long-range bipartisan support, it also made the United States an unreliable negotiator of arms control agreements. The Soviets could reasonably look for opportunities to play one part of the American political system off against the other and then complain when one administration did not continue or stand behind agreements negotiated by the previous one.

If this was the overall problem, the plausible options for modernizing the U.S. ICBM force seemed three in number. One possibility was to try to modify and improve the dense-pack basing mode for the MX—primarily by using multiple shelters (although in a much smaller land area than had been the case in the Carter administration's MPS system). This would assume that the MX was the future U.S. ICBM force, and thus that the basing improvements needed for long-run survivability were to be made for the MX system. Such an approach would probably have somewhat deemphasized the role of fratricide among attacking warheads as a method of assuring MX survivability, and would have instead emphasized the hardness of the shelters and the role of deception as the missiles were moved among shelters within the limited land area. But the issues involved in assessing the degree of hardness that could be attained, the types of attacks that might be planned against such an MX deployment, and the measures and countermeasures that would be involved (including, probably, the need for ballistic missile defense) were quite complicated—in many ways even more complicated than the arguments about electronic measures and countermeasures needed to protect the continuous-patrol aircraft that had taken place during the Townes Committee's deliberations two years previously. Further, there was no assurance that congressional approval could be obtained for this sort of approach.

Alternatively, one might consider canceling the MX altogether and developing a small, single-warhead ICBM in its place. During the intervening two years since the first Townes Committee's deliberations, this option had begun to appear somewhat more attractive. The Scowcroft Commission's charter was sufficiently broad to encompass such a solution. Experimental data were now available that indicated the possibility of building mobile launchers sufficiently hardened against nuclear effects that such launchers would have some reasonable survivability even if they were deployed only on large military reservations; their mobility would permit them to move off of such reservations in case of actual attack, thereby further significantly complicating the attacker's problem. Moreover, hardened silos or shelters for small missiles (and there was now also some evidence that significant increases in silo hardening might be plausible) might also provide a reasonable deployment method if an arms control agreement or other factors could limit the number of potential attacking warheads to a sufficiently low level. Whether deployed in hardened mobile launchers or in hard silos, a single-warhead missile was inherently a less attractive target than a large MIRVed

ICBM. These considerations led to the notion that, if the commission's eventual recommendation indicated a shift toward small, single-warhead ICBMs, the arms control approach adopted by the United States should be one that encouraged both sides to move in that direction. (Indeed, the MX itself could be said to have been, in important part, a product of arms control regimes such as SALT I and SALT II that concentrated on limiting the number of launchers and thus created an indirect incentive to put as much capability as possible into each launcher and missile.)

The third option, and the one eventually adopted by the commission, was to proceed with a limited MX deployment in existing silos but to begin promptly the development of a small, single-warhead ICBM, to shift the long-range future of the U.S. ICBM force toward such a small missile, and to shift the arms control approach toward agreements that would promote such an evolution on both sides. This recommendation was thus a first cousin of the package suggested by the majority of the first Townes Committee two years previously, with the important difference that now the solution to the long-run ICBM survivability problem focused on the new small single-warhead ICBM. The reasons for the limited MX deployment's being part of this package were both strategic and political. The strategic advantages included an earlier ability than would be the case with any other program to put at risk Soviet hardened targets and thereby to begin to match, sooner rather than later, the capability that the Soviets had deployed in their SS-18 and SS-19 ICBMs. Of greater importance, however, was the political dimension of the problem. This meant politics in three senses: the politics of Americans dealing with one another (and the need to achieve a domestic consensus); the politics of the United States' dealing with its allies; and the politics of the United States' negotiating with the Soviet Union and deterring it from nuclear blackmail. On all three counts it was felt by the commission that the United States should not unilaterally cancel its only ongoing ICBM modernization program. The importance of putting together a solution that the administration and other MX supporters could endorse, the importance of not asking our allies to deploy intermediate-range land-based systems while we would be canceling our own analogous strategic system on land, and the importance of having some bargaining leverage with the Soviets in the ongoing START talks, all militated against unilateral cancellation.

Early soundings with key members of the House and Senate at the beginning of the commission's deliberations indicated that a package such as the third option might be able to achieve enough support to pass the Congress. This was somewhat surprising, because many members of Congress had already expressed themselves as quite hostile to the idea of placing the MX in existing silos, as had, in fact, many members of the commission themselves. It was felt, however, that such opposition had always occurred in the absence of any clear agreement about a sound direction for the U.S. ICBM program over the long run. The commission came to feel that it was a reasonable bet that, when it was explained that such a deployment was only part of a package that pointed both the U.S. ICBM program and arms control in a very different direction for the long run, an interim MX deployment in silos might be able to obtain the needed support.

In order for such an approach to work, however, a number of members of Congress had to be convinced that the administration was willing to undertake some major changes in its strategic programs, in its approach toward arms control, and in its attitude toward bipartisanship—particularly toward Democrats in the House of Representatives.

Consultations with Congress were early and extensive, including numerous breakfasts at Blair House in which the commission explained the options before it and sought the advice of members of both houses. There were many other meetings individually with senators and representatives and with groups such as the Task Force on National Security of the House Democratic Caucus. The early participation of key Democratic House members—in particular, Aspin, Gore, Dicks, and Foley—was central to this effort.

Following the commission's report and the president's endorsement of it, the administration won its first test vote on the MX in May by a margin of 53 votes in the House, but the coalition in support of the commission's package was still a very fragile one. In the next House vote on July 20, the margin was reduced to 13 votes. By midsummer it became clear to the commission and the administration, as well as to the supporters of the compromise package in the House and Senate, that some further steps were needed in order to hold support.

In the Congress, among some of the most influential of the administration's supporters on this issue, there was particular concern that the administration was not carrying out the commission's recommendations on arms control. Informal discussions took place throughout the summer, and on August 25 Congressman Aspin wrote to the commission urging that it take the lead in developing an approach toward arms control more concrete than the somewhat general suggestions that had been included in the commission report in April. Aspin's letter suggested that there could be some grounds for compromise between those who, in the Congress, had argued against constraints on missile destructive capacity (throw-weight) and those who, in the administration, had argued for quick and sharp throw-weight reductions that would make necessary a major and early reconstruction of the Soviet ICBM force. He thus proposed gradual and phased throw-weight reductions. He also argued that the unique character of bombers and the weapons they carried should be taken into consideration in the U.S. proposal, but that bomber limitations should be balanced against limitations on missile destructive capacity. These two suggestions were central to the idea of forging a compromise on the administration's START position between the administration and a number of skeptical members of Congress.

Shortly thereafter, early in September, Senators Nunn, Cohen, and Percy wrote to the commission, urging upon it a set of ideas compatible with those Aspin had advanced—and setting forth these ideas in the form of a modified version of the "build-down" approach toward arms control that had initially been proposed by Senators Cohen and Nunn. Central to the Nunn-Cohen-Percy approach was the idea that strategic arms modernization might, by appropriate arms control agreements, be channeled into more stabilizing directions. Such an approach differed fundamentally from the notion of a nuclear freeze that would seek altogether to halt strategic arms modernization. Nunn, Cohen, and Percy suggested a "double build-down"—a steady reduction in ballistic missile warheads and a parallel reduction in the aggregate destructive capacity of ballistic missiles (throw-weight) and of bombers and their weapons. Such a build-down approach, it was urged, could be designed to give incentives on both sides to reduce their most destabilizing systems as they modernized their forces; this would mark a departure from trying to use arms control as an effort by either side to dictate the force structure of the other.

The commission, and particularly its chairman, functioned as a sort of matchmaker in many of these consultations between the interested members of Congress and the administration. The six key senators and representatives who had been most involved in these discussions—Nunn, Cohen, Percy, Aspin, Gore, and Dicks —sent to the administration a set of arms control principles that the president endorsed and incorporated in a revised arms control approach announced publicly on October 4.

It is too early at the end of 1983 to assess whether this sequence of events and the approach toward arms control and strategic modernization that it produced will have lasting effect. The events of the late summer and autumn of 1983 have included the Soviet destruction of a Korean airliner, the attack by truck bomb on the U.S. Marine headquarters in Beirut, and the U.S. military action in Grenada. In addition, as the U.S. deployment of Pershing and ground-launched cruise missiles in Europe began, following formal approval by the West German government, the Soviets walked out of the Geneva talks on intermediate-range nuclear forces in late November and also declined in early December to set a date for resuming the Strategic Arms Reduction Talks in 1984. Most seriously for the Alliance, both the Social Democratic party in Germany and the the Labour party in Britain—previously strong supporters of NATO—have turned against the INF modernization. Overreaching all of this uncertainty is the continuing uncertainty about the health of General Secretary Andropov. Indeed the winter of 1984 appears at this point to hold only bleak promise—whatever one's perspective on U.S.–Soviet relations, arms control, or the needs of strategy.

Nevertheless, the effort to work cooperatively with the administration toward a common policy that has been displayed by the group of six members of Congress and a number of their colleagues may have been an important turning point in the U.S. strategic debate and the politics (both intra- and international) of nuclear weapons and arms control. This is not because the Soviets are likely to jump to an early acceptance of the compromise build-

down package worked out by the congressmen and the administration during August and September of 1983, nor because the
small, single-warhead ICBM is clearly assured of a successful and
expeditious development. The problem of producing a positive and
unifying overall national response, as we once did, to a strategic
challenge by the Soviets is difficult, time-consuming, and multifaceted. It will be much harder this time, and our beginning has
not been nearly so smooth as it was in the late 1940s and late
1950s.

This time we must sort out far more basic issues than was the
case either when NATO was formed or in the aftermath of Sputnik. Our ethical dilemmas and disagreements are severe. Technology holds important perils for the survivability of important
types of strategic systems. Thoughtful people disagree about
whether arms control is part of the solution or the problem. Important new strategic questions exist about the vulnerability of our
society's whole infrastructure to very limited (even nonnuclear)
attacks and the vulnerabilities and importance of our tools for the
use of space. There is a major need to adjust the military forces in
our key alliance, NATO, to take advantage of new technology and
improve our conventional forces, while still maintaining the tie—
historically dependent on our nuclear guarantee—to our European allies.

The search through this thicket—the search for a bipartisan
national consensus such as that which built NATO and that which
guided us at the beginning of the 1960s—will be extremely
difficult. But the authors in this volume have at least pointed in
some promising directions. Collectively they have looked unblink-
ingly at the hardest and newest of our strategic problems, not
merely at the comfortable and familiar ones.

However these authors' solutions are assessed, they break
ground. The consensus to come—if such be our blessing—will
have to be formed by working the new fields that they mark.

Notes

Contributors

Index

NOTES

2. Charles Krauthammer: "On Nuclear Morality"

1. "The Pastoral Letter of the U.S. Bishops on War and Peace: The Challenge of Peace: God's Promise and Our Response," reprinted in *Origins* 13, no. 1, May 19, 1983, p. 23.
2. Michael Novak, "Moral Clarity in the Nuclear Age," *National Review,* April 1, 1983.
3. "The Pastoral Letter," p. 13.
4. Speech to the House of Commons, 1955.
5. Albert Wohlstetter, "Bishops, Statesmen, and Other Strategists on the Bombing of Innocents," *Commentary* (June 1983): 15–35.
6. "The Pastoral Letter," p. 19.
7. John Paul II, Message to UN Special Session, 1983, p. 3.
8. Jonathan Schell, *The Fate of the Earth* (New York: Knopf, 1982).
9. Ibid., p. 219.
10. "The Pastoral Letter," p. 18.
11. Novak, p. 383.
12. "The Pastoral Letter," p. 14.
13. McGeorge Bundy, George Kennan, Robert McNamara, and Gerard Smith, "Nuclear Weapons and the Atlantic Alliance," *Foreign Affairs* 60 (1982).

3. Patrick Glynn: "The Moral Case for the Arms Buildup"

1. Robert Scheer, *With Enough Shovels: Reagan, Bush, and Nuclear War* (New York: Random House, 1982), p. 3.
2. "The Pastoral Letter of the U.S. Bishops on War and Peace: The Challenge of Peace: God's Promise and Our Response," reprinted in *Origins* 13, no. 1, May 19, 1983, p. 23.
3. Alain C. Enthoven and Wayne K. Wayne, *How Much Is Enough? Shaping the Defense Program 1961–69,* quoted in Lawrence Freedman, *The Evolution of Nuclear Strategy* (New York: St. Martin's Press, 1983), p. 246.
4. Bernard Brodie, *Strategy in the Missile Age* (Princeton, N.J.: Princeton University Press, 1965), p. 9.
5. Thomas W. Wolfe, *The SALT Experience* (Cambridge, Mass.: Ballinger, 1979), pp. 136–37.
6. Freedman, p. 378.
7. Leon Wieseltier, "Nuclear War, Nuclear Peace," *The New Republic,* January 10 & 17, 1983, pp. 7–38.
8. Quoted in Freedman, p. 257.

9. Gen. Maj. A. S. Milovidov, ed., *The Philosophical Heritage of V. I. Lenin and the Problems of Contemporary War (A Soviet View)*, quoted in Joseph D. Douglass, Jr., and Amoretta M. Hoeber, *Soviet Strategy for Nuclear War*, forward by Eugene V. Rostow (Stanford, Calif.: Hoover Institution Press, 1979), p. 10.

10. Ibid., p. 16.

11. Col. M. P. Skirdo, "Leadership in Modern War," *Selected Soviet Military Writings 1970–75*, tr. U.S. Air Force (Washington, D.C.: U.S. Government Printing Office, n.d.), pp. 151–52.

12. Freedman, p. 258.

13. Ibid., p. 248.

14. "The Real Paul Warnke," *The New Republic*, March 26, 1977, p. 23.

15. Jerome H. Kahan, "Arms Interaction and Arms Control," reprinted from Jerome H. Kahan, *Security in the Nuclear Age: Developing U.S. Strategic Arms Policy* (1975), in John F. Reichart and Steven R. Sturm, eds., *American Defense Policy*, 5th ed. (Baltimore and London: The Johns Hopkins University Press, 1982), p. 396.

16. Seymour Weiss, ". . . But Let's Not Overlook the Hurdles," *The Wall Street Journal*, April 8, 1983, p. 20: "Euphemistically described as the Moscow system, the Soviet ABM defense provides protection to a substantial portion of the western USSR, containing about 75 percent of Soviet population and industry and a substantial portion of Soviet military capabilities."

17. Henry Kissinger, *Years of Upheaval* (Boston and Toronto: Little, Brown, 1982), p. 261.

18. "Soviet ABM Breakout," *The Wall Street Journal*, August 16, 1983, p. 32; cf. Rowland Evans and Robert Novak, "A 'Smoking Gun' in Siberia," *Washington Post*, August 17, 1983.

19. For a fuller description of the apolitical character of assured destruction thinking, see Wendell John Coats, Jr., "The Ideology of Arms Control," *Journal of Contemporary Studies* 5, no. 3 (Summer 1982): 5–15.

20. Richard Smoke, "The Evolution of American Defense Policy," in Reichart and Sturm, eds., p. 121. Reprinted, with revisions, from "National Security Affairs," in *Handbook of Political Science*, vol. 8, *International Politics*, ed. Fred I. Greenstein and Nelson W. Polsby (Reading, Mass.: Addison-Wesley, 1975).

21. Peter W. Rodman, "The Missiles of October: Twenty Years Later," *Commentary*, October 1982, pp. 39–45.

22. Wolfe, pp. 332–33, n79.

23. Ibid., pp. 136–37.

24. *Report of the President's Commission on Strategic Forces* (Washington, D.C.: U.S. Government Printing Office, 1983), pp. 7ff.

25. Elmo R. Zumwalt, Jr., "Heritage of Weakness," in W. Scott Thompson, ed., *National Security in the 1980s: From Weakness to Strength* (San Francisco: Institute for Contemporary Studies, 1980), p. 24; cf. Harold Brown, *Thinking about National Security: Defense and Foreign Policy in a Dangerous World* (Boulder, Colo.: Westview Press, 1983), pp. 66–67.

26. See Gerard Smith, *Doubletalk: The Story of the First Strategic Arms Limitation Talks* (Garden City, N.Y.: Doubleday, 1980), pp. 323–61.

27. U.S. Department of Defense, *Soviet Military Power*, 2nd. ed. (Washington, D.C.: U.S. Government Printing Office, 1983), pp. 6, 7, 78, 80.

28. See U.S. Department of Defense, *Soviet Military Power* (Washington, D.C.: U.S. Government Printing Office, 1981), pp. 9–13; idem, *Soviet Military Power*, 2nd. ed. (Washington, D.C.: U.S. Government Printing Office, 1983), pp. 73–74; Caspar W. Weinberger, Secretary of Defense, *Annual Report to Congress, Fiscal Year 1983* (Washington, D.C.: U.S. Government Printing Office, 1983), pp. I-5, I-20, II-26–29; International Institute for Strategic Studies, *The Military Balance, 1982–83* (London: International Institute for Strategic Studies, 1982), pp. 12–13.

29. McGeorge Bundy, "The Bishops and the Bomb," *The New York Review of Books,* June 16, 1983, p. 8.

30. Ibid., p. 4.

31. For an elaboration of the relevance of this distinction to the concept of deterrence, see Brent Scowcroft's chapter in this volume.

32. Theodore Draper, "How Not to Think about Nuclear War," *The New York Review of Books,* July 15, 1982, p. 42.

33. "The Pastoral Letter," p. 13.

34. See Richard Grenier, "The Horror, the Horror" (rev. of Anton Antonov-Ovseyenko, *The Time of Stalin: Portrait of a Tyranny),* *The New Republic,* May 26, 1982, pp. 27–32.

35. *Report to the Congress on Forced Labor in the USSR,* U.S. Department of State, February 9, 1983; quoted in Arnold Beichman and Mikhail S. Bernstam, *Andropov: New Challenge to the West,* introduction by Robert Conquest (New York: Stein and Day, 1983), pp. 184–85, 239–40n. See also David Satter, "The System of Forced Labor in Russia," *The Wall Street Journal,* June 25, 1982, p. 26; cf. Beichman and Bernstam. On the number of political victims in psychiatric hospitals, see Sidney Bloch and Peter Reddaway, *Psychiatric Terror: How Soviet Psychiatry Is Used to Suppress Dissent* (New York: Basic Books, 1977), pp. 258–63; cf. "Psychiatric Abuse in the USSR: Statistical Survey, July 1982," *Freedom Appeals,* September/October 1983, p. 42.

36. See Michael Barry, "Afghanistan—Another Cambodia?" *Commentary,* August 1982, pp. 29–37; Rosanne Klass, "Soviet Terror in Afghanistan," *Freedom at Issue,* March–April 1983, pp. 3–5.

5. Brent Scowcroft: "Understanding the U.S. Strategic Arsenal"

1. Guilio Douhet, *The Command of the Air,* trans. Dino Ferrari (New York: Coward McCann, 1942).

2. A comprehensive review and analysis of the effects of strategic bombing in World War II is contained in the 316 "volumes" of the *U.S. Strategic Bombing Survey.*

3. For a more complete description of the various theories, see Herman Kahn, *On Thermonuclear War* (Princeton, N.J.: Princeton University Press, 1961).

4. For a discussion of the reception the Douhet thesis received in various countries, see Bernard Brodie, *Strategy in the Missile Age* (Princeton, N.J.: Princeton University Press, 1959), pp. 71ff.

5. Even with extreme accuracy, military planners could be expected to fire two warheads against each target to compensate for the possibility that one of them might malfunction in some manner (i.e., compensating for less than perfect reliability).

9. Colin S. Gray: "Arms Control: Problems"

1. Bernard Brodie, *War and Politics* (New York: Macmillan, 1973), p. 452.

2. See Robert Osgood, *Limited War Revisited* (Boulder, Colo.: Westview, 1979); Stephen Peter Rosen, "Vietnam and the American Theory of Limited War," *International Security* 7, no. 2 (Fall 1982): 83–113.

3. Superior examples of the arms control literature of that period were Donald G. Brennan, ed., *Arms Control, Disarmament, and National Security* (New York: Braziller, 1961); Thomas C. Schelling and Morton H. Halperin, *Strategy and Arms Control* (New York: Twentieth Century Fund, 1961).

4. Useful, though less than fundamental, analyses include Christoph Bertram, *The Future of Arms Control: Part II, Arms Control and Technological Change: Elements of a New Approach,* Adelphi Papers no. 146 (London: IISS, Summer 1978); Richard Burt, "A Glass Half Empty," *Foreign Policy,* no. 36 (Fall 1979): 33–48; Barry Blechman, "Do Negotiated Arms Limitations

Have a Future?" *Foreign Affairs* 59, no. 1 (Fall 1980): 102–25; Richard Burt, "The Relevance of Arms Control in the 1980s," *Daedalus* 110, no. 1 (Winter 1981): 159–77.

5. Whereas the Reagan administration addressed defense planning questions prior to settling upon preferred arms control positions, it is a matter of public record that the Carter administration in 1977 hastened to design and present new arms control policies before it had determined its defense policy story.

6. See Robert P. Berman and John C. Baker, *Soviet Strategic Forces* (Washington, D.C.: Brookings, 1982).

7. Notwithstanding its status as the principal unit of account through ten years of SALT activity, a precise agreed definition of what is and is not a "launcher" has yet to be achieved.

8. As John Steinbruner has written, "The principal problem is no longer the size of the nuclear establishments but rather the safe management of complex interactions between them. The opportunity for preventing the creation of large destructive capabilities has been lost" ("Fears of War, Programs for Peace," *The Brookings Review* 1, no. 1 [Fall 1982]: 10).

9. See John D. Steinbruner, "Nuclear Decapitation," *Foreign Policy,* no. 45 (Winter 1981–82): 16–28; Desmond Ball, *Can Nuclear War Be Controlled?* Adelphi Papers no. 169 (London: IISS, Autumn 1981).

10. See Colin S. Gray and Donald G. Brennan, *Common Interests and Arms Control,* HI–3218–P (Croton-on-Hudson, N.Y.: Hudson Institute, August 1980).

11. I have discussed this matter in some detail in *Strategic Studies and Public Policy: The American Experience* (Lexington, Ky.: The University of Kentucky Press, 1982), pp. 72–79.

12. The historical evidence on the negative political ramifications of intensive arms competition is not at all persuasive. The period of most rapid change in the terms of the Soviet-American strategic balance coincided with the brief era of détente, while the complex multinational naval competitions of the nineteenth and early twentieth centuries similarly seem not to support the logical proposition that intensive military competition greatly aggravates political relations. Bernard Brodie wrote as follows: "In the nineteenth century, continued building was the only way of preventing a sudden overthrow of naval position, and the period of greatest rapidity of transition showed no marked exacerbation of animosities between the major maritime Powers. Compared to the Anglo-German naval rivalry of the years preceding the World War, when naval materiel had attained a relative degree of stability, the political atmosphere of the latter part of the nineteenth century as reflected in naval competition might be said to have been placid" *(Sea Power in the Machine Age* [Princeton, N.J.: Princeton University Press, 1941], p. 255).

13. See Jack L. Snyder, *The Soviet Strategic Culture: Implications for Limited Nuclear Operations,* R–2154–AF (Santa Monica, Calif.: Rand, September 1977); Ken Booth, *Strategy and Ethnocentrism* (London: Croom Helm, 1979); Colin S. Gray, "National Style in Strategy: The American Example," *International Security* 6, no. 4 (Spring 1982): 21–48.

14. Jonathan Schell, *The Fate of the Earth* (New York: Knopf, 1982), pt. III.

15. Prepared statement in U.S. Senate Committee on Foreign Relations, *The SALT II Treaty, Hearings,* pt. 3, 96th Cong., 1st sess. (Washington, D.C.: U.S. Government Printing Office, 1979), p. 166.

16. See Colin S. Gray, "Strategic Stability Reconsidered," *Daedalus* 109, no. 4 (Fall 1980): 135–54.

17. Robert J. Ranger, *Arms and Politics, 1958–1978: Arms Control in a Changing Political Context* (Toronto: Macmillan of Canada, 1979). Also see Johan J. Holst, "Strategic Arms Control and Stability: A Retrospective Look," in *Why ABM? Policy Issues in the Missile Defense Controversy,* ed. Johan J. Holst and William Schneider, Jr. (New York: Pergamon, 1969), ch. 12.

18. Richard Burt, "Reassessing the Strategic Balance," *International Security* 5, no. 1 (Summer 1980): 51–52.

19. See Kenneth L. Adelman, "Rafshooning the Armageddon: Selling SALT," *Policy Review*, no. 9 (Summer 1979): 85–102.

20. Early in 1983, this was the situation with respect to the official position on the MX ICBM.

21. Laurence Martin, *The Two-Edged Sword: Armed Force in the Modern World* (London: Weidenfeld and Nicolson, 1982), pp. 72, 73.

22. Writing about naval competition in the late nineteenth century, with reference to hypothetical arms control agreements, Bernard Brodie gave the opinion that "it is very likely that a more costly and politically more dangerous competition was avoided because the Powers permitted the building to go on steadily, subject only to self-imposed restraints, which in a period of such rapid obsolescence of new material were certain to be real" *(Sea Power in the Machine Age*, p. 254). Brodie would probably have disagreed, but this author believes that the judgment quoted here is salient to the superpower arms competition of the 1980s.

23. See John Erickson, "The Soviet View of Deterrence: A General Survey," *Survival* 24, no. 6 (November/December 1982): 242–51; John J. Dziak, *Soviet Perceptions of Military Power: The Interaction of Theory and Practice* (New York: Crane, Russak, 1981).

24. See Jake Garn, "The Suppression of Information Concerning Soviet SALT Violations," *Policy Review*, no. 9 (Summer 1979): 11–32; David S. Sullivan, *The Bitter Fruit of SALT: A Record of Soviet Duplicity* (Houston, Tex.: Texas Policy Institute, 1982).

25. Lest the arms control process as a whole be endangered, with the negative implications of that for Soviet-American political relations in general, the United States has placed itself in the position of being a reluctant accomplice in Soviet illegality. This is not to endorse every wild or ill-considered charge of Soviet cheating that has been leveled by American critics. Most, but not all, of the evidence of illegality is ambiguous.

26. With reference to "yellow rain," two commentators have argued as follows: "If the Soviet Union would cheat on an agreement which offers it little or no military advantage, what would happen in a really important area like strategic nuclear arms limitation, or force reductions in Europe? Coming as it did at a time when its revelation risked both détente and the SALT II treaty, both of which Moscow wanted, this violation suggests a cosmic cynicism toward international law" (Paul Bracken and Martin Shubik, *Strategic War: What Are the Questions and Who Should Ask Them?* Working Paper no. 50 [New Haven, Conn.: Yale School of Organization and Management, April 1982], p. 18).

10. Amory B. Lovins and L. Hunter Lovins: "Reducing Vulnerability: The Energy Jugular"

1. Republished as A. B. and L. H. Lovins, *Brittle Power: Energy Strategy for National Security* (Andover, Mass.: Brick House, 1982); translations forthcoming, including Japanese (Tokyo: Jiji Tsushin, 1983). This brief summary of the book's major findings cannot do justice to its rich technical background, documented by three technical appendices and more than 1,200 references. Classification review and extensive peer review of the substantially identical FEMA report ensured that the analysis would not provide a cookbook for the malicious.

2. The main terminals at Ras Tanura and Ju'aymah are highly vulnerable: "Even a near miss at Ras Tanura could ignite successive oil tank explosions and damage the basic pumping infrastructure" (Senate Committee on Foreign Relations, "The Proposed AWACS/F-15 Enhancement Sale to Saudi Arabia" [Washington, D.C.: U.S. Government Printing Office, September 1981]). Supplementary pipeline capacity meant to diversify Saudi oil-shipping capabilities will be equally fragile. Certain components without which the terminals cannot load oil into tankers are among the largest metal fabrications in the world, and only a handful of plants can build them. Ayatollah Khomeini of Iran has recently threatened to attack the terminals (Y. M. Ibrahim, "Iran Threatens Persian Gulf's Oil Shipments," *The Wall Street*

Journal, September 20, 1983, p. 31). Iran has already bombed Iraq's main refinery, and Iraq has bombed Iran's main oil terminal.

3. See, e.g., W. J. Broad, "Nuclear Pulse," *Science* 212 (1980): 1009–12; E. J. Lerner, "Electromagnetic Pulses: Potential Crippler," *IEEE Spectrum* (May 1981): 41–46, and "EMPs and Nuclear Power," *IEEE Spectrum* (June 1981): 48–49.

4. For example, the Canvey Island LNG terminal on the Thames below London has on four occasions narrowly avoided involvement in nearby oil spills and fires, one arising from an IRA bombing of a nearby kerosene tank. A $4 billion LNG plant in Arzew, Algeria, narrowly escaped destruction one night a few years ago when a gas cloud from a leaking tank drifted through it and dispersed without igniting.

5. See, e.g., U.S. General Accounting Office, *Liquefied Energy Gases Safety,* 3 vols., EMD–78–28, July 28, 1978; B. R. Williamson and L. R. B. Mann, "Thermal Hazards from Propane (LPG) Fireballs," *Combustion Science and Technology* 25 (1981): 141–45.

6. *The Economist,* April 12, 1980, p. 52.

7. M. M. Stephens, *Vulnerability of Total Petroleum Systems,* DAHC20–70–C–0316, report to Defense Civil Preparedness Agency (Work Unit 4362A), May 1973, p. 38; idem, "The Oil and Natural Gas Industries: A Potential Target of Terrorists," in *Terrorism: Threat, Reality, Response,* ed. R. Kupperman and D. Trent (Stanford, Calif.: Hoover Institution Press, 1979), p. 208.

8. Office of Technology Assessment, *The Effects of Nuclear War,* OTA–NS–89, May 1979, p. 64. The Soviet concentration is even heavier (A. M. Katz, *Life after Nuclear War* [Cambridge, Mass.: Ballinger, 1981], pp. 317ff).

9. "Tosco Says Refinery Was Hit by Sabotage, Dampening Earnings," *The Wall Street Journal,* April 4, 1980, p. 6.

10. For example, a Shell gasoline pipeline in Oakland, California, was damaged in 1969; a Puerto Rican gasoline pipeline was sheared by ground shock from a bomb in 1975; and the Trans-Alaska pipeline was lightly damaged by bombs in 1977 and 1978. In 1974, twenty Kentucky gas pipelines and two of their cooling towers were dynamited.

11. U.S. General Accounting Office, *Key Crude Oil and Products Pipelines Are Vulnerable to Disruptions,* EMD–9–63, August 27, 1979.

12. Ibid., p. 30.

13. Most noticeably in Central America and in southern Africa, where Soviet limpet mines are a trademark of the African National Congress's periodic attacks on South African power lines, power plants, and substations; see, e.g., *Los Angeles Times,* July 21, 1981, p. I:1, and July 22, 1981, p. I:2.

14. Federal Bureau of Investigation, *Bomb Summary 1978, Uniform Crime Reports* (Washington, D.C.: U.S. Government Printing Office, 1979).

15. A. B. and L. H. Lovins, *Energy/War: Breaking the Nuclear Link* (New York: Harper, 1981); A. B. Lovins, "Nuclear Weapons and Power-Reactor Plutonium," *Nature* 283 (1980): 817–23.

16. This can be inferred from fault and event trees in U.S. Nuclear Regulatory Commission, *Reactor Safety Study,* NUREG–75–014, October 1975.

17. S. Fetter and K. Tsipis, "Catastrophic Releases of Radioactivity," *Scientific American* 244, no. 4 (April 1981): 41–47; J. P. Holdren, letter in response (Energy and Resources Group, University of California at Berkeley), March 27, 1981; B. Ramberg, *The Destruction of Nuclear Energy Facilities in War* (Lexington, Mass.: Heath, 1980).

18. Ibid. This implies, incidentally, that a *non*nuclear NATO/Warsaw Pact conflict on the North German plain would probably release fallout equivalent to that from thousands of tactical warheads, just from collateral damage to the four large reactors already sited there.

19. Quoted in R. Drobnick and S. Enzer, "Future Environments of International Trade: A

Summary and Report of the Fourth Twenty Year Forecast Project," F—42 (Los Angeles: Center for Futures Research, University of Southern California, March 1981).

20. "The Case for Emergency Power," *Electrical Construction and Maintenance* (New York: McGraw-Hill, December 1965).

21. U.S. Department of Energy, *Energy Insider* 3, no. 19 (September 15, 1980).

22. Lovins and Lovins, *Brittle Power*, app. 3; R. Stobaugh and D. Yergin, eds., *Energy Future* (New York: Ballantine, 1979); Solar Energy Research Institute, *A New Prosperity* (Andover, Mass.: Brick House, 1981).

23. Solar Energy Research Institute, op. cit.; A. B. and L. H. Lovins, F. Krause, and W. Bach, *Least-Cost Energy: Solving the CO₂ Problem* (Andover, Mass.: Brick House, 1982); D. Olivier et al., *Energy-Efficient Futures: Opening the Solar Option* (London: Earth Resources Research, Ltd., 1983); A. B. and L. H. Lovins, "Electric Utilities: Key to Capitalizing the Energy Transition," *Technological Forecasting and Social Change* 22 (1982): 153—66.

24. Energy Information Administration data show 1979—82 savings of 7.82 q/y (quadrillion BTU per year), over half of it from improved technical efficiency. Fossil fuel supply fell 1.00 q/y, nonrenewable supply 0.63 q/y (coal rose 0.80 but oil and gas fell 1.79). Renewable supply increased 0.34 q/y, so total U.S. supply fell 0.29 q/y—both excluding wood, which rose about 0.5 q/y. With the fluctuating hydroelectric output smoothed, the net total increase was somewhat under 0.1 q/y.

25. In 1980, nuclear power delivered 230 TW-h of electricity with a heat content of 0.785 q. Assuming average efficiency of 45 percent in houses and 75 percent in industry, the 2.0—2.4 q of wood burned delivered about 1.35—1.56 q, or 400—460 TW-h of heat. In 1982, nuclear power delivered 0.90 q and wood probably 1.5—1.8 q.

26. Lovins and Lovins, *Brittle Power*, ch. 17.

11. Robert Kupperman: "Vulnerable America"

1. For more information, see Robert Kupperman, et al., "Terror, the Strategic Tool: Response and Control," *The Annals* (September 1982): 24—38.

2. For more information, see Robert Kupperman, Richard Wilcox, and Harvey Smith, "Crisis Management: Some Opportunities," *Science Magazine* (February 7, 1975): 404—10; Roxanne Hiltz and Murray Turoff, *Network Nation: Human Communication via Computer* (Reading, Mass.: Addison-Wesley, 1978).

12. Hans Mark: "Arms Control and Space Technology"

1. Speech by President Carter at the Kennedy Space Center on October 1, 1978.

2. A. Einstein, "Zur Quantentheorie der Strahlung" ("On the Quantum Theory of Radiation"), *Physikalische Zeitschrift* 18 (1917): 121.

3. T. H. Maiman, "Stimulated Optical Emission in Fluorescent Solids, I: Theoretical Considerations," *Physical Review* 123 (1961): 1145; T. H. Maiman, R. H. Hoskin, I. J. D'Haenes, C. K. Azawa, and V. Evtuhov, "Stimulated Optical Emission in Fluorescent Solids, II: Spectroscopy and Stimulated Emission in Ruby," *Physical Review* 123 (1961): 1151.

4. N. C. Christofilos, "The Argus Experiment," *Journal of Geophysical Research* 64 (1959): 869.

5. Hans Mark, "Technology and the Strategic Balance" (based on the Charles H. Davis Lecture delivered at the U.S. Naval War College, May 6, 1981), *Technology in Society* 4 (1982): 15—32.

6. Hans Mark, "Our Heritage in Applied Research" (based on the Robert Henry Thurston Lecture delivered at the annual meeting of the American Society of Mechanical Engineers, November 1982), *Mechanical Engineering* 105 (1983): 37—41.

13. Newt Gingrich and John Madison: "Space and National Defense"

1. Jerry Pournelle, "The Decisive Frontier: Space," *Omni* 4 (November 1981): 139.

2. Carl von Clausewitz, *On War,* trans. and ed. Michael Howard and Peter Paret (Princeton, N.J.: Princeton University Press, 1976), pp. 134–36.

3. Interview with Marcia S. Smith, Congressional Research Service, Washington, D.C., January 21, 1983.

4. Robert B. Giffen, *U.S. Space System Survivability: Strategic Alternatives for the 1990's* (Washington, D.C.: National Defense University Press, 1982), p. 19.

5. James J. Haggerty, "Military in Space," *Aerospace* 20 (Spring 1982): 3.

6. "The Soviet Military Space Program," *International Defense Review* 21 (February 1982): 149.

7. Interview with Marcia S. Smith.

8. K. L. Eichelberger, "A New Duel: Antisatellite Combat in Space," *Naval War College Review* 35 (May–June 1982): 41.

9. Giffen, p. 19.

10. Eichelberger, p. 42.

11. Giffen, p. 21.

12. Interview with Hans Mark, deputy administrator, National Aeronautics and Space Administration, Washington, D.C., January 20, 1983.

13. Dan Goure, "Space Conflict Strategies," *Defense & Foreign Affairs* 19 (August–September 1981): 38.

14. Dino A. Lorenzini and Charles L. Fox, "2001: A U.S. Space Force," *Naval War College Review* 34 (March–April 1981): 61.

15. Giffen, p. 53.

CONTRIBUTORS

RICHARD BURT was sworn in as assistant secretary of state for European affairs in February 1983, after having served as director of the Bureau of Politico-Military Affairs at the Department of State. Previously, he was the national security affairs correspondent for *The New York Times* covering foreign policy and defense issues in Washington, D.C., and the assistant director of the International Institute for Strategic Studies in London.

NEWT GINGRICH, a Republican from Georgia, is serving his third term in the U.S. House of Representatives. He is a member of the House Administration Committee, the Public Works and Transportation Committee (along with its subcommittee on aviation), and the U.S. House Military Reform Caucus. With Mark Florio, he co-wrote "A Post-Weber Model of Bureaucracy" for the volume *A Government's Role in Solving Societal Problems* (1982), and his articles have appeared in *The Futurist, Defense Science, Human Events, First Monday*, and *Conservative Digest*.

PATRICK GLYNN is co-editor of the *Journal of Contemporary Studies* and acting executive director of the Institute for Contemporary Studies. His articles and reviews have appeared in a number of magazines, including *The New Republic* and *Commentary*.

COLIN S. GRAY is president of the National Institute for Public Policy. Formerly director of national security studies at the Hudson Institute, he currently is a member of the General Advisory Committee of the U.S. Arms Control and Disarmament Agency. Dr. Gray also serves on the editorial boards of *Orbis* and *International Security Review* and has written extensively on U.S., Soviet, and NATO defense policies; his books include *The Geopolitics of the Nuclear Era* (1977), *The MX ICBM and National Security* (1982), *Strategic Studies and Public Policy: The American Experience* (1982), *American Military Space Policy: Information Systems, Weapon Systems, and Arms Control* (1983), and *Nuclear Strategy and National Style* (forthcoming).

CHARLES KRAUTHAMMER is a senior editor at *The New Republic* and contributing essayist to *Time*. He was formerly special assistant and speech writer to vice-president Walter F. Mondale.

ROBERT KUPPERMAN is executive director in scientific and technical affairs for the Center for Strategic and International Studies. He has held a number of positions in the United States government, including that of assistant director for the Office of Emergency Preparedness; deputy assistant director for military and economic affairs, and later chief scientist, for the U.S. Arms Control and Disarmament Agency; and transition director for the Federal Emergency Management Agency. Among his latest works are *Terrorism: Threat, Reality, Response* (with D. M. Trent, 1979), *Congress and Terrorism: A Report to the Sergeant-at-Arms of the United States Senate* (1981), *Ballistic Missile Defense: A Potential Arms-Control Initiative* (with others, 1981), and *Strategic Requirements for the Army in the Year 2000* (with others, 1983).

AMORY B. LOVINS, a physicist, is director of research at Rocky Mountain Institute, a nonprofit foundation exploring the links between energy, land, water, security, and economics. A former Oxford don and twice Regents' Lecturer at the University of California, he has also been Grauer Lecturer at the University of British Columbia, Distinguished Visiting Professor at the University of Colorado, and Luce Visiting Professor at Dartmouth College. He served in 1980–81 on the Energy Research Advisory Board of the U.S. Department of Energy and has published numerous technical papers and a dozen books, including *Soft Energy Paths* (1977) and, with his wife Hunter, *Brittle Power: Energy Strategy for National Security* (1982), a Defense Civil Preparedness Agency study on which their chapter is based.

L. HUNTER LOVINS, Esq., is a member of the California Bar, a sociologist and political scientist, and president of Rocky Mountain Institute. She also helped to establish and was for six years assistant director of the California Conservation Project, an urban forestry group. In 1982 she was Luce Visiting Professor at Dartmouth College, during which time she and her husband Amory won a Mitchell Prize for an essay on reallocating utility capital. Together, the Lovinses have served as consultants to a wide range of governmental and private sector clients, and currently they are policy advisors to Friends of the Earth. A 16mm film on their work, "Lovins on the Soft Path," received (among other awards) the American Film Festival's "Best of Category (Energy)."

JOHN MADISON, an American Political Science Association Congressional Fellow working as a staff member in Representative Newt Gingrich's office, is also manager of the Program Support Office in the Office of Aeronautics and Space Technology at NASA headquarters in Washington, D.C., helping to develop NASA's long-range plans for aeronautics and space research and technology programs. He has managed various aircraft and rocket propulsion research and technology programs for NASA, the navy, and the air force for the past nineteen years.

HANS MARK is the deputy administrator of NASA. From 1977 to 1981 he served first as under secretary and later as secretary of the air force. Prior to that he was director of NASA's Ames Research Center and held teaching positions at the University of California and the Massachusetts Institute of Technology. Dr. Mark has published many articles on technical topics and co-authored several books. He is a member of the National Academy of Engineering.

SAM NUNN is a United States senator (D–Ga.). He is the ranking minority member of the Senate Armed Services Committee and also serves as a member of the Intelligence, Governmental Affairs, and Small Business committees. Prior to his election to the Senate in 1972, he practiced law in Perry, Georgia, was legal counsel to the House Armed Services Committee (1962–63), and served two terms in the Georgia House of Representatives (1968–72). He has authored numerous proposals in the national security area that have become law and has written three major reports on the NATO Alliance for the Armed Services Committee.

WILLIAM J. PERRY is a managing director of Hambrecht & Quist, an investment banking firm in San Francisco specializing in high-technology companies. Prior to joining the firm, he held the office of under secretary of defense for research and engineering, during which time he was responsible for all weapon systems procurement and all research and development. Dr. Perry was one of the founders of ESL, Inc., in 1964 and served as its president until 1977, when he entered government service.

MICHAEL QUINLAN, a British career civil servant, is currently permanent secretary at the Department of Employment in London. Most of his career has, however, been in the defense field, particularly in United Kingdom and NATO security policy. From 1977 to 1981 he was deputy under secretary of state (policy and programmes) in the Ministry of Defence and was deeply involved in nuclear issues under both Labour and Conservative governments. He also headed the U.K. delegation in the NATO High-Level Group that developed the NATO plans for Pershing II and cruise missile deployment in Europe.

BRENT SCOWCROFT is vice-chairman of Kissinger Associates, Inc., an international business consulting firm. A retired lieutenant-general in the United States Air Force, he was formerly national security adviser to President Ford and now serves as chairman of the President's Commission on Strategic Forces.

WALTER B. SLOCOMBE is a member of the Washington, D.C., law firm of Caplin & Drysdale, Chartered. During the Carter administration, he was deputy under secretary for policy planning (1979–81) and the principal deputy assistant secretary of defense for international security affairs (1977–79), serving concurrently as director of the Defense Department SALT Task Force. Mr. Slocombe has also been a research associate at the International Institute for Strategic Studies in London and a member of the Program Analysis Staff of the National Security Council.

R. JAMES WOOLSEY is a partner in the law firm of Shea & Gardner, Washington, D.C. From 1977–79 he was under secretary of the navy, prior to which he served the United States government in a number of capacities, including general counsel to the U.S. Senate Committee on Armed Services, member of the National Security Council staff, and advisor on the U.S. delegation to the Strategic Arms Limitation Talks (1969–70). In 1981 he was a member of the first Townes Committee dealing with MX missile basing, and in 1983 he served both on the President's Commission on Strategic Forces (the Scowcroft Commission) and as delegate-at-large to the Strategic Arms Reduction Talks with the Soviet Union.

INDEX